THE ROUGH GUIDE to

Food

written by
George Miller and Katharine Reeve

with a foreword by
Guy Watson

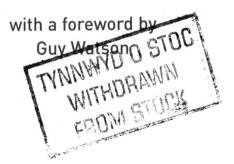

ROUGH
GUIDES

www.roughguides.com

Credits

The Rough Guide to Food

Managing Editor: Peter Buckley
Design & layout: George Miller
Diagrams: Gemma Matthews
Proofreading: Andrew McCulloch
Production: Rebecca Short

Rough Guides Reference

Editors: Peter Buckley, Tracy Hopkins,
Matthew Milton,
Joe Staines, Ruth Tidball
Director: Andrew Lockett

Publishing information

This first edition of *The Rough Guide to Food*
published 2009 by Rough Guides Ltd,
80 Strand, London WC2R 0RL
375 Hudson Street, New York 10014
Email: mail@roughguides.co.uk

Distributed by the Penguin Group
Penguin Books Ltd, 80 Strand, London WC2R 0RL
Penguin Group (USA), 375 Hudson Street, NY 10014, USA
Penguin Group (Australia), 250 Camberwell Road, Camberwell, Victoria 3124, Australia
Penguin Group (Canada), 90 Eglinton Avenue East, Suite 700, Toronto, ON, M4P 2Y3
Penguin Group (New Zealand), Cnr Rosedale and Airborne Roads, Albany, Auckland,
New Zealand

Printed and bound in China
Typeset in Din, Minion and Myriad

320 pages; includes index

A catalogue record for this book is available from the British Library

ISBN 13: 978-1-84836-001-3

1 3 5 7 9 8 6 4 2

Contents

About this book

In the time we've spent writing this book, the food landscape has changed dramatically. The world's financial systems have collapsed, exposing our vulnerability to the effects of globalization; international food shortages and food price rises have led to changes in our shopping habits and even riots; our appetite for ethically and naturally produced food such as Fairtrade and organic, which has been gaining ground over the last decade, is being severely tested in the new climate of the credit crunch.

So clearly there are wider issues at stake than just personal enjoyment or nourishment from food. The food industry is responsible for much environmental damage (see **Climate change and food miles**) and leaves behind a heavy carbon footprint because of its intensive farming methods (see **Farming today**), as well as its heavy reliance on pesticides (see **All in the soil**) and energy-intensive manufacturing and retailing. Increasingly, what we eat is controlled by a handful of giant transnational corporations which answer to shareholders, not the public or even national governments (see **Global trade**), as seen in the great biotechnology experiment that is genetically modified foods (see **GM and the future of food**). Organic farming (see **Organic food**) and Fairtrade (see **Free trade or Fairtrade?**) seem to offer alternatives, but are they all they're cracked up to be?

At the same time, in the UK and US the seemingly unstoppable growth of obesity threatens to stretch government finances to the limit, as health costs soar just to manage the life-threatening diseases caused by us eating too much processed food. So what is healthy eating? We tackle the hidden dangers in our food, including the shocking state of children's diets in this country (see **What is healthy food?**).

To cap it all, we are probably less well informed about food than we've ever been and do not trust our main sources of information on the subject: the government, supermarkets and the media. It's no wonder we're confused about food. The big businesses of the food industry thrive on our confusion about the origin of our food and healthy eating, but some critics argue that it needn't be this hard. Michael Pollan, author of *In Defence of Food*, thinks eating well can be boiled down to four simple guidelines:

1. Don't eat anything your great-grandmother would not recognize as food.
2. Don't buy anything with more than five ingredients.
3. Only eat at a table; eat slowly and communally.
4. Distrust any food claiming health benefits.

Being better informed will help us take back control of what we eat from the likes of Tesco and Sainsbury's and give us real choices; this book will help you distinguish the good from the bad in the supermarket (see **The supermarkets**). It also shows you where your food really comes from and explores the sustainable alternatives to industrial-scale food production and slogging round the supermarkets.

In **Real food** we hear from the people who are championing a return to carefully produced, high-quality real food and highlight small producers and shops dedicated to offering you a better choice (see **The directory**). Cooking from scratch, so long in the doldrums, is making a comeback; more of us are starting to buy local and discover the pleasures of farmers' markets and the super-fresh food on offer in vegetable box deliveries; some of us are even growing our own fruit and veg (see **Grow your own**). We are poised to start to enjoy real food again. We just need to be shown where to start. That is the aim of this book.

❚❚We have a right to know how our food is produced ... consumers should be able to get accurate and unbiased information about what they are buying and how it was produced.**❚❚**

Peter Singer,
The Ethics of What We Eat

About the authors

Authors **George Miller** and **Katharine Reeve** are food fanatics from Devon (the heartland of organic food activists and food angst).

George grew up in the west of Scotland at a time when vegetables (if you don't count chips) were still quite a rare sight. He realized how enjoyable food could be while studying in France, and later discovered the delights of simply prepared fresh foods while living in Greece. The first meal he remembers learning to cook was spaghetti bolognaise and chocolate mousse. He is an omnivore, but draws the line at Marmite and tripe. Formerly Editorial Director of Granta Books, he is now a freelance editor, translator and podcaster (for publishers and literary festivals).

Katharine grew up in rural Norfolk and has grown her own vegetables intermittently since the age of nine. A keen home-cook since childhood forays into *Italian food: the basics*, she was an early organic vegetable box adopter and collects vintage cookbooks. Her idea of a good weekend is tracking down small producers and new food markets. She has worked as a non-fiction commissioning editor in publishing, most recently as Editorial Director at OUP, and is now teaches creative writing at Bath Spa University.

Acknowledgements

A list of all the people who talked to us about their particular interest in and knowledge of food would be too long to include here, but thanks are especially due to: Greenpeace, Guy Watson, Meg Rivers' Cakes, Justin Kerswell at Viva!, Geoff Sayers at The Well-Hung Meat Company, Steven Macatonia at Union Hand-Roasted, Sainsbury's, CIWF, Donald Hay, St Stephen's Primary School, Bath, Department of English and Creative Studies at Bath Spa University, Bananalink, Pesticide Action Network, Brown Cow, Olives et Al, Liberation Nuts and Paul A. Young.

We would like to thank Andrew Lockett at Rough Guides for commissioning the book and Peter Buckley for helping us come in to land with the manuscript. Gemma Matthews deserves a special mention for the no-nonsense way she tackled often tricky diagrams and for providing an invaluable InDesign drop-in clinic.

Part I

The food chain

How it began

Human history is founded on farming. It was farming which enabled people to put down roots in fixed communities and enabled those communities to develop into complex societies. When the harvest went well, any surpluses could be stored for times of shortage, thereby allowing populations to grow. And as they grew, these early farming communities absorbed their hunter-gatherer neighbours or simply outstripped them. The human urge to innovate led to technological innovations such as the plough (see box on p.5) and the wheel, which made agriculture still more productive.

Societies which were capable of producing a valuable grain surplus came to develop bureaucracies to keep account of it. Unromantic though it is, the first writing systems in Mesopotamia didn't record the scribes' innermost thoughts but grain harvests and sheep numbers.

The **warm period** that began after the end of the last Ice Age around 8500 BC created the right climatic conditions for farming to develop. The first traces of agriculture found by archaeologists are in the **Fertile Crescent** in the Middle East (see map on p.4). From here it spread slowly and sporadically in the course of the millennia that followed.

The advantages of agriculture seem obvious to us: compared to hunting and gathering, cultivation of the land could provide a food supply ten or even a hundred times greater. But the development of farming was not a foregone conclusion. (Even today there are still hunter-gatherers, such as the !Kung bush people of the Kalahari, who live on a varied diet which includes over a hundred different types of plant.) In fact, early farming came at a price: like all agriculture before the age of the tractor and the combine harvester, it was back-breaking work, and studies of human remains have revealed that, along with a more stable, settled existence,

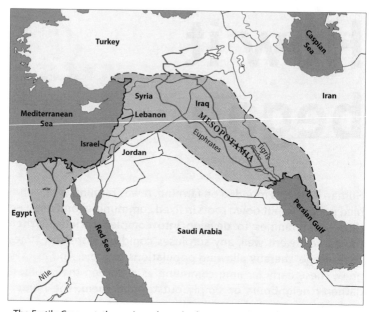

The Fertile Crescent, the region where the first traces of prehistoric agriculture have been found.

early farmers also had health problems from eating a limited, cultivated diet. They were smaller and less well nourished than their hunter-gatherer contemporaries. Studies of modern-day hunter-gatherers suggest that our ancestors had to work a good deal less hard to feed themselves than farmers did; after all, their varied meals were laid on by nature, as long as they knew how to track them down.

Prehistoric farming didn't replace hunter-gatherer societies overnight. Agriculture involved a trade-off: your diet was more monotonous and working in the fields was harder work than collecting leaves and berries, but in the long run it was a more reliable way to support a growing population. Whereas a population reliant on nature's larder could quickly deplete its supply and find itself forced to up sticks or go hungry, agriculture offered the prosect of stability. Not for nothing do we talk of settling down in terms of "putting down roots".

The first cultivated crops were **wheat** and **barley** (traces of emmer wheat from around 8500 BC have been found in the Fertile Crescent), but the process of domesticating all the major food crops (selectively breeding plants to adapt them to our needs and local conditions) took millennia. Olives, figs and grapes were not domesticated until around 4000 BC and strawberries have only been cultivated since the Middle Ages. The reason for this is that some plants take to domestication more readily than others: wild wheat and barley ears evolved to "shatter" in order to reproduce by distributing their seeds, but a single, naturally occurring gene mutation is all it took for the plant to retain its seeds in a form that mankind could harvest and re-sow. An apple or pear tree, on the other hand, requires knowledge of the technique of grafting and therefore a much greater intuitive understanding of plant biology – coupled with experimentation and patience – in order to bear fruit. By Roman times, almost all of the major crops we know today were being grown somewhere in the world:

Plough on

The plough is an invention older than the wheel by as much as a thousand years, and its impact on human history has been just as profound. By turning over the soil, this simple device brought nutrients closer to the surface and returned crop residues, weeds and the goodness they contained to the soil. The ancient Egyptians tied their ploughs to the horns of their oxen, and the Greeks added

wheels to theirs, making them easier to steer. In the Americas, meanwhile, the absence of large domesticated draught animals such as oxen meant they had to make do with digging sticks to till the soil, which limited the type of land on which crops could be grown.

The process of tilling the land has left a deep impression on our culture and our language: every time we talk of ploughing back profits, having a furrowed brow, or a harrowing experience or even a ploughman's lunch, we're harking back to our agricultural roots. But in the last twenty years there have been growing signs that ploughing's days are numbered. This is because ploughing, especially with a state-of-the-art 500hp tractor, is a major contributor to **soil erosion** and a cause of **flooding**. Long term, it degrades the quality of the soil, as became apparent in the US during the years of the **Dust Bowl** in the 1930s, when drought caused recently ploughed-up grassland soil to dry up and simply blow away. With it went the livelihoods of thousands of farming families.

New **low-impact systems** for preparing the soil are increasingly popular, such as no-till, min-till and lo-till, which, as their names suggest, do not churn up a foot of topsoil, but merely "tickle" it, disturbing it just enough to plant the seed. Though yields dip initially, with careful management they recover to former levels. These systems also encourage bird life, attracted to stubble fields which remain unploughed over the winter.

maize in Mexico, soya beans in China, sorghum in Africa. The "big three" – **maize, wheat** and **rice** – were already well established, and since these cereals are toxic if eaten raw, the birth of agriculture also meant the development of cooking.

The **domestication of animals** had begun even earlier than that of wheat (see box below). Again, inhabitants of the Fertile Crescent were fortunate in having several species suitable for domestication readily available: sheep, pigs, goats and cattle. Other continents could offer no appropriate candidates: the majority of large mammals rule themselves out for domestication for any number of reasons; many are simply too bad-tempered (zebras, for example, bite and don't let go), too prone to panic (gazelles) or too reluctant to breed in captivity.

Agriculture advances

The Greeks and Romans understood that growing the same crop in a field year after year led to diminishing returns and so allowed fields to lie fallow every other year, but it was only in the Middle Ages that the full benefits of **crop rotation** became apparent. By growing wheat or rye in one field, pea or bean crops in another and leaving a third fallow, medieval farmers could increase the output from their land, and in doing so, improve the health of the people. The Middle Ages also saw other technological advances in agriculture, such as watermills for milling grain and the widespread use of the more effective "heavy plough" pulled by horses in the recently developed harness, rather than lumbering oxen.

Animal tamers: domesticating animals

Species	Date domesticated (BC)	Place domesticated
Dog	10,000	SW Asia, China, N America
Sheep	8000	SW Asia
Goat	8000	SW Asia
Pig	8000	China, SW Asia
Cow	6000	SW Asia, India, N Africa
Horse	4000	Ukraine

Dates and places shown are the earliest for which there is evidence.

Agriculture changed little until the eighteenth century, when the enclosure of land and new tools such as the metal plough and Jethro Tull's seed-drill helped bring about the first **agricultural revolution**. A four-crop rotation system devised in Holland encouraged **animal husbandry**, since turnips were one of the four crops and could be used as animal feed. The animals' manure in turn fed the soil.

In the Victorian period steamships and refrigeration meant agricultural goods could be traded on an international scale. By the second half of the nineteenth century, millions of **food miles** had already being clocked up: the US was exporting cereals from its vast former grasslands from which millions of buffalo and native North Americans had been cleared, and South America and Australia were exporting refrigerated meat by the shipload.

The wars and since

World War I highlighted the fact that Britain had become dangerously dependent on imports to feed itself; well over half the food the country consumed was imported in the early decades of last century. This was clearly unsustainable in time of war, so the government launched a major drive to make British farming more productive. Farmers were lauded as national heroes during both world wars, and in the post-war world they seemed to be able to do no wrong, as yields increased year on year through the miracle of chemical fertilizers and heavy machinery. By 1945, three-quarters of food Britain consumed was home-grown, thanks in part to the vastly increased the amount of land under arable cultivation.

Mechanization continued apace post-war, encouraged by generous state loans. In the 1940s, 90% of cows were hand-milked. By 1960 only 10% were. The emphasis of the government's post-war agriculture policy, expressed in the 1947 Agriculture Act, was on stability and efficiency. Agriculture would not be left to chance and the market. Stability would come through guaranteeing prices and assuring farmers there would be a market for their food. Efficiency would result from the widespread adoption of new scientific methods of farming. In 1973 the UK took the momentous step of joining the EEC, which has had a profound effect of food policy ever since. This is the era we are still living in today (see pp.21–23).

All in the soil

Sixty years ago, with memories of wartime food shortages still vivid, a new industrial approach to agriculture was developed to create plentiful, affordable food for all. Traditional practices of mixed farming and careful land management were pushed aside to make way for the new chemical fertilizers and pesticides, which promised a high-yield, low-maintenance monoculture (single crop) method of farming.

The problem we face today is that half a century of intensive farming has robbed the soil of its nutrients, leaving it in such a degraded state that soil erosion is now a major global problem, reducing both the land fit for agriculture and crop yields. Globally, as we get richer we are eating nearly our own body weight in meat each year, putting ever more pressure on the land to provide the vast amounts of crops needed for animal feed.

Agricultural land is also under threat from a new pressure: the demand for biofuel crops (see pp.122–124). We are at a crossroads with a variety of options before us, such as GM foods (see pp.144–154), meat reduction and organic and low-input farming.

Soil is a vital part of the Earth's structure and essential to our well-being. Without healthy soil we would starve: nearly everything we eat either grows in soil or is fed on what grows in it. And almost all vegetation relies on it for water and nutrients. But soil is extremely slow to replenish itself: it takes between a hundred and a thousand years to form just one centimetre of new soil. Conversely, it can be destroyed within a generation through unsustainable farming practices, climate change and other human intervention such as building and pollution. Soil is therefore effectively a **non-renewable resource** which needs protecting.

Science magazine has called soil one of the most complicated bio-materials on the planet, as it is a composite of minerals (rock-weathering products, many of them created by the last Ice Age) and organic matter (decomposing plant material) as well as the product of complex interactions between climate, geology, plants, biological activity, time and human action.

A top layer of **humus** contains most of the organic matter. Humus is the key to healthy soil and is responsible for its capacity to retain a large percentage of water. The next layer down consists of tiny particles of decayed leaves, twigs and animal remains. Insoluble minerals are also found here, whereas soluble minerals are found in the subsequent layer as they leach down. Underpinning all this, 1–10m below the surface, is the bedrock. Humus and poly-saccharide gums, produced by the soil's micro-organisms, glue soil particles together to resist erosion and form the soil's crumb structure. It is the aerated nature of soil which allows roots to penetrate it and plants to grow.

//We stand, in most places on Earth, only six inches from desolation, for that is the thickness of the topsoil layer upon which the entire life of the planet depends.//

R. Neil Sampson,
Farmland or Wasteland,
1981

//Organic matter is one of the most important components of soil ... Changing farming methods have reduced organic matter concentrations in some soils.//

The Environment
Agency, 2008

It's a bug's life

There are around five billion living organisms in just one teaspoonful of healthy soil and 10,000 different species. Bacteria's function centres around the metabolic processes within the soil. Fungi break down most of the organic matter and in some cases also help the uptake of nutrients into plant roots. Micro-organisms are essential to soil function: they create structure, convert organic matter into humus, protect against erosion and aid water retention, drainage, aeration and compaction resistance. Larger soil life includes the familiar earthworms. There are 25 species of earth-worms in Britain and they can live for up to five years. During this time they eat their way through enormous amounts of soil each day to create a network of pores, which helps drainage and aeration. Other soil life such as mites and beetles break up organic matter and help recycle nutrients – working with the microscopic protozoa and nematodes to feed off the bacteria and fungi and in so doing **releasing nitrogen** and minerals back into the soil for plant use.

The biological life of soil is responsible for its fertility. It releases minerals from the sub-soil, fixes atmospheric nutrients into the soil and transports nutrients directly to plant roots. But all this is threatened by the barrage of fertilizers and pesticides which we've been pouring onto the soil over the last fifty years. Inorganic fertilizer suppresses soil life, unlike organic matter, killing off bacteria and fungi, disrupting the delicate balance of soil life and leaving it less fertile. This in turn encourages the increased use of chemicals to encourage plant growth in compromised soil.

When soil gets sick

A fertile soil with plenty of microbial life is capable of supplying all our mineral needs. Intensive farming has severely depleted soil life and its mineral content: nutrient levels in soil fell dramatically between 1940 and 1991 to the extent that fruit and vegetable mineral levels are now 15–76% lower than in 1940. This has implications for our health, too; our bodies need a regular supply of seven **key macro-minerals**: calcium, chloride, magnesium, phosphorus, potassium, sodium, and sulphur for good health (plus a range of trace minerals including boron, cobalt, copper, chromium, iodine, iron, manganese, selenium and zinc).

In 2001 the European Commission indicated that soil loss and declining soil fertility were a major threat to sustainable development, because they diminish the viability of agricultural land. It has been estimated that 52 million hectares of land in the EU (16% of the total land area) are affected by **soil degradation**. Soil problems have global consequences for **food security, poverty reduction, water protection** and **biodiversity**. Soil

Pasture

Only a few decades ago our countryside was full of mixed farms which grew crops and also reared livestock. Today's industrial approach has led to **monocultures** (concentration on a single crop-type), which put intense pressure on the soil, sustained in the short term by increased chemical use. The reduction in soil quality is discernible in the meat we eat: the iron content of meat has dropped by over 70% since 1940, putting us at an increased risk of anaemia (see p.189).

Pasturelands need high-quality soil in order to pass on essential nutrients to animals through the grass they eat. In the past, permanent pasture meadows remained unploughed and therefore retained a great variety of flowers and grasses.

Organic farmers plant clover alongside grass to increase soil fertility. Pasture fields are grazed for part of the year and then the grass is cut to be dried for hay, or packaged and fermented for silage. **Intensive livestock farming** creates the conditions for disease and poor soil quality through continuous grazing by the same species of livestock season after season.

Soil facts

▶ **Soil is the top layer of dynamic material** on the surface of the Earth in which plants grow. Without soil cover, there would only be barren rock or sand.

▶ **Plants take up nutrients** (especially nitrogen, calcium, phosphorus, potassium and iron) from the soil through their roots.

▶ **Soil retains and filters water** reducing the risk of pollution and flooding.

▶ **75% of land in the UK is agricultural** But only 16% is classed as top quality.

▶ **Only one-tenth of the Earth's surface is ploughable, arable land** Another 8% is used as pasture for grazing animals.

degradation has often been cited as the most frequent cause of cultural decline and total **civilization collapse** in the past. Today, with well over six-and-a-half billion inhabitants on Earth, the consequences of inaction are likely to be felt globally. Here are the warning signs of sick soil:

▶ **Compaction** reduces the pore space between soil particles, diminishing its capacity to absorb water and air. This is caused by the use of heavy machinery, or dense stocking rates typical in intensive farming, which subject soils to extensive pressure. Compaction alone can drastically reduce crop yields.

▶ **Contamination** occurs through the introduction to the soil of chemical compounds, biological organisms or other materials which negatively affect or alter soil function. It can occur through deposition from the atmosphere (acid rain), deliberate application (fertilizer), spillage, leakage or illegal dumping.

▶ **Reduced biodiversity** can have drastic consequences for soil fertility, as many of the key process underpinning these functions depend on soil life.

▶ **Loss of organic matter** adversely affects key soil functions and fertility. A Swiss trial found organic land had much greater levels of soil microbial mass and soil particle stability. The European Soil Bureau estimates that 75% of southern Europe is at pre-desertification stage.

▶ **Erosion** is the final stage of soil degradation. A recent UK government survey suggests that 44% of arable land is prone to erosion. Soil has always been eroded by wind and water, but human activity has greatly accelerated post-war to the point that is it a serious threat to food production worldwide. In China and India combined, more than twelve million square kilometres have been severely eroded since 1945 through deforestation, overgrazing and farming. In parts of the Mediterranean, the erosion rate is as high as 20cm per century and in Africa it's up to 2m per century.

Carbon footprints in the soil

Twenty percent of the UK's **greenhouse gas emissions** are the result of food production and farming. Soil contains about twice as much carbon as the atmosphere and vegetation combined, making soil protection a key component of the fight against climate change. England's soils have been losing carbon at the rate of four million tonnes a year for the past 25 years.

Agricultural activity has been releasing soil carbon for the last 10,000 years, but most emissions have occurred over the last century, mainly as a result of ploughing. Emissions tripled between 1945 and 1986. Recent rises in temperatures have encouraged greater microbial activity and faster decay of organic matter, in turn creating greater gas emissions.

Nitrous oxide fertilizers are the largest source of carbon dioxide emissions in agriculture and the single largest source of the deadly nitrous oxide, which has 296 times more impact than CO_2. Nearly half of the food eaten globally is produced with nitrogen fertilizer and its use worldwide is growing fast. Artificial fertilizers increase greenhouse gas emissions at all stages:

▶ **Greenhouse gas emissions** from the manufacturing and transport of nitrogen fertilizer are estimated at 6.7 tonnes CO_2 equivalent per tonne.

▶ Chemical fertilizers are made from finite **fossil fuel** supplies.

▶ Production of fertilizer is an **energy-intensive** process, accounting for nearly 2% of the world's total energy consumption.

▶ **Lime applications** are needed to counteract the acidifying effect of the fertilizer on the soil. The manufacture of lime produces more carbon dioxide.

▶ **Fertilizers suppress soil micro-organisms** that oxidize atmospheric methane.

▶ Artificial fertilizers cause plants to produce weak root systems. This means less carbon is built up in the soil, causing an on-going **net loss of carbon** from the soil.

By contrast, **organic farming is climate friendly**: life-cycle analyses by the UK Government have found that organic farming generally uses 26% less energy than intensive farming to produce the same amount of food (29% less energy for wheat, 38% less for milk and 35% less for beef).

The coming of the chemicals

Nitrogen makes up 78% of the air we breathe. It is also a key element in **plant growth**, since nitrogen is a component of chlorophyll, which is vital to photosynthesis. Air-borne nitrogen requires "fixing" in the soil through certain plants which are able to extract it, such as alfalfa, clover, beans and peas.

Historically, farmers returned nitrogen to the soil through rotting organic matter, or else (less ecologically sound) they abandoned exhausted fields for newly cleared tracts with higher nitrogen levels. In the late nineteenth century, supplements in the form of sodium nitrate from Chilean mines were shipped to Europe for use in both agriculture and munitions. But these sources were finite. A British chemist, Sir William Crookes, warned in 1898 "we are drawing on the Earth's capital, and our drafts will not perpetually be honoured". In other words, food shortages loomed for the growing populations of the industrialized west.

A world-changing breakthrough came in 1909 when German chemist **Fritz Haber** combined hydrogen and nitrogen in high-temperature, high-pressure conditions. Through this process he successfully created ammonia, which could be converted into fertilizer in the form of a soluble salt which farmers could spread on their land. Ammonium nitrate's explosive properties also boosted the German armaments industry in World War I.

The so-called **Haber–Bosch process** has been described as the most important invention of the twentieth century. As if by magic, harvests could be increased four-fold. When China foresaw a food crisis in the 1970s, for example, it responded by building vast ammonium nitrate plants. China's economic miracle owes a debt to the Haber–Bosch process. In fact, without Haber's process the Earth would be able to sustain two billion fewer people. In other words, around one-third of human life today owes its existence to Fritz Haber.

Hero or villain? Fritz Haber's work earned him the Nobel Prize for Chemistry in 1918, though he was also a pioneer in the field of chemical warfare. Poison gas, he wrote, turns "warfare into chess".

Nitrogen: solution or problem?

"Bread from air" was the boast at the start of last century when nitrates were first synthesized. One big biochemical company today calls it "truly a superstar of food production". While it is undoubtedly true that nitrogen fertilizers have boosted harvests, the extra food comes at a price:

▶ Nitrogen fertilizers have been criticized for producing plants that are **poor in nutrients**, prone to disease and therefore need more pesticide treatment.

▶ When nitrogen fertilizer is introduced into the soil, microbes have to work hard to break it down. They need energy in order to do this, and obtain that energy from the available soil organic matter or humus. This leads ultimately to a "**burning out** of the soil".

▶ Nitrogen fertilizers contribute to **soil degradation and water pollution**. Defra (the Department for Environment, Food and Rural Affairs) has identified high (and rising) levels of nitrates in water, much of which comes from agricultural land in the form of "run-off".

▶ Over time, nitrogen residues can have a devastating effect on the **environment**. They can cause algaes to bloom in lakes and suffocate fish; they combine with water in the atmosphere and fall back to Earth as acid rain; and damage ecosystems.

▶ The world is suffering a **nitrogen imbalance**: most of the northern hemisphere has too much nitrogen and Africa's soil is severely depleted.

Pesticides
The hidden extras on your plate

"Pesticide" is a catch-all terms for the vast array of chemicals that are available to farmers, including weedkillers, fungicides and seed treatments. Around the world an estimated three billion kilogrammes of pesticides are sprayed on crops each year, much of it to meet supermarkets' demand for cosmetically perfect produce. Pesticide production is big business ($32 billion in 2006) and the industry is dominated by multinational chemical giants such as BASF, Bayer, DuPont and Monsanto. They have vast research and marketing budgets, and a keen interest in promoting GM crops (see Chapter 10).

Chemical pesticides have been in widespread use only since the end of World War II (indeed, their development went hand in hand with developments in chemical warfare). Post-war, as part of the drive to increase domestic food production, the chemical companies were given free rein by governments to bring new products to market, and regulation of the industry's impact on human health in the UK remained by voluntary agreement until 1986.

What's your poison?

Non-organic UK farmers currently have access to over 350 pesticides. In 2006, arable crops in the UK were treated with nearly 20,000 tonnes of pesticides. By the time it is harvested, the average wheat crop will have received three applications of weed-killer, three of fungicide and one each of growth regulator and insecticide. Fruit crops can receive many more sprayings than that. Treatments are also given to crops after they are harvested in order to prolong their life and prevent damage by pests while in storage. All the while, **pesticide resistance** is rising alarmingly, leading manufacturers to increase the toxicity of the chemicals they sell.

The impact of pesticides

The sheer ubiquity of artificial chemicals in the environment and our food makes it difficult to isolate particular effects on our health. But as scientists learn more about the toxicity of pesticides more questions are being raised about their safety.

▶**Fatalities and poisonings** The World Health Organization (WHO) estimates there are 220,000 pesticide-related deaths and up to 26 million direct poisonings worldwide each year, many the result of inadequate training or safety regimes in developing countries. Closer to home, there is growing evidence of health problems suffered by those who live near agricultural land treated with pesticides.

▶ **Persistent Organic Pollutants** These are some of the most pernicious chemical substances ever created, including DDT, dioxins, PCBs (polychlorinated biphenyls) and Chlordane (traces of DDT, see p.18, have been found in polar bears). They have been linked to cancers and birth abnormalities. An international treaty banned twelve POPs in 2003 (the "dirty dozen") but they continue to pose a threat to people and wildlife because POPs accumulate in the food we eat. They remain in the body's fatty tissue and "biomagnify", which means they become more pronounced the higher up the food chain they go.

▶ **Pesticide residues in food** Pesticide sprays leave residues in our food. Residues have been detected in up to 30% of food tested in the UK. Washing and peeling can help in the case of fruit and veg, but traces of up to eight different pesticides have been found on single pieces of fruit, such as grapes and pears, for sale in the UK. Pesticides have been linked to a host of diseases and ailments, from allergies to cancers.

▶ **Killers, by design** Pesticides have been carefully designed by scientists to disrupt nervous and reproductive systems of insects; the problem is they may also harm humans too. There are a great many unknowns regarding the effects of these chemicals on humans. Pesticides have been linked to rising male infertility. A 2005 Washington State University study exposed pregnant rats to fungicides and pesticides. Their subsequent male offspring had a sperm count reduced by 20%; these effects were passed onto the majority of subsequent generations. Dr Michael Skinner, who led the research team, said: "The hazards of environmental toxins are much more pronounced that we realized."

Testing for pesticides

The **Pesticide Residues Committee** (PRC) is the body entrusted by the UK government with testing food for chemical contamination. The PRC tests a range of everyday foods every quarter and publishes its findings, but it has come under fire in the past for not taking action quickly enough when the **Maximum Residue Levels** (MRL) have been exceeded and

for testing too few samples to give a true picture of the extent of residues in food. The committee tends

While we in the West may worry about pesticide residues on our fresh fruit, this African boy is using an old pesticide container to draw water from a well, with potentially fatal consequences.

Babies and young children: at particular risk?

Weight for weight, they eat almost twice the amount of fruit and vegetables as adults, three times the amount of bread and cereals and five times the amount of dairy produce. The very foods which form a large part of the early diet of Western children – apples, bananas and pears – contain the highest **pesticide residues** (see p.102). It is only in the last decade that the results of increased research into the effects of pesticides on the highly sensitive **endocrine (hormone) system** at key stages in development have shown in many cases that these can interfere with normal endocrine signalling and function even at ultra-low levels. Other research has indicated that foetuses and children exposed to residues may be affected detrimentally as regards the development of their organs, immune and nervous systems. Some of the pesticides commonly used in 2007 are known to pass through the placenta.

There is also some suggestion that the concentrations of sufferers of childhood bone marrow disease, aplastic anaemia and related immune system conditions could be linked to rural pesticide use. The Royal Commission on Environmental Pollution's 2005 report on crop-spraying noted that the Government's Advisory Committee on Pesticides gave "little recognition" to the fact that "there could be important differences in the susceptibility of individuals within the human population".

Concern about food purity and toxic chemicals leads three-quarters of new parents to buy organic food for the first time. Such has been the demand for organic baby food that Sainsbury's has withdrawn its non-organic own-label baby food range.

to return a "no cause for concern" verdict, even when samples exceed the MRL or multiple pesticide traces are found in a single sample.

The battle over the significance of chemical residues is a fierce one, as it relates directly to people's attitude to intensive large-scale agriculture. Responses range from treating residues as an irrelevance to human health to treating them as a potential time bomb, since we are all building up a store of a wide variety of chemicals in our bodies (the so-called **cocktail effect** argument).

The chemical industry is large and powerful and is able to counter objections to particular pesticides with new, improved formulas. And the pesticide testing bodies have no resources to test for all chemicals or the combined effect of pesticides in the human body. Pesticides which share the same "toxicological mode of action" might be expected to have a compound effect in the body, but it has been calculated that even to test for the potential effects of all combinations of two dozen common chemicals would cost $3 trillion. At least you can be sure of one thing: organic samples (in all but a tiny fraction of cases of accidental contamination) are residue-free.

DDT: an early environmental victory

DDT was the first synthetic pesticide of the modern age. Used first against mosquitoes to combat malaria, its often indiscriminate agricultural use took off after World War II. US biologist **Rachel Carson** was appalled by the poison's effect on the environment, especially wildlife, and in 1962 published *Silent Spring*, a book which provided a powerful impetus for the fledgling environmental movement. Carson's book tapped into public distrust of sprayed chemicals to such an extent that *Time* magazine called Carson one of the hundred most influential people of the twentieth century. The book led to the banning of the agricultural use of DDT in the US in 1972, the first major victory for US environmental campaigners. (Britain waited till 1984 to implement a ban.)

However, DDT has a half-life of up to fifteen years, which means traces of it are still in the soil and are still being found. Most of us have DDT residues stored in our body fat. Links to cancer are claimed but not conclusively proven, but the WHO rates it as "moderately hazardous".

From sheep dip to Gulf War syndrome

Organophosphate pesticides have been in widespread use since the 1960s (for example in sheep dip) and currently account for 38% of all pesticides worldwide. They are also among the most controversial. The World Health Organization describes their effects: "Organophosphates inhibit the destruction of the neurotransmitter such that the neurons are constantly being stimulated and the message is repeatedly transmitted from one neuron to the next ... organophosphates can cause change in heart rate, tremors, muscle weakness or paralysis, restlessness, mental

Discarded pesticide containers on a dump site. The disposal of obsolete pesticides is a big problem, especially in Africa.

confusion, loss of memory, convulsions and coma."

A 1951 report recommending they be labelled "deadly poison" was ignored for a quarter of a century. In the 1980s and 90s farm workers who had been exposed to low levels of organophosphates over a long period began reporting symptoms similar to those in the WHO list. The UK government has commissioned research into their effects, but maintains that organophosphates are safe. (When the government withdraws a pesticide licence, it becomes liable for substantial compensation claims from the manufacturer.) Organophosphate nerve gas is also the suspected cause of Gulf War syndrome.

> **//** It is simply impossible to predict the effects of lifetime exposure to chemicals and physical agents that are not part of the biological experience of man. **//**
>
> Rachel Carson

Taking on the pesticides industry: the EU ban

"No groups of the population are exposed to residues in food at levels that threaten their health." European Crop Protection Association, 2008

Nearly forty pesticides which we were promised were safe have been banned or withdrawn from use over the past decade. The EU's top ten insecticides are considered hazardous by the World Health Organization (WHO) and use of insecticides has more than doubled over the past decade within the EU. The EU recently succeeded in banning a highly toxic nerve poison, endosulfan (a persistent organochlorine), against a three-year legal challenge by a group of agrichemical firms led by Bayer CropScience.

In 2006, after extensive new research, the EU recommended a ban on a further 23 pesticides: those officially recognized as being carcinogenic, mutagenic (altering genetic information resulting in subsequent mutations), reprotoxic (affecting fertility) or endocrine disrupting (responsible for birth defects) all of which have been found to be present as residues in food. Others, including the UK, fought the proposed ban. The research showed that of over 60,000 food samples (including baby foods), 40% contained pesticide residues and a further 3% contained levels in excess of EC MRLs. Some countries immediately banned some of the named pesticides.

With each new pesticide costing about £150 million to launch onto the market, the industry body, the European Crop Protection Association (ecpa.eu), lobbied aggressively against the ban. But how reassuring is their stance: "just as coffee and alcohol are hazardous at high doses, normal use [of agro-chemicals] poses no risk to health"? They also warned that banning dangerous pesticides would lead to food price rises. In November 2008, despite strong industry opposition, MEPs backed the ban and additionally voted to end most plane-spraying.

Is there a better way?

There certainly seems to be a good argument for seeking alternatives to pesticides when you consider that that only an estimated 0.01% of pesticides applied actually reach their intended target. The remaining 99.99% ends up elsewhere in the environment. Organic farming makes do with just four pesticides (see p.100). Beneficial parasites and predators can also help combat pests as can crop rotation, maintaining soil fertility and controlling planting time and crop density. **Integrated Pest Management** is an ecological method of pest control that doesn't rule out chemical pesticides, but aims to use them as just one element in the armoury. For further information on pesticides, see:

Pesticides Residue Committee pesticides.gov.uk/prc_home.asp This body keeps an eye on the residue levels of the foods you eat (they're listed by supermarket and brand in their quarterly reports).

The Pesticides Action Network pan-uk.org Independent, non-profit organization which provides the latest news and research on pesticide abuses and problems. They work with other organizations such as Friends of the Earth to support farmers who want to farm without pesticides, reduce stockpile pollution and raise awareness of the problems of pesticide use.

Denmark: setting a good example

In the 1990s the Danes got tough on pesticide use and banned all but 78 of them. High taxes were imposed on the permitted pesticides, but simultaneously an information campaign showed farmers that if they sprayed less, savings on pesticides would more than compensate for slightly lower crop yields.

As a result Denmark has reduced its use of agro-chemicals by more than half. The Danish government has been actively encouraging organic farming for two decades and the Danes are currently the biggest consumers of organic produce in Europe.

Farming today

It's telling that when the industry magazine, *Farmers Weekly*, chose the top twenty influential people in UK agriculture, number one spot went not to a British or international politician but to Tesco boss Sir Terry Leahy. The magazine dubbed him "the man farmers love to hate", but given that Tesco controls 30% of the grocery market in Britain, Leahy is the man the majority of farmers have to please. Farmers find themselves caught between retailers who are unwilling to pass on rising production costs to their customers and a public who are ever more concerned about food quality, provenance, the environment and animal welfare, but still hooked on cheap food. When farmers look to the future and express guarded optimism it is generally because of the growing demand for food due to rising world population and the new market for biofuels. Hope is also being placed in biotech (see Chapter 10).

"Weed it and reap": farming in the age of the subsidy

EU farm subsidy policy may not be high on anyone's list of riveting reading, but it has had a profound effect on the state of agriculture, so here's just as much as you need to know: subsidies for agriculture were part of the EEC (as it was then called) right from the start. France wouldn't let Germany have access to its markets for industrial goods without an agreement on farm prices to protect French agriculture. From the early 1960s, the **Common Agricultural Policy** (CAP) developed into a many-tentacled beast that affected all aspects of European food production.

Under the CAP, farmers were encouraged to grow certain crops through guarantees of a minimum level of payment for them. At the same time, imports from outside the EU were subject to tariffs and quotas, which penalized farmers from other parts of the world. The result was overproduction of basic commodities in the 1970s and 80s, the infamous **butter mountains** and **wine lakes**. The EU's answer to paying farmers to grow too much was "set-aside", in other words, paying them not to grow so much.

The CAP has devoured a vast proportion of the EU's (vast) total budget (up to 61%). It still accounts for 40% of the budget (€55bn per annum) and the fact that France has taken the lion's share year after year has fuelled the wrath of many a British Eurosceptic. The CAP has been subject to fierce criticism throughout its life – for distorting the market, for penalizing farmers in the developing world through import tariffs and

Red tractor: reassurance for shoppers?

The Red Tractor British Farm Standard scheme is one of more than two dozen potentially confusing **food assurance schemes**. It was launched in 2000 by the food and farming industries. The Red Tractor logo itself is owned by the National Farmers' Union (NFU), which licenses it to other bodies. It guarantees that food bearing its label has been produced to **basic food safety and hygiene standards** as well as **animal welfare** and **environmental criteria**. Currently nearly eighty thousand British farms use the mark. The scheme seeks to give quality and traceability reassurance to the consumer, but has been widely criticized for having little true value. In December 2000, the Government's Advisory Committee on Consumer Products and the Environment felt it was "not clear that the schemes involved merited the claims being made ... They appeared to incorporate only minimum legal requirements on the environment." Compassion in World Farming maintain that the Red Tractor "is not a guarantee of good animal welfare and allows intensive production."

Take chicken farming for example: the Red Tractor scheme places greatest emphasis on **biosecurity** such as salmonella prevention and disinfection. But vaccination programmes are permitted and beak trimming allowed. There is no mention of letting birds perch or peck, only space to "walk, turn, sit, preen, flap/stretch their wings and dustbathe".

Many people concerned with animal welfare have come to the conclusion that the Red Tractor is a welfare-lite scheme. See views for and against here:

Red Tractor redtractor.org.uk

Compassion in World Farming ciwf.org.uk

rewarding the big players over the small. (And the EU also still subsidizes tobacco farming to the tune of one-third of a billion euros a year.) In the US, agricultural policy has followed a similar pattern.

When it comes to harvesting healthy Euro-subsidies, it has always helped to be a big player. It's reckoned that 80% of the cash available goes to just 20% of the EU's farmers. Some large farms and estates qualify for annual awards well over £1 million. The Co-op Group, which owns the UK's biggest commercial farm group, Farmcare Ltd, got £2.4 million in 2008. The Queen had to make do with £400,000 for her Sandringham Estates.

Recent reforms have "decoupled" subsidies from production, Eurospeak for offering a payment according to size and environmental stewardship of the land rather than output. Such things as food safety and animal welfare are also part of the deal. While some parts of the CAP have yet to be reformed, the main shift is towards viewing funds as contributing to the rural economy in its broadest sense, rather just to the production of commodities.

The UK and most other EU governments have been very reluctant to divulge who has benefited most from EU subsidies, but freedom of information legislation means that there should soon be much more detail available about how much multinational food giants such as Tate and Lyle and Nestlé and members of the royal family have gained from subsidies. It's measured in millions. Find out who gets what from the CAP, and see which countries aren't refusing to let on:

Farm Subsidy farmsubsidy.org

The organic alternative

There is a good deal of confusion over what organic agriculture actually is. Most people think of it more in terms of what it *doesn't* do (use pesticides or chemical fertilizers) rather than what it does. Just as the term "conventional farming" is very broad, organic is also a broad church

How now, brown cow: an organic success story

Brown Cow Farm is an award-winning beef and dairy farm in Somerset run by husband-and-wife team, Clive and Judith Freane. They explained to Rough Guides their reasons for going organic: "It was following the BSE crisis in the mid-1990s that we decided that, as parents of very young children, the only way we wanted to produce food was organically." That way, they could be certain it was safe and traceable, a guarantee offered by no other system. So out went the pesticides and the chemical fertilizers, and they've never looked back since. Their meat has been acclaimed by the likes of Jamie Oliver and Raymond Blanc, and frequently elicits the response "it's the best I've ever tasted".

Judith and Clive run a dairy herd of one hundred Guernsey cows, which produces the rich, creamy milk they use in their yoghurts. The Guernseys also provide the calves that go into their beef enterprise. In conventional farming, these males calves would normally be killed at birth. Pre-war, their mixed dairy and beef system would have been the norm, but the revelation that flavoursome beef could be produced from what was regarded as a dairy breed, Judith explains, "tipped the beef industry upside down".

To what do they attribute the exceptional quality of their beef? Judith believes it's due to a number of factors, including their careful stock breeding, concern for animal welfare and the balanced nutrition the animals get. The meat is hung and butchered on site, too, giving Brown Cow complete control over the quality of their beef. There have also been other benefits on the farm, such as the dramatic increase in the bio-diversity of its flora and fauna, including herons, buzzards and kingfishers.

It may be based in an idyllic setting, but Brown Cow is a modern forward-thinking business, which is looking to extend its brand with a new products such as a range of leather luggage. You can find Brown Cow on-line, at David Lidgate's butchers in London and at local farmers' markets.

Brown Cow Organics, Perridge Farm, Pilton, Somerset, browncoworganics.co.uk

David Lidgate, Holland Park Avenue, W11 ▷ 020 7727 8243

(including, for example, biodynamic growers who plant according to the phases of the moon). A more generally agreed set of **aims and principles**, though, is set out by the International Federation of Organic Agriculture Movements (ifoam.org):

▶ To produce sufficient quantities of **high-quality food**, fibre and other products.

▶ To work compatibly with **natural cycles and living systems** through the soil, plants and animals in the entire production system.

▶ To recognize the wider **social and ecological impact** of the organic system.

▶ To maintain and increase **long-term fertility and biological activity of soils** without reliance on chemical inputs.

▶ To maintain and encourage **biodiversity** through the use of sustainable production systems and the protection of wildlife habitats.

▶ To maintain and conserve **genetic diversity**.

▶ To promote the responsible use and **conservation of water** and aquatic life.

▶ To use, as far as possible, **renewable resources** and avoid pollution and waste.

▶ To foster **local and regional** production and distribution.

▶ To create a harmonious **balance** between **crop production and animal husbandry**.

Organic livestock: small but growing

	Organic Animals	% of UK total	
Poultry	4,421,000	2.5	Organically produced
Sheep	747,000	2.1	
Cattle	245,000	2.4	Conventionally produced
Pigs	33,000	0.7	

Estimated number of organically reared animals and animals "in conversion" in the UK (2007).

▶ To provide living conditions that allows animals to express the basic aspects of their **innate behaviour**.

▶ To use biodegradable, **recyclable and recycled packaging**.

▶ To provide everyone involved in organic farming and processing with a **quality of life** that satisfies their basic needs, within a safe, secure and healthy working environment.

▶ To support the establishment of a **production, processing and distribution chain** which is socially just and ecologically responsible.

▶ To recognize the importance of, and protect and learn from, **indigenous knowledge** and **traditional farming** systems.

It takes at least two years for a farm to qualify as organic, during which time it is said to be **"in conversion"**. (Food labelled as "in conversion" is not fully organic, but on its way, and therefore tends to cost more than conventionally grown produce.) At present, 3.5% of agricultural land in the UK is organic or in conversion. Most of it is pasture or woodland. The areas with the highest percentage of organic land are the South West and Wales, which unsurprisingly is where most of the organic meat comes from.

In 1984 there were fewer than three hundred organic farms in the UK and the retail value of organic products was estimated at around £1 million. By the end of 2004 there were over 4300 organic farms UK, the market for organic food in the UK was the third largest in the world with over £1 billion in retail sales. Now it's rapidly heading towards £2 billion.

Defra has a plan to encourage organic food production with the aim that UK producers will be able to supply at least 70% of the domestic organic market with indigenous products by 2010. When the plan was published in 2002, only one-third of all organic products consumed here was home-produced. By 2005, the Soil Association estimated that that figure had risen to two-thirds.

External forces may put a brake on the growth of organic farming, however. While prices for conventionally grown wheat remain high, the incentive to put land into conversion may be weak. Likewise, biofuel crops are attracting farmers. At the same time, rising grain prices push up the production cost of organic meat, since organic animals must be fed almost exclusively on organic feed. (When organic feedstuffs are in short supply, Defra permits pigs and poultry to be fed up to 10% non-organic feed, though this has to be reduced to 5% from January 2010.)

Horticulture
Everything in the garden's rosy?

Whereas there are only a handful of main cereal crops grown in the UK, horticulture is much more diverse agricultural sector, embracing many different crops in the three major areas of **salad**, **field vegetables** and **fruit**: as many as three hundred major and three thousand minor horticultural products are estimated to be grown in the UK. Many farmers have turned away from common vegetables such as beans, peas and sprouts, as the profit margins are so slim; in the past decade the percentage of British land devoted to vegetable growing has shrunk by around one-quarter and with it the UK's veg self-sufficiency has gone from 71%

Hydroponics: tomatoes from the rainy north

Ever wondered why there are so many identical Dutch tomatoes in the supermarkets all year round? Holland is after all a small northern European country rather than a sun-kissed southern one. The answer is **hydroponics**, the science of growing plants without soil. In the hydroponic system, plants are grown in large, computer-controlled greenhouses in which the light, heat, humidity and water and nutrients needed by plants are all minutely regulated. Plant nutrition comes from a constant drip-feed of synthetic nitrogen fertilizer.

Hydroponics first took off after World War II, when cheap polythene suitable for greenhouses became available. Because hydroponic systems are expensive to set up and manage, they only make economic sense if you're growing **expensive crops** such as tomatoes, aubergines, strawberries, herbs and flowers. Hydroponics produce higher yields than field crops, as plants can be crowded together, their growth more tightly controlled and the growing season prolonged. Websites excitedly mention the possibility of growing food hydroponically in space.

Hydroponics produces food that is big, regular and bland, which suits the supermarkets, with their preference for uniformity, colour and appearance over taste and texture. Though hydroponics may at first look clean and green – after all, the absence of soil means no soil diseases to worry about and indoor environments make pests easier to keep at bay with fewer pesticides – it is nonetheless a system based on **high-energy inputs and chemicals**. Organic hydroponics are theoretically possible, though markedly at odds with the ethos of a cycle of production in harmony with nature. Interestingly, hydroponic advocates, who get excited about the "plump, juicy, unblemished fruit" which they can grow, rarely mention *taste* as a reason to adopt the system.

England's disappearing orchards

The apple is the quintessential English fruit. Well over two thousand varieties have been grown here over the centuries, often lovingly bred by growers who adapt the fruit to the soil and climate of a specific location. Many have highly evocative names that reveal their origins such as Keswick Codlin, Kentish Fillbasket and Yorkshire Greening. They vary greatly in taste, too: the pitmaster's pineapple tastes mildly of pineapple and the oaken pin has a hint of nutmeg.

But a visit to your local supermarket will often give the impression that the apple is a non-native fruit imported from France, New Zealand or South Africa and only available in half a dozen big, cosmetically perfect varieties such as Golden Delicious, Granny Smith, Gala and Fuji. Supermarkets are after as streamlined a supply chain as possible. They want rock-bottom prices, and regular, good-looking fruit – and lots of it. Small consignments of quirkily named and irregularly shaped fruit are just too much trouble.

The result of this has been a **drastic decline** in both the diversity of varieties grown and the number of orchards in the country. In the decade from 1990, as world apple production rose by one-third, English apple orchards shrank to half of their former extent and four hundred growers went out of business. Production has now dropped to less than one-quarter of the level it stood at just after World War II. Kent, the "garden of England", has lost a shocking 85% of its orchards in fifty years.

Even during English apple season, British supermarkets' commitment to stocking home-grown apples is more impressive in their marketing claims than in reality. A 2005 survey by Friends of the Earth found that only a little over one-third of apples in supermarkets were British. And what goes for apples also goes for those other traditional British orchard fruits: pears, plums and cherries.

▶ Declining English apple sales matter not only because of loss of livelihoods, heritage and flavours, but also because of the effect of the **landscape and wildlife habitats**; orchards are home to species of bats, woodpeckers and owls that are rare elsewhere in the countryside.

to 60% (fruit has remained static at 11%). The only areas which seem to be holding up strongly are the country's favourite vegetable, the carrot (we eat ten billion of them a year in the UK), and asparagus, which has a short season.

Naturally, horticulture is a seasonal industry, which means it is highly dependent on casual labour, much of which comes from Eastern Europe. "Were there not migrant workers in food and agriculture," according to union leader Jack Dromey, "food and agriculture would be in very serious difficulty." But it's not a sector with a good track record for the treatment of its employees. Farmers, who keep their permanent staff levels to a minimum, depend on so-called gangmasters to recruit

▶ The English apple season starts in July and runs through till spring, and many varieties have excellent storing properties and will **keep for months** if wrapped and stored in a cool place. Bramleys can keep for up to twelve months.

▶ **Common Ground** is an organization which campaigns for local distinctiveness and organizes a national Apple Day each year on 21 October.

What you can do: Stop buying tasteless imports and choose home-produced apples whenever you can. **Farm shops** and **farmers' markets** are a good source. Accept the fact that they won't be cosmetically perfect; it's a small price to pay for the superior taste. If you have space in your garden, get hold of the *Apple Source Book* (Hodder & Stoughton, 2007) and plant your own apple tree. The book is a

"celebration of nearly 3000 varieties of apple we can grow in these islands, with their distinctive flavours, uses, places of origin, stories and associated customs". It contains recipes, lists nurseries which sell apple trees and even has hints on cider-making.

The Brogdale Horticultural Trust, Kent brogdale.org is the home to the National Fruit Collection, the largest collection of varieties of fruit trees in the world.

Common Ground
commonground.org.uk

and supply the casual workers who harvest, sort and pack their fruit and vegetables.

Some **migrant workers** in the UK have reported shocking abuses of their rights, such as instances of wages being withheld, summary dismissals and appalling living conditions. Some commentators, such as Felicity Lawrence in her book *Not on the Label*, have compared its worst excesses to a form of modern-day slavery. Supermarkets, meanwhile, have tended to look the other way until abuses are splashed all over the front covers of newspapers. The unfortunate reality for the industry is that it is the supermarkets' relentless pressure to drive costs down which gives rise to these labour practices in the first place.

It was the drowning of twenty-three Chinese cockle-pickers in Morecambe Bay in 2004 that led the government to crack down on gang-masters and introduce a licensing authority with the power to put the worst offenders throughout the agricultural and fisheries industries out of business.

Livestock
Casting a long shadow

As a species we are consuming more meat than ever before: world per capita meat consumption has doubled since the 1960s and, on current projections, by 2050 it will have doubled again. Throughout most of human history it was very different; the majority of people were peasants and the bulk of their diets were made up of staple grains. But meat has a long association with affluence; as western societies have become wealthier since the war, they have spent ever more on meat, and now developing nations with more disposable income are catching up fast. Their diets are changing to resemble that of the west, which means more meat (especially chicken and pork), dairy and eggs. Worldwide, average meat consumption is currently around a quarter pound per person per day, though Americans chomp their way through twice that much.

In the developed world, meanwhile, after health warnings about the dangers of eating too much red meat, our appetite for meat seems to be levelling off. In the last 25 years demand for beef and lamb has declined, but there has been a jump in demand for chicken worldwide. Meat-eating remains woven into our lives socially and economically. One person in five on Earth is engaged in some way with livestock, and production is increasingly taking place on vast industrial-scale farms, especially in south-east Asia and South America.

Our growing carnivorousness has a massive **environmental impact**: to produce the 52 billion animals the world's population eats each year, we already use 30% of the Earth's ice-free land. Cattle convert calories in their feed into calories in their flesh at a ratio as poor as ten to one (ten kilos of feed to produce one kilo of meat). So one-third of the global grain harvest now goes into animal feed, and animals now consume far more protein edible by humans in the form of grains than they provide.

Not only is livestock production resource-intensive, it also plays a major role in **greenhouse gas emissions** and environmental degradation. Nearly one-fifth of total greenhouse gas emissions are due to livestock production, and livestock account for four-fifths of total agricultural emissions. A report in 2006 by the UN's Food and Agriculture Organization, *Livestock's Long Shadow*, reckoned that the livestock industry's effect on climate, the environment and biodiversity was "truly enormous". It calculated, for example, that animal waste was probably the largest cause of water pollution in the developing world and a larger contributor of greenhouse gases than all road transport. Methane gas, which ruminants such as cattle and sheep emit as part of their digestive process, is 21 times more potent as a greenhouse gas than CO_2.

Download the UN report, *Livestock's Long Shadow*, here:

Food and Agriculture Organization of the United Nations fao.org

Losing touch with our food

In the past we lived in much closer proximity to animals, often under the same roof in so-called "long houses". Animals were a necessary part of everyday life. Ruminants, thanks to their double stomachs, were able to access the energy in cellulose in grass and hay, which other animals could not, and they – along with pigs, which acted as waste disposal units – provided vital fertility for the soil in the form of dung. Wandering pigs were a familiar hazard in towns for centuries and keeping animals was a normal part of most people's experience until after World War II.

That close connection has been progressively lost in recent decades, to the extent that many children now have difficulty telling which animal a pork chop or a beefburger comes from, though admittedly some meat products disguise their origins so skilfully, only scientific analysis could reveal the truth. More worryingly, certain southern states in the US object to farm animals being classified as sentient beings and prefer to categorize them as "agricultural goods". (In the EU, farm animals have been recognized as sentient beings, but only since 1997.)

With such huge demand for meat products, it's perhaps unsurprising that much livestock production has become an industrial process that turns out standardized units. The trend has been towards selective breeding and confinement to make the management of animals easier and cheaper. Livestock production is increasingly in the hands of the ever more powerful breeders, most of whom are closely linked to the agro-industrial giants and who provide the "genetic material" for the growers.

Since the longer you have to feed an animal before it reaches its slaughter weight, the more it costs, the emphasis has been on shortening the fattening-up time. Like a couch potato, an animal that is confined and has nothing to do but eat gains weight more rapidly than one which is roaming around a farm. And, like a bodybuilder, its feed can be supplemented with growth hormones. Two generations ago, cattle would have been slaughtered at four to five years. A generation ago that had dropped to two to three years. Today, thanks to their grain-and-drug-enriched diet, they don't live beyond about sixteen months.

All this means, of course, profound changes to animals' natural environments and behaviour. Intensive farming leads to a host of problems: **crowding**, which makes animals more prone to disease and fighting; **confinement**, which stresses animals and alters their behaviour; and **selective breeding**, which can further strain animals' physiology. One-third of chickens, overwhelmed by the weight of their rapidly expanding bodies, which are selectively bred to maximize the development of profitable breast meat, become lame before they are slaughtered.

Animal welfare

Concern for how animals are treated is nothing new, but as the industrial scale and methods of livestock farming have become the norm in the last few decades, those concerns have grown significantly. There is a moral difference, many people believe, between eating meat from animals reared as naturally as possible and from those whose lives are nasty, brutish and short. A frequent claim of the meat industry is that "we are simply giving the public what they want at the price they want it". However, a 2005 survey of over 2500 UK citizens' attitudes to animal welfare revealed that:

▶ 67% believed that the level of **farm animal welfare** in the EU is poor or very poor, and more than three-quarters of people believe more needs to be done to raise standards.

▶ The species for which the level of welfare was believed to be very poor were: **broiler chickens** (71%); laying hens (64%); turkeys (56%); and pigs (49%).

▶ 85% would like to see manufacturers put more **animal welfare information** on the label.

There are many campaign organizations, such as Viva! and PETA, fighting for better welfare standards for animals. Prominent among them is **Compassion in World Farming** (CIWF), which campaigns to improve the treatment of farm animals around the world. They are concerned with issues such as the welfare of animals in factory farming, the long distances animals are transported to slaughter, inhumane methods of slaughter and the honest labelling of food so that consumers can make informed choices. CIWF advocate eating less meat, to lessen the environmental impact of livestock farming and the pressure on the system to pump out tonnes of low-cost, low-welfare meat.

People for the Ethical Treatment of Animals peta.org.uk

Viva! (Vegetarians' International Voice for Animals) viva.org.uk

Born free?

The **Farm Animals Welfare Council** was set up by the UK government in 1979 to monitor the welfare of animals and advise on policy. They have a long list of topics for future investigation including several, such as the welfare of indoor pigs and the link between animal disease and welfare, which surprisingly they have never investigated in their thirty-year existence.

The Council have set out "five freedoms", which they would like to see applied to all stages of an animal's life, from birth to slaughterhouse. They are more an expression of an ideal rather than a code of conduct, though their inadequacy faced with a cynical industry is demonstrated by a pig-keeping website which declared that "stalls and tethers" system provided four out of five freedoms and are therefore a pretty good deal.

▶ **Freedom from hunger and thirst** by ready access to fresh water and a diet to maintain full health and vigour.

▶ **Freedom from discomfort** by providing an appropriate environment including shelter and a comfortable resting area.

▶ **Freedom from pain, injury or disease** by prevention or rapid diagnosis and treatment.

▶ **Freedom to express normal behaviour** by providing sufficient space, proper facilities and company of the animal's own kind.

▶ **Freedom from fear and distress** by ensuring conditions and treatment which avoid mental suffering.

Cows: milk and methane

Our hunting ancestors in the Pleistocene age more than ten thousand years ago stalked the great aurochs, cattle which stood six feet at the shoulder. These wild cattle feature prominently in twenty thousand years of cave paintings, suggesting the privileged place they held in early human cultures, and cows have been the objects of reverence for many cultures since.

It is ironic, therefore, that their modern relatives bred by man for over eight thousand years are – after humans and thanks to humans – probably the most destructive creatures on the planet. An astonishing 30% of the

Holsteins: the ultimate milk machine

In traditional farming, cows were "dual-purpose" – bred for both their milk and meat. However, pressure to maximize milk yields has led to specialization and the über-cow that is the Holstein (92% of all cows in the UK are Holstein bred).

But even if they look like the black-and-white cows of a child's farmyard, Holsteins have a tough life, milked two or three times a day and often back in calf within one hundred days of giving birth. In its lifetime of three "lactation cycles" these mobile milk machines will give around 26,000 litres of milk before being sold off to be processed as cheap mince that may well end up in your hamburger.

In the past decade the UK's dairy herd has shrunk by over half a million cows as farmers, demoralized by low milk prices, desert the industry. Meanwhile, milk output per cow has risen dramatically from 5500 litres per cow per year to almost 7000 litres.

Cows need to produce calves in order to produce milk. Female calves go on to become dairy cows themselves, but male calves face one of three possible fates. The first is to be shot at birth as an undesirable by-product of the dairy industry. Or they may be fattened up as "**dairy beef**", the sort of animal that becomes economy mince as its meat isn't good enough to be sold as prime beef. (Holstein calves don't put on weight to produce prime beef in the way that broad-backed cattle do, yet don't cost much less to rear.) Some bull calves (a minority) will be reared as **veal**, a fourteen-week existence. Now it will be on straw in a pen rather than in the notorious veal crates, which were banned in the UK in 1990.

Rare breeds: more than museum pieces?

Many rare breeds of British farm animal have declined to the brink of extinction in the past few decades. But are rare breeds anything more than just quaint museum pieces cherished out of nostalgia for our rural past? Yes, according to the **Rare Breeds Survival Trust**, which is working to ensure the survival of around seventy traditional British breeds, including the Soay and Hebridean sheep (pictured below) and Tamworth pigs. The RBST recognizes that to make it in the twenty-first century, farm animals have to be commercially viable, not just cute in photographs (though some of them are undeniably that, too). It champions native breeds which offer exceptional and distinctive quality in their meat, wool or milk.

For example, the "Cotswold Lion" is the imposing longwool sheep on whose fleecy back the wealth of the Cotswolds was built in the Middle Ages. The breed went into decline when the wool industry's focus moved north during the industrial revolution and it took a concerted effort to save it from extinction in the twentieth century.

Farming rare breeds takes knowledge and passion, which are likely to go hand in hand with concern for animal welfare and so are well worth seeking out. The meat often tastes infinitely superior to standard production-line breeds, too. The RBST has details on its website of butchers which stock meat from rare breeds as well as approved farm parks where you can see the animals:

Rare Breeds Survival Trust rbst.org.uk

world's grain goes to feed them. A cow's methane "emissions" have been calculated to produce in a year 70% of the harmful greenhouse gases of the average Toyota Landcruiser. Reconciling global demand for beef with stemming environmental damage to the planet is one of the greatest challenges facing agriculture and politics.

Sheep

At the beginning of the sixteenth century, sheep outnumbered people in England by three to one. Today that position is more or less reversed, but the UK still has the largest flock of any European country (24 million). Sheep are well suited to much of the UK's hilly terrain where no other crop or livestock would thrive. Nonetheless, and despite being about nineteen thousand kilometres away, over half the fresh lamb on British supermarket shelves comes from New Zealand, by far the world's largest lamb exporter. The UK is by far its biggest customer. Sheep are allowed to graze almost everywhere in the world where they are reared – there are no ovine equivalent of the intensive cattle and pig production units.

Pigs

Pigs are the ultimate waste disposal units, omnivores that people have fed on surpluses and waste for millennia. Though popularly characterized as slothful and gluttonous, pigs are highly intelligent and sociable animals which, left to their own devices, will happily spend many hours each day foraging for food and interacting with each other.

Contrast this with the system of "**stalls and tethers**", which is now banned in the UK, to confine and restrict movement of sows during their sixteen-week pregnancy. The animals spend most of their time lying down in a narrow stall (known as a "gestation crate" in the US), only rising to feed and urinate. A confined animal can develop leg sores and atypical behaviour through boredom, such as bar biting and repeatedly nosing the concrete floor. Tethering was banned in the EU in 2006 but an EU-wide

Bacon sarnie anyone?

"Rearing the pigs outside with lots of space to forage means the meat becomes very flavoursome." *Roger Newton, Norfolk Pig Farmer and Waitrose supplier*

Intensively farmed pigs have not benefited from the Hugh or Jamie effect yet; kept inside in windowless sheds with metal or concrete floors, they lead pretty dreadful lives. Sows are incarcerated in clamp-like **farrowing crates**, so they can barely move. Pork sourced outside the UK will have been produced without being subject to the sow-stall ban (tiny spaces they're allocated while pregnant) and piglets are often castrated without anaesthetic.

False economies: Asda's 2p sausage (cheaper than dog food) represented the nadir of Britain's cheap food culture when it was launched in summer 2008. Along with Tesco's £2 chicken, it speaks volumes about our disregard for the lives of other species and for our own health. When he tested it for the *Daily Mail*, chef Rowley Leigh found it "completely bland, it just takes up some space in your mouth." No wonder, it only contained 34% pork. But, he added, "there is a more serious question about the morality of cheap food."

For 25p each you can get an M&S sausage made of 93% British pork. Nutritionally as well as ethically, it's better to eat one high-quality sausage with lots of mashed potato and vegetables than two of the Asda ones, which are full of fat and filler ingredients. (Asda has the worst animal welfare record; M&S the best. See p.220.)

ban on solitary confinement for sows will have to wait till 2013, though the UK and some Scandinavian countries have already implemented it. Though not tethered, the majority of British pigs are kept indoors and their tails are docked (cut off) in order to stop tail-biting, which results from over-crowding.

Pig farmers in the EU don't receive subsidies, so they are dependent on the price they receive from the retailer and wholesaler. Although bacon is a £1 billion business in the UK, the British pig industry is in crisis. Pigs need to be fed all year round; they can't be put out to grass in the spring like sheep and cattle. As feeding swill (catering waste products) to pigs is now illegal for fears of contamination, pig farmers have been especially vulnerable to recent grain price rises. At the same time, the supermarkets are reluctant to put their prices up, especially when there is abundant imported pork available. As a result,

> **// The breeding sow should be thought of, and treated as, a valuable piece of machinery whose function is to pump out baby pigs like a sausage machine. //**
>
> J. Taylor,
> Wall's Meat
> Company Ltd,
> 1978

Happy pigs at Norwood organic farm (left) and a confined sow on a factory farm (right). Which would you take your children to see?

▶ **Waitrose** runs its own farm, Leckford (bought by the eponymous John Lewis in 1928) and sources its meat carefully from high-welfare suppliers. It has the best record for pig welfare, followed by M&S, and both of their own-label pork comes from pigs which are allowed to give birth and live outside (Waitrose's standard sausages come from pigs born outside but raised inside spacious airy sheds with straw to sleep on).

▶ **Tesco, Sainsbury's and Morrisons** have very poor pig welfare records so don't buy your bacon and sausages from them until their policies change. Contact them and ask what they're doing about pig welfare standards or better still try an online organic delivery instead.

Bringing home the bacon: what can you do?

Imported pig meat is likely to have been produced to a lower welfare standard than British pork. According to industry estimates, some 70% of imported meat would not qualify as legal if it had been produced in the UK. The problem is that up to half the bacon, ham and sausages we eat is outside the home where it is much harder to tell where something comes from. If you're concerned about pig welfare standards, the best bet is to buy organic British pork.

more and more British farmers are abandoning the industry and the national pig herd of 400,000 breeding sows is less than half the size it was a little over a decade ago. Already one-quarter of the bacon eaten in the UK comes from Denmark, a trend that seems likely to continue.

In the **organic system** pigs are reared outdoors for virtually all their lives. In the most intensive system by contrast the animals are kept in fattening units on slats and may never see daylight. Three-quarters of British pigs are reared indoors. They are slaughtered at the age of six months if they are to be pork and eight to nine months if they are to be turned into bacon. Compassion in World Farming believes that, just as there are labels to make plain that eggs come from caged hens, there should also be an "industrially produced pork" designation on packs to help inform consumer choice.

The chicken and the egg

Our appetite for chicken is insatiable. The birds which began their association with humans as red jungle fowl many millennia ago now provide half of the meat eaten in the UK. In the guise of chicken tikka masala, it's supplanted roast beef as our new national dish, and the chicken nugget (battered, mechanically recovered meat and skin) has replaced beef as the US's favourite meat. Britons now eat their way through 800 million chickens each year – more than a whole chicken every month for each of us. To feed this demand, chickens outnumber people in western Europe by a ratio of three to one. (In the US, it's seven to one.) Altogether there are six-and-a-half billion chickens reared in the EU annually.

Of all farmed animals, intensively reared chickens probably get the toughest deal: the shortest lives (as little as 42 days), the densest stocking (up to 50,000 birds in a shed) and the most dismal conditions, where their only possible activity is feeding. Billions of male chicks are gassed or crushed alive at birth as they are unsuitable for egg or meat production.

Just as cattle are divided into beef and milk animals, chickens are reared for either eggs or meat (**broilers**). A century ago, a chicken would have had a few years as an egg-layer and then been killed for the pot. In the 1920s, specialization took over: birds were either kept for maximum laying or else were quickly fattened up for meat. The following decade industrial-scale chicken processing began – production-line techniques for slaughter and butchering.

Unfortunately for them, chickens have what the industry calls a good "**conversion rate**" of feed to meat. Intensively reared broilers are expected to reach their killing weight at around seven weeks, twice as fast as thirty years ago. By the time they do, the birds have become obese and often lame as a result. A 2008 study found that a quarter of intensively reared broiler chickens had difficulty walking. Some fail to make the grade because their hearts give out too soon.

In 2012 it will become illegal to keep conventional battery-caged egg-laying hens in the EU, although the UK poultry industry is trying to get a five-year extension to this date. Even after the battery-cage ban, the birds will still be caged; it's just that the cages offer a few more mod cons (such as a perch, a nest and material to peck in) and a bit more floor space. Research suggests that the difference in production costs between a battery egg and a free-range one is as little as 1.5p, a small price to pay, you might think, given the suffering it prevents.

In 2008 Hugh Fearnley-Whittingstall launched a Channel 4 campaign, "Chicken Out!", to make people aware of the conditions in which broiler chickens were kept. In the month following the programme, sales of intensively reared birds dropped and demand for free-range eggs outstripped supply, though the industry claimed this was merely in line with the underlying trend. Nonetheless, free-range chicken is still a small percentage of the sixteen million chickens Britons buy each week.

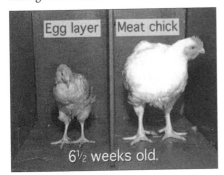

Egg layer | Meat chick

6½ weeks old.

By six-and-a-half weeks, the broiler bird (right), bred and fed for super-fast growth, is significantly larger than the egg-laying chicken (left). These broilers are basically obese chickens: they have a greater fat content than protein content.

When the food chain snaps: food scares

From a human point of view, animal diseases fall into one of two categories: those which humans can catch (salmonella, BSE and avian flu) and those which are confined to the animal population (blue tongue, foot and mouth). Modern methods of animal rearing – lots of genetically identical animals kept in close proximity – are widely believed to play a part in spreading animal disease.

▶ **Salmonella** Following a threefold increase in poultry-related salmonella cases in the space of a year, junior health minister Edwina Curry told a TV reporter in 1988: "Most of the egg production in this country, sadly, is now affected with salmonella." Egg sales instantly plummetted by 60% and the government had to step in to offer poultry farmers compensation for millions of unsold eggs and two million slaughtered hens. The government subsequently introduced legislation to improve hygiene in hen houses and imposed tighter controls on the sale of eggs.

The chances of catching salmonella (symptoms include fever, diarrhoea and vomiting) remain slim, since the bacteria are killed off by thorough cooking, but the risk increases if you are a child or elderly. A 2003 survey found that 0.03% of British eggs contained salmonella. The possibility of finding salmonella in imported eggs, which often find there way into the catering trade, is higher. The FSA recommends pasteurized eggs for dishes which require uncooked egg since that process kills off the bacteria.

▶ **BSE** Better known as **Mad Cow Disease** on account of its effect on cattle's behaviour, BSE is a deadly neurological condition which most commonly affects cattle over the age of five. The first recorded cases in the UK were in 1986. Thereafter, the number of cases built to a peak in 1992. As a result, British beef was banned from Europe for a decade and remains banned in many parts of the world (including the US and Australia).

Although no meat has ever been found to be contaminated with the disease, there were over 180,000 cases of BSE in the UK up to 2006. It was the result of feeding vegetarian cows agro-industrial by-products in the form of meat and bonemeal. Though that practice is now banned in the EU, two-and-a-half million tonnes of the stuff were being fed to livestock before the ban.

In 1996 a strong link was established between BSE and **variant Creutzfeldt-Jakob Disease** (vCJD), a degenerative neurological disease in humans. The likeliest way of contracting the disease was through eating infected animal tissue; the most infective parts of the animal are the brain and the spinal cord, which can find their way into foodstuffs as "mechanically recovered meat".

▶ **Foot and Mouth Disease** The 2001 outbreak in the UK led to apocalyptic scenes in the countryside: huge pyres of slaughtered cattle, which could be smelled for miles around, the army mobilized, horror stories of leaking lorries transporting carcasses and the wholesale closure of the countryside to visitors. The outbreak started when illegally imported meat infected with the disease found its way into pigswill (made of catering waste). Unlike the last major outbreak in the

late 1960s, animals were transported further and more often, so the disease spread much more rapidly before it was detected. The total cost to the UK taxpayer was almost £3 billion and it's estimated that the tourism industry probably sustained an equally large loss. In all, around six-and-a-half billion animals were slaughtered as a consequence of the outbreak.

▶ **Bluetongue disease** is a severe, highly infectious virus spread by midges, which can affect cattle, goats and especially sheep. Previously not found in Europe, it began its northward advance through southern Europe from the late-1990s as summers grew warmer and the midge extended its territory. The first British cases were recorded in East Anglia and the South East in the autumn of 2007, leading to the establishment of surveillance and protection zones. Outbreaks are hard to control and mean a suspension of meat exports for farmers in affected areas.

▶ **Bird flu** is a viral infection which is highly contagious among bird populations (it can also infect pigs). It was first identified in the late-nineteenth century. Research published in *Nature* in 2005 claimed that the deadly flu of 1918–19, which killed fifty million people, was probably avian in origin. There have been some highly publicized cases in which the **H5N1** strain has crossed the **species barrier** and infected humans with fatal consequences – the first was in Hong Kong in 1997. At that time, an eminent microbiologist warned that a pandemic was "only one or two mutational events away". Since then, the virus has spread among bird populations and been found in over fifty countries in worldwide.

Although there have been over two hundred human fatalities from H5N1 since 1997, the virus has not yet succeeded in mutating into a form that enables it to pass between humans, though the WHO takes the possibility of that happening very seriously and the UK government has an emergency action plan at the ready. Each time the H5N1 strain, which is now well established in parts of Asia, affects a human it improves its chances of transmitting itself among the human population. Since the first case of H5N1 in February 2007 at **Bernard Matthews**' intensive turkey plant in Suffolk, over a quarter of a million birds have been gassed in an attempt to stop the spread of the disease in the UK. Intensive poultry-keeping allows the virus to experiment with more mutations; food writer Joanna Blythman compared the situation to an "overcrowded nursery of wheezy toddlers when the latest bug comes knocking".

The UK's Chief Medical Officer, Sir Liam Donaldson, said in 2006: "We do not know what the virus is that will cause pandemic flu. What we do know is that Mother Nature has the recipe book and it's just a matter of time before she starts cooking."

Find out more

World Health Organization who.int/csr/disease/avian_influenza

The poultry industry would need an area the size of the Lake District devoted entirely to chicken farming to satisfy the UK's appetite for chicken from a free-range system (if that situation should ever arise), and would much rather convince us of enhanced welfare standards as a modification to the existing intensive system.

A Tesco spokesman responded to criticism of their notorious £2 chicken by saying said "No one should feel guilty for buying a chicken just because it is good value. The only reduction we make is in the price – not the welfare." But the link between cheap meat and poor animal welfare is a well-established one. At the time of writing, the Tesco £2 chicken is still on sale.

Freedom food: monitoring chicken factories

Freedom Food is the RSPCA's farm assurance and food-labelling scheme, dedicated, it says, "to improving the lives of as many farm animals as possible, including chickens". Their criteria for the Freedom Food mark on chickens include:

▶ a ban on **growth-promoting antibiotics** in the chicken feed

▶ **stocking density** of under 20 birds per m² (25% more than industry norm)

▶ **no mutilation** of chickens allowed

▶ an **enriched environment** including places for birds to perch and objects for them to peck at

▶ at least 8 hours' **access to the outdoors** for free-range birds

▶ well-trained staff and **humane slaughter practices**

Indoor-reared birds bearing the Freedom Food mark are priced between intensive birds and fully free-range ones. Critics of this scheme argue that it misleads consumers, who assume animals are allowed to live free-range outdoors. The CIWF clarifies that Freedom Food "does not guarantee animals are free-range", but the scheme does ensure greater space for intensively farmed animals kept indoors. Supporters say that it does the best it can, working within the existing system to improve standards. You can find their Good Chicken Guide at:

RSPCA rspca.org.uk

Thinking outside the coop: what can you do?

Opt for free-range or, better still, organic chicken. Avoid "standard grade" chicken; the standard is very low. Sadly, most of the chicken on sale today falls into this category. (Don't be misled by pictures of fields and hills on the label.) At present – though through consumer pressure this may change – Waitrose and Marks & Spencer are the only supermarkets which do not sell any so-called "standard grade" birds. Also try local butchers and farm shops for free-range and organic chicken.

For a devastating exposé of the international chicken system, see:

Planet Chicken Hattie Ellis (Hodder and Stoughton, 2007)

Wild and healthy alternatives: venison and beyond

Remains found in caves where *Homo erectus* – the first primate to use tools and walk upright – dwelt half a million years ago suggest that 70% of his diet was venison (he was also partial to otter and rhino). In the Middle Ages, hunting became the aristocratic leisure activity of choice and deer the nobility's preferred quarry. (The word "venison" originally meant any meat acquired through hunting.)

Today there are just three hundred UK deer farms (or "parks") producing around five thousand red and fallow deer each year, a tiny industry compared to beef or chicken. Most animals are slaughtered on the farm at between one and two years, avoiding stressful journeys to the abattoir. Venison is higher in iron than any other red meat, lower in cholesterol and free from antibiotics and growth promoters. That, together with the fact that it is almost always free-range and often priced lower than good quality beef, make it a meat well worth trying.

There are also some UK farmers who have given up on trying to make conventional animal husbandry profitable and have begun experimenting with exotic species such as water buffalo for their meat and milk. And in these credit crunch times, rabbit and even squirrel have started appearing at farmers' markets.

While none of these species is likely to replace the old favourites in your local supermarket, growing interest in them and in rare breeds (see box p.35) can only be a good thing as it encourages us to see meat not simply as bland, cheap protein, but as part of our ongoing relationship with animals and the environment.

British Deer Farmers' Association bdfa.co.uk

The future of farming
The return of food security

Less than a decade ago, abundant cheap food and huge surpluses meant that it was possible to seriously discuss a **post-agricultural future** in which farmers in rich countries such as Britain simply looked after the rural environment and were paid to restore the damage that intensive agriculture had done. Tourism, is was often said, is worth more in purely financial terms to the rural economy than farming. Cheap food could be imported from countries where it cost less to produce. The very notion of "**food security**" – a country's ability to satisfy its own food requirements – seemed old-fashioned, reminiscent of an age when we feared U-boats in the Channel. Today, however, food security has returned with a vengeance and is likely to rival energy security as a hot political question in the future. In the last decade, the proportion of the UK's food which is home-produced has dropped by 14% to 60%, yet Defra in 2006 was still confidently declaring that "self-sufficiency makes little sense in a world of interrelated international markets". There are three main reasons not to be so complacent:

▶ There is much more **international competition** for food than a decade ago (see pp.118–119).

▶ There is also competition for crops from **biofuels**. As environmentalist George Monbiot has said: "Those who worry about the scale and intensity of today's agriculture should consider what farming will look like when it is run by the oil industry." (See pp.122–124.)

▶ **Climate change** has also made the supply of food more volatile. Though it has had less of an impact than the other two factors so far, this will increase in the future (see Chapter 8).

All this means that food is turning back into what it was throughout much of history – a **strategic asset**, not just a tradable commodity. Along with food security, the new buzzword is **sustainability**, that is, the ability of our food system to be much less reliant on finite oil resources and able to continue into the future without bankrupting the environment. All this means change for the producers of our food.

More and more small farmers are calling it a day, leaving the industry to the industrial-scale producers. In 1900, 12% of the working population worked on the land. That had dropped to barely 2% a century later.

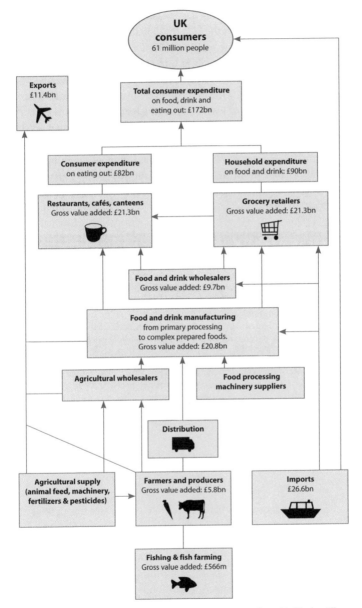

FARMING TODAY

UK consumers
61 million people

Exports
£11.4bn

Total consumer expenditure
on food, drink and
eating out: £172bn

Consumer expenditure
on eating out: £82bn

Household expenditure
on food and drink: £90bn

Restaurants, cafés, canteens
Gross value added: £21.3bn

Grocery retailers
Gross value added: £21.3bn

Food and drink wholesalers
Gross value added: £9.7bn

Food and drink manufacturing
from primary processing
to complex prepared foods.
Gross value added: £20.8bn

Agricultural wholesalers

**Food processing
machinery suppliers**

Distribution

Agricultural supply
(animal feed, machinery,
fertilizers & pesticides)

Farmers and producers
Gross value added: £5.8bn

Imports
£26.6bn

Fishing & fish farming
Gross value added: £566m

The UK food chain, 2007. The UK produces 60% of its food. "Gross value added" is the difference between the value of goods and services and the cost of raw materials. It reveals how little of the ultimate value of food goes to UK farmers. The whole chain accounts for 18% of the UK's total greenhouse gas emissions.

45

Even on a shorter time-scale the decline is significant; in 1990, there were 474,000 agricultural jobs in the UK. By 2005 there were just 340,000, well over half of whom are now aged over 55. Only 4% are under 35. One-quarter of them have another job to bring in cash since average earnings for full-time farm workers was just £13,000 in 2007, and over half have already diversified into a wide range of tourism and leisure activities.

All sectors of traditional livestock farming have shrunk in the past dec-ade, but none more so than dairy. Many farmers have given up on dairy farming after years when milk prices dictated by the big dairy companies and supermarkets were too low to be viable (often less than production cost). And because profit margins are already so tight, it only takes one crisis – such as the BSE crisis or foot and mouth – to force thousands of farmers out of business.

Fairtrade for UK farmers?

Tesco now makes more profit in less than five minutes than most UK farms make in a year (in 2005 average farm income was £17,500) and yet they, like Morrisons, Asda and Sainsbury's, grind down the supply price to often below the cost of production, forcing farmers out of business and reducing UK food security. The Competition Commission Report of 2000 confirmed this: "The burden of cost increases in the supply chain has fallen disproportionately heavily on small suppliers such as farmers".

According to Richard Hirst of the National Farmers' Union: "If growers can't have a bigger share of the retail value to reward them for their work, they'll go and do something else. Five years ago growers were receiving 41% of the retail value, now it's 20%." But the government's answer seems to be that farmers should turn to more intensive systems to lower their unit costs, which is hardly a sustainable solution. M&S and Waitrose, meanwhile, win praise for paying suppliers a fair price.

Fishing

The sea covers more than 70% of the globe and is a vitally important natural resource for fishing, biological diversity and climate regulation. Over half of the Earth's surface is covered by "deep sea", oceans over 3000m in depth. Around 64% is known as the "high seas", areas beyond national jurisdiction and therefore particularly vulnerable to exploitation and mismanagement. We have only recently woken up to the fact that for the last fifty years we have been squandering this resource. In the words of the United Nations, "the impact of humans on the sea can be devastating."

Fruits of the sea

Whereas on land we have to cultivate vegetables, meat and wheat to produce food, the sea, lakes and rivers offer a self-replenishing naturally occurring resource – fish. Fishing involves either hunting wild fish at the artisanal or industrial level (with ever more technologically sophisticated equipment) or harvesting fish artificially grown in controlled farm environments (aquaculture). Methods vary according to the fishery, ranging from a small hook attached to a line to the industrial techniques of midwater trawls or massive purse seines operated by 70m fishing vessels.

Fish is now widely recognized as a healthy source of nutrition as it is protein-rich, naturally low in saturated fat and rich in polyunsaturated fats, particularly the **omega-3 fatty acids** eicosapentaenoic acid (EPA) and docosapentaenoic acid (DHA) as well as vitamins and essential minerals including iron, zinc, iodine and selenium.

Over 20% of the global population live in coastal areas and, especially in developing countries, the sea is a crucial food source. Population shifts combined with dietary changes in the developed world have led to greater fish consumption, so that we are now eating five times the amount our grandparents ate in the 1950s. Traditional fishing would never have been able to supply this demand; the reality of the fish on your plate is that it was probably reared on a fish farm or caught in distant seas by a massive

Greenpeace activists stage an action in the North Sea against a Norwegian trawler in a campaign to establish marine reserves to protect cod and other marine life.

industrial trawler – a fish factory – with hi-tech detection devices, mile-long nets and vast freezers. The fishing industry that feeds our appetite for fish has overfished stocks to the extent that many species are at the lowest levels since records began.

Any more fish in the sea?

Overfishing is now at crisis levels. The UN Food and Agriculture Organization (FAO) has reported that nearly 70% of the world's fish stocks are now fully fished, overfished or depleted. "The fishing industry and politicians have ignored the scientists and continued to batter cod stocks," according to Greenpeace. What this means in practice is that once-plentiful fish species such as cod are now classified as **vulnerable or near to extinction**. And fish longevity and slow reproduction cycles make it difficult for them to recover once they have reached such a low point. After years of failing to face up to the serious drops in fish stocks (cod, hake, haddock and tuna levels are 10% of 1950s levels) and refusal to reduce the fishing industry (propped up for years by enormous subsidies from vote-conscious politicians and a powerful fishing lobby), we currently have a global fishing fleet which has twice the capacity needed to catch what the ocean can sustainably produce.

The warming sea

Climate change will bring warmer seas, which will in turn lead to the movement of certain temperature-sensitive fish species such as herring to other areas, thereby removing the main food source for other species such as cod. Warmer seas will also reduce plankton, another source of food for fish, and lessen the ability of oceans to hold dissolved carbon dioxide, reducing the supply of this vital part of the food chain and increasing the amount in the atmosphere, further exacerbating the temperature rise. Changes in wind patterns will lead to more tropical storms and changes in surface currents will affect the delicate marine ecosystem at deeper levels. Research into Alaskan and Canadian salmon has shown that warmer seas are already having an impact; unusual temperature changes can lead to mass mortality of certain fish species.

New technology over the past twenty years has on the one hand led to more efficient fishing with fish-finding devices, onboard freezing and the capacity to remain at sea for up to a year, but it also created the possibility of overfishing.

Ironically, when tuna and cod are at critical levels, they tend to huddle together making them easy targets for hi-tech fishing boats whose scanners can spot their distinctive shapes on their screens. Our childhood memories of skate and plaice and cod and chips by the sea will not be shared by our own children: cod is on the verge of commercial collapse and common skate is virtually extinct.

Choosing your tuna

Tuna, being an oily fish, has high levels of beneficial omega-3 oils. Fresh tuna is the most nutritious, followed by tinned albacore tuna and then skipjack and yellowfin. Tinned tuna remains one of the cheapest, easiest ways of getting fish oils into your diet whether it's in a tuna and sweetcorn pasta sauce for children or Tonno e Fagioli, a simple white-bean salad. Tinned tuna is big business (50% of all canned fish is skipjack): the UK is the second biggest market worldwide, after the US, and canned tuna accounts for 20% by weight of all fish eaten here. Because of this, consumers have the power to reduce destructive fishing methods such as **purse-seine nets** and FADs (fish aggregation devices, which lure fish into a huge net), which are used by many fleets to increase their catch, but are also responsible for wiping out thousands of sharks, turtles and juvenile tuna. A 2008 Greenpeace canned fish ranking put bestselling John West firmly at the bottom for sustainability and Sainsbury's (pole-and- line caught) own-label far ahead of other supermarkets. Tesco's own-label fared poorly as a result of lack of consumer information and unsustainability.

Fish4Ever is a company dedicated to sustainable fishing and dolphin-, albatross-, turtle- and shark-friendly methods. They avoid spawning areas and by-catch, and prepare the fish using traditional techniques. Test results for dioxins and mercury (damaging to children and pregnant women) show the range has between zero and only just traceable levels. You can buy their basic skipjack (around £1 a can) or Ortiz-like (albacore white) canned tuna, as well as peppered mackerel, smoked kippers and anchovies. Available in some supermarkets, health food shops and delis. (fish-4-ever.com)

Bycatch

Along with the damage caused to the seabed by their rollers and metal nets, "bycatch" is one of the main side-effects of industrial sea fishing. Of the total fish catch, about three-quarters is thrown away as bycatch because it is either too small or the wrong species. Market forces and non-selective fishing techniques are the main causes of this environmentally disastrous aspect of modern fishing. Every year hundreds of thousands of marine mammals, turtles and seabirds are killed needlessly in fishing gears, something which the World Wildlife Fund (WWF) is campaigning to halt. It has had some success in certain areas through its promotion of dolphin-, turtle- and seabird-friendly devices, and in campaigning for bans on damaging practices in areas where conservation of endangered species is a particularly acute concern.

Jellyfish and chips?

▶ **Continued overfishing** threatens to leave the UK with waters populated with nothing but jellyfish and algae, as many fish are on their way to becoming extinct.

▶ Global fishing yields **declined by 13%** in a decade (1994–2005).

▶ Preventing fishing in protected areas **boosted biodiversity** by 23% and increased catches in nearby areas.

▶ Currently less than 1% of global ocean is **effectively protected**.

▶ **All commercial fish stocks will have collapsed** by 2048 if the current trend continues.

The MCS's "Silent Seas" report found that only eight of the total of 47 fish stocks found around the British Isles remain in a healthy state.

In 2004, 68% of the fish we consumed in the UK was **imported** (see below). Prepared and preserved fish products were the largest category at 36%, and frozen fillets made up a quarter of the total. Cod – mainly from Iceland – continues to account for almost half of all whitefish consumption. The majority of fish imported comes from Iceland, Norway and Denmark. Most UK fish exports (over 200,000 tonnes p.a.) go to the Netherlands, France and Spain.

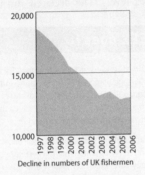

Decline in numbers of UK fishermen

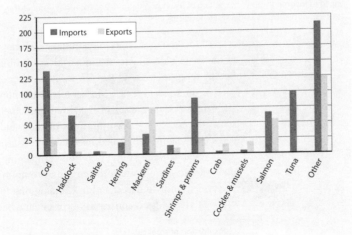

Who controls the seas?

Lack of cooperation, vested interests, mutual mistrust and the inherent difficulties of policing remote waters have created a situation in which sustainability in fishing remains a distant aim rather than a reality. Government bodies (the UK fishing industry is overseen by Defra) and other organizations are currently working at national, regional and international levels to gain agreement over how to manage the sea.

Fishing quotas (the amount of fish a fisherman is allowed to catch) and temporary fishery closures are negotiated at national level between government and industry, and then set annually by the EU, based on fish stock levels. The declared aim is to safeguard stocks and make fishing

EEZ does it

The UN ended historic free-for-all fishing in 1994 with the establishment of exclusive 200-mile fishing territories around individual countries, creating **Exclusive Economic Zones** (EEZs). Today 86 coastal states have economic jurisdiction up to the 200-mile limit, meaning that around 99% of the world's major fisheries now fall under a particular nation's jurisdiction.

Each state determines the total allowable catch for each fish species within its zone and estimates its own harvest capacity. Coastal states are obliged to assess what they can catch themselves and give neighbouring states and land-locked countries access to any surplus. This "fencing-off" of the sea has led to problems over historically fished areas. Norway and Iceland closed their waters to foreign fleets, leaving the UK fishing industry in trouble, as it was no longer able to fish for cod in the waters up to the Arctic. It did enable poorer West African countries to receive much-needed income through the selling of fishing rights to richer countries – but at the price of depleting essential staple food supplies.

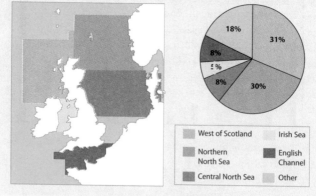

Proportion of total catch

West of Scotland Irish Sea
Northern North Sea English Channel
Central North Sea Other

sustainable. But the EU promotes the interests of the powerful European fishing industry and negotiates deals to enable fleets to fish in far-off waters, when they are not able to fish their own either because of fishing bans, reduced quotas or uneconomic stocks.

Setting quotas is a delicate balancing act between consumer demand and fishermen's livelihoods on one hand, and the survival of fish species on the other. Quota trends are towards fewer days at sea to reduce the quantity of fish caught and subsidies are paid to fisher-men to compensate for lost income. Critics say that paying out large subsidies to keep fishermen relatively compliant is propping up the industry artificially and sustaining over-capacity. Fishermen blame current restrictions for wrecking their industry while scientists believe that reckless overfishing is reducing the potential for a fishing industry at all.

Internationally, the UN provides guidance as well as a forum for legislation and deal-brokering to promote global cooperation over fishing. Its role became increasingly important once the freedom of the seas notion was final-ly displaced by twentieth-century economic imperatives. In 1945, the US unilaterally decided to lay claim to parts of resource-rich seas, prompting other countries to follow suit and produc-ing a race for resources. On 1 November 1967 Malta's Ambassador to the United Nations, Arvid Pardo, called for "an effective international regime over the seabed and the ocean floor beyond a clearly defined national jurisdiction". This eventually led to the adoption in 1982 of the United Nations Convention on the Law of the Sea (UNCLOS).

If we were to meet the FSA's suggested intake levels, the Royal Commission on Environmental Pollution estimates the present total level of fish consumption in the UK would need to increase by over 40%, with oily fish consumption increasing by over 200%.

Greenpeace

Modern fishing with modern technology is the most destructive activity on Earth ... Overfishing threatens to deprive developing countries of food to put delicacies on the tables of rich countries.

Charles Clover,
The End of the Line

Out at sea, out of sight

There are many disquieting stories behind the food on our plates: prawns for the traditional Spanish paella you may eat on holiday are actually caught by Spanish fishing fleets in African waters, access to which has been bought by the EU from various African governments, leaving local

Last orders for cod and chips?

The UK has traditionally fished for cod, but once plentiful North Sea supplies are fast becoming a distant memory. Stocks are rapidly dwindling and fishing reductions have failed to prevent their decline, since around 80% of cod landed internationally are juvenile cod aged one to three which have not yet spawned.

The fishing industry continues to argue for the right to fish cod, despite the recommendations of scientists, who warn that cod is "outside safe biological limits", meaning there is not enough breeding stock to stop the species disappearing. The Great Banks northwest **Atlantic cod crisis** saw a once profitable fishery collapse in the 1990s through overfishing. Years later, it still shows no signs of recovery.

There are some sources of cod which are sustainable: Pacific cod from the Bering Sea and Aleutian Islands fishery was certified as an environmentally responsible by the MSC in 2006. Cod stocks are looking healthier in the north-east Arctic, Icelandic and Faroese waters, but it would be all too easy to repeat the mistakes of the Great Banks when fishermen seized on the first sign of cod recovering, to catch many young fish and thereby destroyed any chance of the species recovering.

Cod and chips is not the only traditional dish which may be on the way out; **eel and mash**'s days are numbered too. Eel numbers are at 2% of pre-1980s levels due to overexploitation, poor water quality and disease.

▶ Cod can live **twenty years** and grow to 1.5m.

▶ Most are caught between two and four years. Cod only reach optimal breeding **maturity** at five years.

▶ They **spawn** from January to April, as they prefer cold water.

▶ Females produce up to **four million eggs** but 98% get eaten before hatching, mostly by herring.

▶ **Coley** (or saithe) and **Alaskan pollack** are good substitutes for cod as they are in plentiful supply and mostly sustainably fished.

fishermen with reduced catches. On an environmental note, these prawns comprise just 15% of the total catch, the rest (fish) being mostly thrown back as bycatch. Prawn catches have also been declining over the past twenty years: French fishing trawlers which were catching 150 tonnes in 1983 are now coming away with just 40 tonnes a year.

Whereas for consumers in Europe seafood is a luxury, for West Africans, it is one of the main sources of nutrition and income. Dr Callum Roberts of York University, a leading expert on marine reserves, said of a five-year deal whereby an EU fleet of around 250 boats can fish Mauritania's waters for a fee of £54 million a year: "Foreign trawlers are strip-mining African waters of their fisheries resources. It's a scandal. It's almost international piracy."

Some countries have woken up to the serious implications of selling fishing rights in their own waters. Morocco and Namibia reclaimed their territorial rights from EU trawlers in 2001 and 1992 respectively. But EU fishing trawlers, having depleted their own stocks, are forced further afield to countries which don't yet realize the impact fishing rights will have on their own food or are willing to trade them for short-term income.

//As fishing stocks collapse in other oceans, global fleets are moving en masse to the Pacific, rather than fixing the problems in their own waters.//

Greenpeace

Illegal (sometimes known as "black") fishing is still widespread and further erodes already depleted fish supplies in the sea. High value stocks like tuna are particularly targeted. The Environmental Justice Foundation (ejfoundation.org) has highlighted the inequities suffered by poorer West African countries as a result of "pirate fishing".

Shellfish

UK waters still produce large quantities of shellfish **bivalves** (mussels, oysters and clams) and **crustaceans** (crabs lobsters, nephrops and crawfish). Crab and highly prized scallops are the main wild landings and mussels by far the largest category of farmed shellfish. Coldwater prawns are imported from Iceland, Greenland, Norway and Canada and warmwater prawns are mainly imported from Thailand, India and Ecuador. Most of our home-grown shellfish is exported to France and Spain.

▶ **Brown crab** This is the heaviest British crab and can grow up to a width of about 30cm. They are found in waters down to 100m and are sustainable due to the low-impact method of fishing using traditional pots and are stunned humanely before cooking. Avoid eating crab or other shellfish caught by other methods such as dredge, net or beam trawl as these are extremely damaging to the seabed and create large quantities of bycatch. Crab is best eaten between April and November and is sourced from Cromer in Norfolk or Brixham in Devon.

▶ **Scallops** The Lyme Bay scallop industry was worth £2m until the government decided in June 2008 to close 10% (sixty nautical square miles) of Lyme Bay to fishing to protect marine wildlife. This was the result of a five-year battle between fishermen (who wanted a fifteen-mile

limit) and environmentalists, such as the Devon Wildlife Trust, who said that "dredging for scallops is like collecting mushrooms with a JCB". Bottom-trawling and dredging had been destroying the rare coral reef in the bay for years. The South West Inshore Fishermen's Association criticized the government, saying "it should pay attention to the economic and social costs as well as to the marine environment." Diver-caught scallops may be more expensive, but perhaps this is the price we have to pay to eat delicious seafood and protect the environment in which it grows.

▶ **Mussels** These can be farmed (rope-grown) or harvested from the sea and are a healthy, sustainable source of seafood (and protein). In Scotland, mussels are predominantly rope-grown, a method which entails suspending ropes from floating buoys in areas that have naturally occurring mussels in the water. The mussels will then colonize the ropes where they can be collected by hand when they reach the right size.

The real price of prawns

Wild Prawns are one of the most valuable forms of seafood. Trawling is the most commonly used method for catching cold-water prawns, accounting for about one-third of the world's bycatch; as much as 10kgs of bycatch is discarded for every kilo of prawn landed. Generally those from Iceland have been caught in well-managed fisheries. For a clearer conscience, choose pot-caught prawns, which not only taste better but also reduce bycatch drastically. The pot fishery in Loch Torridon, northwest Scotland, is certified as environmentally responsible by the MSC, but its catch is shipped to Spain. The coldwater prawn trawl fishery from West Greenland sought certification to the MSC environmental standard for sustainable fishing in 2008.

Most warm-water or tiger prawns are **farmed**. The unacceptable levels of bycatch in trawl-caught prawns would be one of the main reasons for choosing farmed prawns, but there are many ethical and environmental issues to consider. Commercial prawn farming started in the 1970s and had exploded into a global industry by the late 1990s to meet increasing consumer demand from the US (the largest importer), Europe (especially the UK, France, Spain and Italy) and Japan. Today 75% of prawns come from Asia; we in the UK eat three times as many prawns as in 2002 and the price has halved.

The new intensive prawn farms would be unrecognizable to the traditional low-density Asian fish farmers of a century ago. It is now seen as an attractive industry with low set-up costs and high profits. It takes four to six months for a prawn to grow to marketable size, allowing farms to produce two harvests a year. But there are also risks: higher stocking densities leave farmers susceptible to repeated outbreaks of disease which, despite frequent pesticide and antibiotic applications, can wipe out a whole prawn population and make ponds unusable for a year. Critics highlight the unethical nature of prawn farming practices: contamination of drinking water is a problem as farms discharge antibiotics, pesticides and disinfectants into the environment. China absorbs most of its production in

Fisherman's friend

"There is only one rule – find the freshest produce you can and let it speak for itself – the main star is the fish." Mitch Tonks

Fish chefs Rick Stein and, more recently, Mitch Tonks (pictured) have reinvented British fish and shellfish cooking by encouraging us to enjoy simply cooked fresh fish and get beyond the fish fingers and chip shops of our youth. Now seared tuna, spiky lime and chilli scallops, or crab linguine with garlic, parsley and red chilli are on the menu. Mitch recommends keeping it simple with both kit (a cast iron ridged grill pan and a very sharp knife) and cooking method. See his book *Fresh: Great Simple Seafood* (Penguin, 2004) for more ideas.

Mitch built up his knowledge of fish and suppliers as a fishmonger before starting the well-known FishWorks restaurants (FishWorks.co.uk) and later moving on to a new restaurant, The Seahorse, on the harbourside in Dartmouth, Devon. He is a firm believer in the need for sustainable sourcing of fish and thinks we should demand our fish is caught ethically and "not mass-trawled by factory ships."

the home market, which is just as well since the EU banned their prawns in 2002 over the use of leukaemia-causing chloramphenicol and cancer-causing nitrofuran. These once-common antibiotics have turned up in Indian supplies, too.

There is also an environmental and human cost. Coastal mangrove forests from Bangladesh to Indonesia have been cut back to create aqua-culture ponds and rice fields have been turned over to prawn ponds with attendant salinated water (they cannot be used for rice again and drinking water can be affected). In Vietnam, more than 80% of original mangrove cover has been deforested in the last fifty years. The disappear-ance of mangroves, which protect low-lying coastlines is linked to the rising death tolls from tropical storms. If this all seems too much, then next time you want to grill tiger prawns, choose organic varieties from Ecuador or sustainably farmed prawns from Madagascar. Waitrose and M&S are good sources.

Farmed fish

The broilers of the sea?

Ever wondered where those crayfish in your lunchtime sandwich came from? Well, it's highly unlikely they ever swam in the open sea. With wild fish stocks in serious decline, new large-scale aquaculture might be the answer. Aquaculture does have clear benefits in providing affordable, sus-tainable fish, with the added benefit of minimal bycatch, so environmental groups give it a cautious thumbs-up.

There has been a dra-matic increase in fish farming since the mid-1980s from China to Chile, Ecuador to Scotland, and it is now the fastest grow-ing meat-producing food sector. The UN Food and Agriculture Organization predicts that by 2010 half

A typical Greek fish farm

of our fish will be farmed (it stood at 43% in 2008) and that much of it will come from Asia. The new fish farming techniques developed in the 1980s saw salmon, once a luxury food, became cheaper and ubiquitous on fish counters and in restaurants. Atlantic salmon stocks have halved in the last twenty years and disappeared from three hundred of its two thousand traditional breeding areas. Ninety

> **// Aquaculture is increasingly going to supply the world's fish needs – we have to accept that, and work to make it sustainable. //**
> Soil Association

percent of all salmon are to be found in only four countries: Scotland, Ireland, Norway and Iceland. The original bland, fatty fillets of farmed salmon of the 1990s seem tired in comparison with the new fish farms of the twenty-first century. An Australian company, CleanSeas, has invested vast sums in its attempts to farm high-value tuna at sea, and exotic, newly farmed species such as tilapia and barramundi are available now in our supermarkets and restaurants.

Tilapia: the new cod on the block?

Farmed tilapia, being sustainably reared and with no concerns over stocks, appears to be the perfect solution to boosting fish supplies while we allow wild species time to recover. Researchers tip it as potentially one of the most important farmed seafood products of the century. The tilapia is a firm white fish which won't fall apart on the barbecue and makes a decent replacement for red snapper in Asian fish curries.

Tilapia are also herbivores and therefore do not require feed based on wild fish, although some fish oil may be included in the feed. However, chefs allegedly hate it because it has such an unfishy taste, and medical research has suggested that farmed tilapia have poor levels of omega-3 fatty acids.

▶ **Freshwater fish** native to Africa, Central and South America and the West Indies. Tilapia were farmed in ancient Egypt and are now farmed in over 85 countries.

▶ **Sustainable alternative** to cod: tilapia sales are predicted to double between 2002 and 2012.

▶ **Profitable to farm** as they grow quickly throughout the year.

Waitrose has come under fire for selling farmed tilapia from Zimbabwe at a time when much of that country's population was going hungry, though they defended themselves, saying that the farms brought jobs and income to impoverished people. The humble farmed tilapia highlights the complexities and contradictions inherent in much of our imported food.

Farmed and dangerous?

Fish farming remains highly controversial from fish welfare and environmental points of view, especially where fish such as salmon, which roam over vast areas in the wild, are prevented from following their migratory instincts and confined to large cages sunk in the sea, like aquatic battery chickens. These fish are born and grow in controlled environments and never get to swim wild: pens and cages in the northern hemisphere and flooded mangrove swamps and rice paddy fields along the equator.

Greenpeace's research lab at the University of Exeter published a wide-ranging report on global fish farming, *Challenging the Aquaculture Industry on Sustainability* (2008), which highlighted the "serious environmental and social impacts that have resulted from the development and practice of aquaculture and which are reflected across the global industry".

The downside of fish farming:

▶ **Destroys coasts** to make way for ponds.

▶ **Pollutes water** with fæcal waste and excess feed.

▶ **Depletes wild fish stock** (caught for feed and to stock farms).

▶ **Disease and chemical pesticide** results from tight stocking levels (fish can be infested with invisible lice).

▶ **Growth promoters and antibiotics** are widely used to boost profits.

▶ **Escaped farmed fish** breed with wild fish, weakening the species.

▶ **Lice and disease** spread from escaped fish to wild fish.

A farm with 200,000 salmon releases about the same amount of fæcal matter as the untreated sewage of 65,000 people. Many farms in the Pacific northwest stock as many as a million fish and their waste creates an oxygen-deprived environment that has damaged biodiversity up to 200 metres from the cages.

The ethics of feeding wild fish to farmed ones is complex. Salmon on the rapidly expanding Chilean fish farms eat sardines and anchovies before being served up themselves on North American dinner tables.

The tuna of Australian ranches eat pilchard caught off the shores of West Africa. To grow one kilo of prawns takes two kilos of feed, while a kilo of salmon requires three. Charles Clover, author of *The End of the Line*, a book about fishing in decline, calls "the diversion of low-value fish from the mouths of people in developing countries into the mouths of well-fed fish in the developed world" an "obscenity". It may be possible to get around this problem – at least in principle – as the Soil Association hopes, with their directive to all its certified organic fish farms, that by 2010 they must feed 100% sustainable fish to their salmon, either as off-cuts from fish processing, or as fish certified as sustainable by the MSC. But if the growth of fish farming is constrained by the availability of wild fish as feed, how sustainable can farming really be in the long run?

Toxic fish: contamination in the food chain

Although fish is generally a healthy food, **marine pollutants** can make it less good for us. Transport ships and oil tankers carrying toxic cargoes along international sea routes have long been the cause of pollution in the marine ecosystem. Major spillages make the headlines with their potent images of seabirds coated in oil and choking to death. There are many forms of pollution which affect the quality of seawater and the health of sealife; some of them are slow and silent until it is too late: agricultural fertilizers and pesticides, sewage, chemical waste, plastic bags, bottles and the ever-increasing numbers of inhalers. Wildlife groups estimate that around one million seabirds and a hundred thousand marine mammals and turtles die each year as a result of marine pollution. Many have been found to have plastic litter in their stomachs (see p.223).

Fish can absorb and accumulate toxins in high concentrations, which are then passed on up the food chain. Polychlorinated biphenyls (PCBs) are prevalent in oily fish, and mercury (which is present in the marine environment) is especially concentrated in large predatory species such as tuna and swordfish. Herring are particularly affected, whereas cod and haddock (and fish fingers) have been found to have very low levels of contaminants. Dioxins are found in herring in relatively large quantities, then salmon and mackerel, and lastly in small quantities in trout.

The reason that mussels and oysters are often a source of food poisoning is not just a result of storing them at the wrong temperature (you should keep them in the coldest part of your fridge at around 4°C) but also because shellfish feed by filtering sea water, making them highly likely to absorb any toxins going.

PCBs and Monsanto

Among the most persistent and damaging marine pollutants have been the chemical PCBs, which have rendered vast areas of water unfit for fish for the last forty years. These phenols were produced mainly for the electrical industry fom the 1920s, before being banned in the 1970s, though warnings about their potent toxicity dated back to the 1940s.

After a number of dramatic incidents in the US, it was accepted that PCBs were highly toxic, probably carcinogenic and certainly persistent in the environment, meaning their damaging effects are long-lived. PCBs had been produced commercially and promoted worldwide by Monsanto (see p.151). PCBs dumped in the Hudson River, New York State between 1947 and 1977 led to a ban on fishing in the area, as fish were found to contain extremely high levels of the toxin. Despite enormous soil removal projects, PCBs are still there and fishing is still banned. The Great Lakes are also still contaminated with PCBs and they have even been found in the Arctic Circle.

Organic fish farms

Organic fish can only be produced in the controlled environment of a fish farm, since there can be no guarantee that wild fish have not been exposed to pollutants and impurities. The sacrifices made to produce a natural product have to be balanced with your desire for food untainted by chemicals and poor welfare practices. The Soil Association are pragmatic about aquaculture and decided in 2006 to work with farms to ensure high standards by extending their certification scheme to organic fish farms. It was a controversial decision that caused a rift in the organization.

Fish carrying the Soil Association label will have been fed sustainably, have lower stocking densities than other farms and will not have been exposed to chemical pesticides. The **Marine Conservation Society** (MCS) supports the organic production of farmed fish and shellfish species as certified by the Soil Association and promotes good practice, including an Environmental Management Plan to monitor and improve the problems commonly found in fish farming. Organic farms such as Graig Farm (see p.303) source their salmon from locations in the Shetland Islands, where salmon are kept in large cages at less than $10kg/m^3$ in the open sea, allowing them shoal and swim properly against sea currents, thereby reducing stress. Intensive fish farms keep 25 to 30kg of fish per cubic metre, while RSPCA Freedom Food guidelines and the MCS recommend a maximum stocking density of 15kg/cubic metre.

So which fish is it OK to eat?

There is no easy answer. As fish populations dip in or out of danger the advice changes. It's not just a matter of picking a non-endangered species; you need to know where and how the fish was caught, as this affects other species. Fish to avoid come from badly managed fisheries with problems of overfishing and/or high levels of bycatch. The **Marine Stewardship Council** (msc.org) certifies sea fisheries for environmental impact. Look out for the MSC labels on packaging and on fish counter labels. They also have detailed advice for shoppers on their website. Here are some currently eco-friendly fish:

▶ **Black bream**

▶ **Brown crab** (pot-caught off south Devon coast)

▶ **Clam** (hand-harvested)

▶ **Cod** (Pacific MSC-certified from Alaska only; avoid Atlantic cod)

▶ **Coley or saithe** (from NE Arctic and combined North Sea stock)

▶ **Dublin Bay prawn/ langoustine** (MSC-certified from Loch Torridon only)

▶ **Herring** (Norwegian only)

▶ **Lobster** (Mexican Baja, Californian and Australian rock)

▶ **Mackerel** (Cornwall)

▶ **Mussel** (hand-harvested or rope-grown)

▶ **Oyster** (sustainably farmed)

▶ **Pilchard or sardine** (from Cornwall)

▶ **Pollack** (line-caught and tagged from Cornwall or MSC-certified from Alaska)

▶ **Prawns** (from NE Arctic only)

▶ **Salmon, Atlantic** (organically farmed) or **Pacific** from Alaska

▶ **Scallop** (diver-caught)

▶ **Seabass** (line-caught; avoid trawl caught)

▶ **Squid**, Atlantic, European

▶ **Tiger prawns** (organically farmed only)

▶ **Tilapia** (sustainably farmed)

▶ **Trout** (organically farmed only)

▶ **Tuna, albacore** (MSC-certified from S and N Pacific)

▶ **Tuna, skipjack** (MSC-certified from Pacific (western and central) and Indian Ocean (pole and line caught only)

And here are some to avoid:

▶ **Monkfish** (from North and North West Spain, Portuguese coast)

▶ **Plaice**

▶ **Salmon** wild Atlantic

▶ **Skates and rays** (except mature cuckoo, spotted and starry rays)

▶ **Swordfish** (seriously overfished)

▶ **Bluefin tuna**

The Marine Conservation Society (MCS) fishonline.org The MCS publishes a UK consumer guide to which fish to buy and which to avoid.

Here today, gone tomorrow: sustainable fishing?

The government's Food Standards Agency (FSA) has been encouraging us for years to eat more fish, but this advice now has to be qualified due to perilously low fish stocks. Newly defined protected areas are being created to develop healthy fish stock reserves, but fishing methods need to become more sustainable. To do this, experts estimate that around 40% of the world's marine environment must be protected and even closed over extended periods while fish stocks are monitored. Fishermen can help by alerting the authorities when they sight spawning grounds so these can be quickly closed, thereby allowing more fish to reach maturity and breed.

Governments are being lobbied to provide **Marine Protected Areas**, designated to help revive stocks from the effects of overfishing. Whereas over 12% of the Earth's land surface is designated as "protected", only 1% of the ocean currently is. When an area off the Isle of Man was closed for fishing, the scallop stock grew to a level twenty times that of nearby waters and scallop catches near to the closed area increased, too.

What can you do?

Our choices are: do nothing and watch prices rise as fish become scarcer, and finally disappear, taking jobs along with them. Alternatively, we could take the long-term view that in order to protect our future fish supplies we might have to switch to different species at certain times and check the label to see if it has been sustainably fished.

Vote with your wallet and send a clear message to the fishing industry and government that you care about sustainably managed stocks. New rules introduced across Europe in 2002 require certain fish and fish products, including salmon, to be labelled with information about the catch area (for example, whether the fish has been caught at sea, in inland waters or farmed) and the production method. This, combined with the accreditation schemes run by marine conservation groups, can help you choose sustainable fish, such as Loch Duart salmon.

Find out more

The End of the Line: How Overfishing is Changing the World and What We Eat
Charles Clover (Ebury Press, 2004)

Bottomfeeder: How the Fish on Our Plates is Killing Our Planet Taras Grescoe
(Macmillan, 2008)

Food processing

The inconvenient truth about food is that as soon as it is harvested or slaughtered, microbes get to work and it begins to go off. Imagine your fridge breaking down on a warm day and think how long its contents would last. To stop food going bad, humans have for millennia used techniques of processing and preserving, from smoking fish and salting meat to drying fruit and pickling vegetables. All of these techniques change both the taste of the food and its nutritional content. But the techniques used by today's big food processors go far beyond these traditional methods, and the transnational corporations which use them rack up profit margins even more impressive than those other giants in the food system, the supermarkets. This chapter looks at some of the ways the food manufacturers process what ends up on our plates and what it means for our health.

The world's first food-canning factory was set up in Bermondsey in 1812 by an engineer called Bryan Donkin. It was a great leap forward for food processing. Before then, there had been few major advances in food preserving techniques since the Middle Ages. The first canned goods to go on sale were more expensive than fresh food and appealed mainly to travellers and the navy. Food hygiene was still poorly understood and a tin of beef weighing over 10lbs could contain plenty of bacteria as well as lumps of unappetizing meat.

By the latter part of the nineteenth century, canning was big business and Australia was shipping millions of tonnes of tinned beef to Britain each year. Mechanization was also taking off in the canning factories across America, bringing costs down and expanding the range of foods available. Taste was a secondary consideration: many of the people who could afford tinned foods had never tasted their fresh equivalents in

Archetypal tinned food, source of dread to past generations of school children and star of one of Monty Python's most famous sketches, Spam® was a creation of the hard times in the 1930s. American GIs spread the fame of this shiny pink pork concoction internationally in World War II. More recently it's been made into sushi and even had a biography devoted to it.

any case. By the late Victorian period, the role of heat treatment in food hygiene was better understood, so the chances of food poisoning were reducing. Processing, especially under a familiar **brand name**, came to represent a certain kind of **dependability**, which it still does today for many consumers.

The modern era of food processing really got under way after World War II. Social patterns began to change; more women were going out to work and had less time to spend in the kitchen. Growing affluence meant fridges and then freezers began to appear in more homes. And food technology held out the prospect of science improving on nature. Today, the limitations of nature have been left far behind. Corn and soya, the two crops that have done most to make the explosion in processed foods possible, are processed, modified and "fractionated" (separated into component parts) in all sorts of novel ways to provide the raw materials in the food manufacturers' box of tricks. Today it's virtually impossible to find a processed food without some derivative of corn or soya (or both) in it, and in the future it may become hard to find non-GM versions as well.

Powerful processors

We are so used to thinking of the supermarkets as the dominant force shaping what we eat that it may come as a surprise to learn that there is a quartet of powerful transnational corporations, whose names few consumers ever hear, which control countless vital aspects of what ends up on the supermarket shelf: from the corn that gets processed as **high-fructose corn syrup** (HFCS) to the chicken that gets put into ready meals, to the soya beans that get broken down into the lecithin that stop the cocoa and cocoa butter from separating in chocolate bars. Much of the world's production of the commodities which are the mainstay of processed foods – **corn, rapeseed, sugar, soya** – pass through their hands and get transformed into the ubiquitous building blocks of innumerable products. So who are these faceless corporations?

> **There are two hundred thousand [UK] farmers, dealing with, basically speaking, three supermarkets, two grain merchants, four fertilizer companies. Not a chance ... they've got power, real power.**
>
> Charles Peers, organic farmer, Oxfordshire

▶ **Cargill** Though not many people know its name, it's hard to find superlatives to do justice to the scale of Cargill, one of the **world's biggest privately owned corporations**, which turned over $120 billion in 2008 and employs around 160,000 people worldwide. From its base in Minneapolis, it controls around 45% of the world's grain trade and it also has significant interests in the international trade in meat, sugar and other types of food processing, as well as owning feed and fertilizer companies. It sells farmers their inputs, and buys up their outputs. It supplies all McDonald's eggs in the US. It owns industrial chocolate plants throughout Europe and also West Africa. And it has recently developed a no-calorie sweetener called Truvia™ in partnership with Coca-Cola (see p.86). It has, in the words of its unofficial biographer, Brewster Keen, "tentacles in every aspect of the global food system". Environmental groups have been critical of Cargill's record, notably over deforestation in South America.

▶ **ADM** (Archer Daniels Midland), though half the size of Cargill, is still a global giant: one of the world's biggest grain traders and wheat, soya, corn and cocoa processors. It is also big in the fields of manufacturing ingredients for food processing, animal feed and sweeteners.

▶ **Bunge** is another mammoth US agribusiness with interests that range from biodiesel and animal feed to mayonnaise.

▶ **Louis Dreyfus**, the only European among the quartet, is a French family firm, a major bulk agricultural commodities trader and a significant owner of international shipping.

These four companies, and others like them, don't just trade in agricultural goods; they pursue the "vertical integration" of the whole food system, buying up smaller players or forming alliances with other companies so as to control all the links in the chain from feed and seed to processing and packaging. They turn cheap subsidized products such as corn and soya beans into higher-value derivatives, which end up in the high-priced cereal boxes or probiotic drinks in the world's shopping trolleys.

Find out more

Food and Water Watch foodandwaterwatch.org/food/pubs/report/cargill **has a 2008 audit of Cargill's record,** *A Corporate Threat to Food and Farming.*

Corporate Watch corporatewatch.org.uk **has reports on many of the big players in the international food system on its site.**

The mega-brands

Brands change hands as transnationals shed interests in particular areas and move into others. Small companies such as Cauldron Foods, which specializes in vegetarian foods, get bought up by giants such as Premier Foods (the UK's biggest food manufacturer), which don't share their ethos but are eager to gain access to another sector of the market. These are some of the biggest players:

▶ **Nestlé** is in the process of repositioning itself as "**the world's foremost nutrition, health and wellness company**". The Swiss giant, though, attributes its success to "added value" products which include: Shreddies, Shredded Wheat, Nescafé, Perrier, Poland Spring, San Pellegrino, Carnation, Nesquik, Coffee-Mate, Ski, Sveltesse, Mövenpick, Lean Cuisine, Buitoni, Aero, After Eight, Blue Riband, Breakaway, Kit-Kat, Quality Street and Smarties. In 2007, it had sales of over £52 billion and net profit of 10%. A recent annual report states that their priorities for future growth include targeting "lower-income consumers in the developing world" and offering luxury and premium products for the affluent west. (See Part II of this book for transnationals' record of trading in the developing world.)

▶ **Unilever** owns Flora, Hellman's, Knorr (its biggest brand at £4 billion), Bertolli, Amora, Ben & Jerry's and Pot Noodle.

▶ **Cadbury Schweppes** is the world's largest confectionery company.

Sweets and soft drinks are very high-profit businesses with low-cost ingredients. Brands include Dr Pepper, 7UP, Snapple, Trident, Hall's and of course the eponymous Cadbury's chocolate.

▶ **Kraft Foods** is the biggest food manufacturer in North America and a major international player. Its brands include Maxwell House, Capri Sun, Philadelphia, Oreo, Shredded Wheat, Ginger Snaps, Ritz, Planters, Toblerone, Milka, Kenco, Côte d'Or and Suchard. It has seven brands with turnovers in excess of $1 billion.

▶ **PepsiCo** chalks up staggering operating profits: in 2006 they were over $7 billion (18% of their turnover). Their brands include Tropicana, Dole, Doritos, Walkers, Pepsi Cola and PJ Smoothies. With their sports drinks, "enhanced" waters, ready-to-drink tea and coffee and "extruded snacks", they are the biggest purveyors of snack foods in the world and they sit, as they say themselves, "squarely in the sweet spot of the food and beverages space – convenience." PepsiCo have five brands which generate over $5bn a year. Aware that the times are changing, PepsiCo devised its own "smart spot" logo and awarded it to 43% of its products which it claims contribute to a "healthier lifestyle".

Behind the scenes at the food factory

Textbooks detailing the myriad techniques of contemporary food processing, their chemical properties and the specialist machinery available to carry them out run to many hundreds of pages. Here are just a few of the things which might have happened to the food you eat:

▶ **Dehydration** Drying foods in the sun is probably the oldest method of preserving. But today, drying is more likely to be carried out using a spray drier. "Liquid foods and slurries" (in no-nonsense industry-speak) is atomized as a spray in a drying chamber. As with many forms of processing, the nutritional content of the food is often reduced, especially vitamins A and D.

▶ **Wet-curing** In meat processing, wet-curing is the process used for most of the bacon we eat. Manufacturers are legally allowed to add up to 10% of the product's weight as water (5% for cooked or cured meats) before it has to be declared on the label. Ham can have even lower percentages of meat; by finely chopping the meat and recombining it with water and preservatives, the meat content can be reduced to as little as 55%. **Recombining** is a favourite technique: many hotdogs turn out to be an amalgam of mechanically recovered chicken, water, pork and an array of other ingredients to bind them together. Poultry and lamb are also prone to bulking out with water, the former in a process known as "**tumbling**" under vacuum with salt and polyphosphates, which help to retain the water in the meat.

▶ **Mechanically recovered meat (MRM)** came to widespread public attention during the 1980s and 90s, when concern about BSE, and its human equivalent vCJD, was intense (see p.40). Carnivores were horrified to discover that they had been eating meat that had been pressure-blasted off stripped animal carcasses, along with parts of the potentially highly infectious spinal cord of cattle. The resulting slurry was then used to bulk out cheap meat products such as pies, burgers and

Unhealthy foods = healthy profits

A 2006 report from Ethical Investment Research Services on the contribution of the global food giants to obesity looked into how much of their revenues derived from unhealthy foods. They defined unhealthy as products which are "high in sugar and/ or fat, and generally nutrient-poor". They included "confectionery, chocolate, sugary cereals, sugary soft drinks, ice cream, some food served at fast food restaurants". The companies below must be hoping that we're not going to discover the joys of beansprouts any day soon.

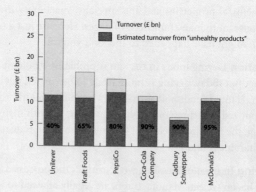

Find out more

Ethical Investment Research Services (EIRIS) Ltd eiris.org *Obesity Concerns in the Food and Beverage Industry*

meat pastes. What was worse, the food processing industry was unable or unwilling to divulge the extent to which MRM from cattle had been used before it was banned in the UK in 1995. Many people know that MRM from beef is now banned; fewer are aware that the use of MRM from poultry and pigs remains legal in the UK. Bisto Gravy for Turkey, for example, lists mechanically recovered turkey on its label.

▶ **Extrusion** Pasta was one of the first foods to be produced by mechanical extrusion process in the 1930s. Today extrusion is the production method of choice for such things as shaped-potato snacks and breakfast cereals. Food generally begins the process in powdered form and is then forced through machines at high temperature and under high pressure before being chopped into pieces of the desired size. Such treatment means that a lot of the vitamins and flavour gets lost along the way and has to be added back in after the product emerges from the machines.

▶ **Frying** One big concern surrounding frying is the amount of fat that the food absorbs during the process. This can be a substantial percentage of the total weight, from 5% in the case of frozen chips to as much as 40% for crisps. To try to reduce this, manufacturers sometimes steam and then dry products after frying. Another big question over frying was raised in 2002 when Swedish researchers found that starchy fried foods such as chips and crisps cooked at above 120°C contained high levels of the potentially carcinogenic substance **acrylamide**. There is not

Robots in disguise. This is the Baker Perkins Cereal Master TX, a state-of-the-art rotary cereal cooker which produces flaked and shredded breakfast cereals. There's an optional coating system if you have want to sugar-glaze. Most manufacturers do.

yet consensus on this question, but the WHO recommends moderating consumption of fried foods for both of the above reasons.

▶ **Irradiation** Advocates of irradiation claim it has been misunderstood and maligned as a food preservation technique. In fact it has been permitted in the UK since 1991 but is not currently used. Irradiated food is food which has been exposed to gamma rays, X-rays or high energy beams with the aim of causing changes in the cellular structure of the irradiated food (and anything that happens to find itself living on it) and thereby the elimination of contaminants. Under UK law seven categories of food are eligible for irradiation: fruit, vegetables, cereals, bulbs and tubers, spices and condiments, fish and shellfish and poultry. However, only one UK licence, for the irradiation of herbs and spices, has so far been granted. The drawbacks of irradiation are vitamin loss, public distrust – perhaps second only to that reserved for GM food – and current unsuitability of the process for meat (those lucky enough to have tried it say it smells "like wet dog"). It also induces flavour changes in dairy products.

Other new techniques may sound like science fiction, but new ways of prolonging the shelf life of foods by altering their chemical make-up are potentially very big business. They include **high-pressure processing**, which aims to kill microbes by applying very high pressure to foods very quickly. Other techniques which have not yet gone into production such as **pulsed electric fields** – in which food is exposed to a high-voltage pulsed electric field between two electrodes – and **low-frequency, high-intensity ultrasound** are being actively explored by the industry.

Bakery fakery

In 1961 bread-making changed forever, thanks to a process developed by the British Baking Industries Research Association in Chorleywood, Hertfordshire, who were "perfecting" an American technique for accelerating the preparation of bread dough. Today the vast majority of bread in the UK is made using the **Chorleywood Bread Process** (CBP). Before CBP, bread-making had continued largely unchanged for centuries. The combination of four ingredients – flour, water, salt and yeast – were all that was required, plus the knowledge and experience of a skilled baker.

Critically, traditional bread-making also took time: the dough had to be worked slowly, then rested to let the yeast develop, and then worked again. Since time is money, the CBP found a way around the lengthy wait by using high-speed mechanical mixers to beat air into the dough. To compensate for the fact that the yeast doesn't have time to multiply, **high-melting-point fats and emulsifiers** go into the mix. It also makes it possible to use British wheat, which has a lower protein content than North American and is cheaper. The **water content** of CPB bread is also higher than traditional bread.

// Scientists and their technological achievements have combined with commercial interests, compliant governments and the public's own indifference to give us the factory bread we now have ... No doubt we deserve it. *//*

Elizabeth David, 1977

Unsurprisingly, the resultant bread has less flavour (or worse, the unpleasant taste of **conditioners and preservatives**), so added ingredients such as sweeteners, syrups, honey and even "artisan bread aroma" additives are often used to mask its shortcomings. If you stand by the sliced bread aisle in a supermarket, the overwhelming smell you will notice is a soft, sweaty sweetness. Nonetheless, one leading food processing textbook boasts that CBP bread is "better in terms of volume, colour and keeping qualities". The first and last are qualities more appealing to the manufacturer than the consumer.

It's true that after the industrial revolution British bread was not always free of adulteration. Eliza Acton, in her marvellously titled *The English*

Traditional bread versus Chorleywood

	Traditional	Chorleywood
Ingredients	Flour, water, 1% yeast, salt	Water, flour, 2.5% yeast, salt, oxidants (ascorbic acid), emulsifiers, fat (lower protein content and more water compared to traditional)
Mixing	Slow mixing (8–15mins); low energy	Fast mixing (<3min) high energy
Proving	3–24hrs at 26°C, including remixing along the way	First proof 10–15min at room temperature. Second proof 45min at 40°C

Marg or butter?

Margarine is manufactured from oil, water and artificial ingredients that mask its lack of taste and hold it all together. It is a highly processed food which, as nutritionist Marion Nestle put it, is basically "soybean oil and food additives. Everything else is theater and greasepaint". Brilliant for the manufacturer, who can make a tidy profit out of water and cheap ingredients, but less good for you.

Margarine sells because of distractingly complicated "healthy" marketing claims and it is true that many margarines have lower saturated fat content than butter; but at what cost? Research shows that margarine additives such as omega-3 are not worth the extra expense as they don't perform as well in this context as in fish. Lower-fat versions need larger quantities of emulsifiers to keep the higher percentage of water bound up with the oils. Yum.

So in preference to marg, choose butter. It's a simple natural food. Butter has the same calorie and total fat content as polyunsaturated marg, far more calcium and vitamin A, and lower salt levels. On the downside, it has 52g of saturated fat per 100g, while marg has 17g. Keep a small amount out of the fridge in a butter dish for spreading; you'll use far less if it's soft.

Bread Book for Domestic Use Adapted to Families of Every Grade (1857), complained that English bread was infamous "both at home and abroad, for its want of genuineness and the faulty mode of preparation" and the addition of potentially poisonous alum (derived from shale) to flour was by no means unknown.

But our nineteenth-century ancestors may have had a better sense of when they were being sold substandard bread and taken their custom elsewhere. Now the vast majority of bread in this country is Chorleywood bread, and more and more of us never get the chance to taste any other sort.

Bread-buying tips

Despite the apparent wealth of choice, supermarkets are not good places to find good bread. If you have to buy your bread in a supermarket, choose a loaf with fewest ingredients, a good crust, rather than something with a long shelf life sealed in a bag. You can spot CBP bread by the emulsifiers, oils, flour treatment agents and sweeteners in the list of ingredients. Supermarket "freshly baked" breads are usually just Chorleywood partially baked pre-mixes finished off on the premises to allow them to boast of an in-store bakery. But you'll be much better off with an artisanal baker (see p.283 for the alternatives to spongy supermarket bread).

Is it safe to eat?

When food manufacturers are surveyed about their concerns, **food safety** regularly tops the list. Unsurprising, since the costs of getting it wrong are spectacular. When in 1990 bottles of Perrier water were found to contain **benzene** from the carbonation process, 280 millions bottles had to be withdrawn worldwide and production was suspended for several months. Sales collapsed and left the company ripe for purchase by Nestlé in 1992. The 2006 Cadbury's product recall of half a million bars of Dairy Milk and other chocolate bars because of **salmonella** contamination took an estimated £5–10 million from the company's bottom line.

In fact, reliable, safe food was the initial promise that the food processors made to their customers in the early twentieth century when many of the companies that have grown into today's mega-brands started out. Those which thrived were the ones who could be depended on to keep delivering the same safe taste year after year. Manufacturers today have complex procedures in place to sample, test and record their production lines, which even include metal detectors to ensure that no foreign objects find their way into your lunchtime pasty and scanners to guarantee that chicken pieces are free from bones. Meats are sprayed to eradicate microbes.

Food safety tends to be viewed as about immediate risks though, rather than a long-term ones. Unlike the link between lung cancer and smoking, the complexity of our diets makes it much harder to establish a simple cause-and-effect relationship between what we eat and the diseases we suffer from. But there have been innumerable studies in the past three decades of the harmful effects of diets based on highly processed foods. And there have been several lawsuits against companies over such things as misleading claims about their products and the presence of **trans fats** (see p.83), which have led to substantial out of court settlements. Food companies' concerns about making their products less bad for us stem at least in part from wanting to avoid class actions further down the line.

Hunt the strawberry

Like medieval alchemists, today's food processors take cheap ingredients and find ever more ingenious ways of creating the products that fill our shelves. The difference is that these modern-day alchemists have succeeded in finding gold where their medieval predecessors failed.

Unsurprisingly, the **flavour** of a product is a critical factor if consumers are going to keep coming back for more. The problem is that processing strips out much of the flavour of raw ingredients. So the **flavour industry** is big business and, because the flavouring is often the one ingredient in the recipe which can't be swapped with another cheap commodity, it's also highly secretive.

Artificial strawberry flavour can contain literally dozens of ingredients. **Natural flavours** are not necessarily purer or healthier than artificial ones; they're just arrived at differently. Both types involve sophisticated chemistry and the result can be identical. A professor of food science at Cornell University told *Fast Food Nation* author Eric Schlosser: "A natural flavour is a flavour that's been derived with an out-of-date technology." In other words, there's probably a slicker way of achieving the same taste without having to bother starting with a real strawberry.

In February 2008, the Food Commission surveyed two dozen widely stocked products that appear from their names and packaging to contain strawberries. Their findings were shocking. They discovered that:

▶ **Nesquik Strawberry Flavour Milk Shake Mix** is strawberry-free and consists largely of sugar

▶ **Asda Great Stuff Strawberry Milk** has less than a teaspoon of strawberries per bottle

▶ **Frijj Strawberry Milk Shake** contains no artificial flavourings, but no strawberries either

▶ **Yoplait's Yop Strawberry Yoghurt** has no strawberries in it

▶ **Alpen Strawberry and Yoghurt Bars** contain only one-third of a gram of strawberries per bar

▶ **Fruit Bowl School Bars** are 45% sugar, and only 1.5% strawberry.

Many of these products are aimed squarely at children and their claims about having a "new fruitier taste" and being "packed with calcium" would understandably mislead parents to think they are buying something much healthier than they are. For the full report on the amazing disappearing strawberry, see:

Food Commission foodcomm.org.uk/latest_flavourings_Feb08.htm

Pick a flavour

▶ **Artificial flavourings** These can be used to create new synthetic flavours (prawn cocktail for example) or cheaply mimic natural ones. Consumers don't like the word "artificial", though, so they frequently appear on the label simply as "flavouring".

▶ **Natural flavourings** In order to count as "natural", a flavouring needs to be **derived from an animal or plant source**, but it can be put through all manner of processes in the lab along the way. And the

Processing: not all bad

Clearspring is a small UK company established in the 1980s to sell traditional foods that support good health, promote sustainable agriculture and provide economic stability for producer communities. Their range has a strong oriental flavour and includes *arame* seaweed (great in salads), *soba* noodles, and such condiments as soya sauce, mirin (sweet sake used in cooking) and tamari, a wheat-free soya sauce brewed to a 500-year-old recipe.

Modern industrial soy sauce is produced from defatted soya flour mixed with hydrochloric acid at high temperature to create hydrolysed vegetable protein to which plenty of salt, caramel and flavourings are added. Clearspring's Shoyu soya sauce is, by contrast, made from naturally fermented whole soya beans and roasted wheat which are slowly aged in cedarwood kegs (see picture).

Clearspring founder Christopher Dawson says: "I will only use a product for my family if there is two hundred years of tradition behind it. You are asking for trouble if you take an isolate from soya – yet so much effort seems to go into taking industry's waste and turning it into new food."

You'll find Clearspring products in many health food shops and supermarkets.

Clearspring clearspring.co.uk

Beware the orange snowmen

Sunny Delight, the orange-flavoured drink, first appeared on the UK's supermarket shelves in 1998. Or rather, it appeared in the refrigerated section next to the fruit juices. This encouraged its reputation as a healthy drink for children, helped along by its multi-million-pound marketing budget. Sunny D took the market by storm. Within a few months it was the third most popular soft drink in the country (after Coke and Pepsi) and it went on to be the twelfth most popular grocery purchase overall. Everyone, it seemed, loved Sunny D.

But then the independent campaign group, the Food Commission, dropped a bombshell: "In fact, it is full of thickeners, colours and flavourings to make it look like a fruit juice, when it's basically just a very sugary drink. Basically, it's just a marketing con." Sunny D's reputation was not helped by reports of a child in Wales turning yellow after drinking it by the litre, at the same time as a Sunny D ad was running in which two Sunny-D-loving snowmen turn orange.

Sales suffered a massive slump and in 2004 Proctor and Gamble sold off the tarnished brand. The new website, which makes much of its parents' panels and its reinvention, is full of boasts of reduced sugar and added vitamins. It's proud of having listened to consumers who didn't want vegetable oil in their fruit drink (were they surprised?), but it still contains starch, thickeners and sweeteners. Rather disarmingly, the website admits that in excessive quantities, the beta-carotene colouring in Sunny D can change the colour of your skin.

The point about Sunny Delight was not that it was worse than many other soft drinks on the shelves (it wasn't), nor that it failed to list its ingredients on the bottles, but that it gave the impression of being a much healthier drink than it was. The soft drinks shelves are still packed with equally dubious concoctions which play up their vitamin content or their no-added-sugar claims. It's legal to call a product with as little as 1% fruit juice a "juice drink". So always check the label.

See p.81 for more on additives. Find out more:

Action on Additives www.actiononadditives.com This campaign aims to list all the foods, drinks and medicines which contain the additives linked to hyperactivity in susceptible children.

Sunny D sunny-d.co.uk Judge the brand re-invention for yourself.

"natural flavouring" in a vanilla product doesn't necessarily come from a vanilla pod. Natural flavourings are the only sort allowed in organic products. Products displaying fruit on the packaging or claiming to be "fruit flavoured" have to declare their fruit content unless it is so small as to be unmeasurable, so a dash of "natural fruit flavouring" gives the manufacturer the best of both worlds – fruity packaging and no need to declare how little fruit content there actually is.

▶ **Named flavourings** Manufacturers know that we will put up less resistance if the flavour in a product seems to come from the ingredient mentioned on the label, such as "natural peach flavour", so this is their preferred choice. Confusingly, though raspberry flavour doesn't have to come from a raspberry, something labelled as "raspberry-flavoured" must.

▶ **Nature-identical flavourings** These have exactly the same chemical composition as natural products, but are made entirely synthetically.

Does it matter?

If a milk shake tastes of strawberry, it encourages your child to drink milk. So maybe it doesn't matter if the flavour comes from a strawberry or out of a chemistry set? The trouble with flavourings, which may in themselves do you no harm, is that they certainly don't do you any good, and yet they mimic ingredients which do: instead of 100g of crushed strawberries in your milk shake, you get a tiny drop of concentrated flavouring. And confused children (and adults) understandably tally up fruit-flavoured, but fruit-free products as part of their "5 A DAY".

Flavourings, by carefully controlling the taste of the product, also enable manufacturers to put in other ingredients, such as starches and sugars, that bulk it out. An insidious long-term effect is that we get so used to the flavourings that manufacturers add to products that we no longer know what the real thing tastes like, and children learn to prefer the more familiar ersatz version. Surveys have found that more people prefer "vanilla flavour" to genuine vanilla from a vanilla pod. Lastly, given that flavourings are the most highly guarded secret ingredient in many foodstuffs, it would be almost impossible to trace the source of an adverse reaction to any particular flavouring cocktail.

Functional and superfoods

Consumer concern over health has increased sales in the new **functional food** and drink category by over 500% in the last decade, as manufacturers' marketing hype promises ever-better disease prevention and health. The government and EU have taken steps to rein this in, though: in 2007 they introduced legislation to end unsubstantiated health claims on food packaging by 2009.

The **functional foods** category (which already encompasses fortified cereals and margarines, but may soon also include snacks and confectionery) has harnessed the power of superfoods, often in the form of added extracts, to sell a new range of expensive, processed products. There is no official definition of **superfoods**, just a vague understanding that they have extremely high concentrations of antioxidants (see p.189), vitamins, minerals and plant chemicals in their raw state (and are therefore more absorbable than in pill or supplement form). Research has shown that such foods can help protect us from heart and other chronic conditions and cancer, but that they should not be seen as a substitute for a balanced mixed diet. Ordinary unprocessed ingredients – inexpensive, nutritious and healthy – are the real superfoods:

Apples and oranges contain high levels of vitamin C as well as pectin, which lowers blood cholesterol levels. **Oily fish** (such as salmon and mackerel) are the best source of omega-3 fatty acids (flaxseed is the best plant source). UK sales of **blueberries** have increased by 132% since 2005, as we discovered that they have the highest concentrations of antioxidants anthocyandins: the most powerful antidote to ageing. **Brazil nuts** are high in selenium and **almonds** in mono-unsaturated fats and vitamin E (make your own organic dark chocolate coated nuts for a semi-healthy sweet treat: cocoa is full of antioxidant flavonoids). **Tea**, especially green tea, is high in antioxidants and the most widely consumed superfood. High levels of the antioxidant lutein, which protects against age-related eye damage and cataracts, are found in broccoli and avocados. **Broccoli** is the ultimate superfood, containing two effective anti-cancer substances sulforaphane and Indole-3-carbinol, as well as high levels of potassium and beta-carotene, which lower the risk of heart disease. There is no need to pay more for "functional" **probiotic drinks** (primarily water and sugar) when live yoghurt has all the easily absorbable calcium and friendly probiotic bacteria (to aid intestinal health) that you need.

Artificial additives: the beginning of the end?

Asda felt that public perception of **food additives** was so negative that it could promote its "Good For You" range under a "no nasties" label. Sandwich chain Pret A Manger has done the same, avoiding "obscure chemicals, additives and preservatives" since their launch. Mounting evidence and a general public distrust of artificial food additives is encouraging manufacturers to reformulate products with more natural ingredients (though some are more natural than others).

The use of food additives is strictly controlled at EU level but decisions are reliant upon scientific research, which in turn is reliant upon funding.

After years of uncertainty the European Food Safety Authority (EFSA) was asked by the European Commission to reassess the safety of all EU-approved food additives using new techniques not available thirty years ago. Many additives are relatively new and their long-term, cumulative impact unknown. EFSA started with **colourings** and one of the first casualties was Red 2G, now banned as a carcinogen.

Researchers from the University of Southampton published an FSA-commissioned study in *The Lancet* in September 2007, which showed the detrimental effects of a cocktail of food colourings and the preservative **sodium benzoate** (used in soft drinks such as Sprite to prevent mold growth), linking these with **hyperactivity** in children. The Southampton study found that sodium benzoate, when mixed with the additive vitamin C in soft drinks, creates the carcinogen, benzene. An earlier WHO review of sodium benzoate claimed it was safe, though they admitted that research backing up this claim was "limited". It is notable that one of the first large non-industry-funded studies returned a negative verdict on additives; other studies are in train.

The disgraced colourings were used in thousands of common foods and had previously been linked with allergic reactions (for example, asthma and eczema). They were frequently found in products aimed at children and teenagers: the yellow colouring, Tartrazine (E102), was found in Tesco's own brand mushy peas; Quinoline Yellow (E104) and Sunset Yellow (E110) was found in Cadbury's Creme Eggs at the time of the study. Red Carmoisine (E122) and Red Ponceau 4R (E124) were also detected (both are banned in the US). Many products contained a combination of these additives, such as Fanta Fruit Twist (made by Coca-Cola), Morrisons Bettabuy orange drink, Skittles sweets and many birthday cakes aimed at young children.

Despite clear evidence about the dangers of the additives studied, the FSA appeared to have given in to pressure from food industry lobbying in giving rather vague advice to parents and not actually banning these substances but asking for voluntary removal by 2009. Many companies remove additives only when bans are in place.

Find out more

Action on Additives Campaign actiononadditives.com This campaign for the removal of artificial colouring additives from food and drink is coordinated by the independent watchdog, The Food Commission. Their website lists products containing additives examined by the Southampton study.

E is for Additives Maurice Hanson with Jill Marsden (Thorsons, 1988) The classic whistleblowing book on the "nasties" in our food. Could do with an update, but still a fascinating read, which takes you through each additive in detail.

Lecithin is more: a guide to some regulars on the label

▶ **Starches** are a vital ingredient in most processed foods. In modified form they can be used to hide "off-flavours" which foods develop as a result of processing. Or they can be added to foods such as yoghurts to bulk them out, especially low-fat varieties. They can soak up water to add weight to a product and even mimic the bulk of fruit or vegetables in everything from potato products to apple pies.

▶ **High-fructose corn syrup** (HFCS) is a product of the US's corn surplus. It has only been present in our diet since 1980, yet it has found its way into a wide variety of foods both sweet and "savoury" and – alarmingly – it has not reduced cane sugar consumption but supplemented it.

▶ **Emulsifiers** have also found their way into many products in the last

"It tastes just like chicken"

The vegetarian organization People for the Ethical Treatment of Animals (PETA) has offered $1 million to "the first person to come up with a method to produce commercially viable quantities of *in vitro* **meat** at competitive prices by 2012". The rules say that the **"meat without feet"** must be chicken, and must taste the same as meat from a real chicken.

In vitro tissue engineering differs from genetic modification (see p.145) in that it tries to **imitate nature**, rather than change it. Stem cells removed from a living animal are cultivated in a nutrient-rich fluid or growth medium, where they are stimulated by electrical impulses. The end product is a boneless, processed meat whose fat content can be controlled.

Peta says: "The result would mimic flesh and could be cooked and eaten. Some promising steps have been made toward this technology, but we're still several years away from having *in vitro* meat be available to the general public."

New Harvest new-harvest.org This is a not-for-profit vegetarian research organization working to develop meat substitutes.

People for the Ethical Treatment of Animals peta.org.uk

two decades. An emulsion is a dispersion of small droplets of one liquid within another, such as oil in water in a salad dressing. Emulsifiers keep the droplets from recombining, thereby allowing manufacturers to add water to products. They are also to be found in baked goods, where they contribute to protein strengthening and aeration, and chocolate, where **lecithin** allows manufacturers to reduce the amount of cocoa butter they use. Sunflower-derived lecithin is beginning to replace soya in the EU as more of the world's soya production goes over to GM.

▶ **Thickeners** Guar gum is an additive extracted from the guar bean which finds its way into a multiplicity of processed dairy products such as yoghurts, ice cream and soft cheese as well as bread, pasta, ham, sausages, prepared fish and pastries. In 2007, nearly two-thirds of EU member countries recalled products contaminated with high dioxin levels in guar gum. **Locust bean gum** and **carageenan** also perform the same function, making you feel full at little extra cost to the manufacturer.

▶ **Trans fats** are produced from oils such as soya or rapeseed which have had hydrogen forced into them to produce solid fats. They're a cheap option for manufacturers, but not good news for consumers. In the words of the Food Standards Agency: "The trans fats found in food containing hydrogenated vegetable oil are harmful and have no known nutritional benefits. They raise the type of cholesterol in the blood that increases the risk of coronary heart disease." One estimate reckoned that 50,000 people a year die prematurely in the EU as a result of consuming a diet rich in trans fatty acids. Trans fats don't currently need to be labelled separately under EU law, but as the US Food and Drug Administration says: "If the ingredient list includes the words 'shortening', 'partially hydrogenated vegetable oil' or 'hydrogenated vegetable oil', the food contains trans fat."

▶ **Preservatives** Unless a food with a long shelf life has been canned, frozen or dried, it will contain preservatives to stop it going bad. Sulphur dioxide, used to preserve dried fruit and inhibit mold growth in wine, has been linked to severe allergic reactions, particularly in asthmatics. Potassium nitrate and nitrite, used in preserved meats, can convert at high temperature to nitrosamines, which are carcinogenic.

In addition, the food processor has it his disposal a whole armoury of other food additives, including acidity regulators, anti-caking, bulking, firming, foaming, gelling, glazing and flour treatment agents, humectants (for moisture), packaging gases and stabilizers.

Artificial sweeteners: sweet poison?

The main reason for using artificial sweeteners in food and drink is to replace (high calorie) sugar with a low-calorie chemical which can help weight loss. The problem is that after thirty years of artificial sweeteners, we've never been fatter. In the US, where soft drinks are drunk in increasingly large servings, there is an epidemic of adult and child obesity. Meanwhile, US milk consumption is down by about 38%, with the largest drop among children. Soft drink manufacturers get them young in the US, where baby bottles are sold with Kool Aid and other soft drink logos; researchers have found instances of these bottles being filled with that brand of drink.

Sweeteners taste like sugar only more so (hundreds of times sweeter but often with an "unnatural" aftertaste) and are therefore added to food and drink in relatively small quantities. Having no food content, these artificially produced chemicals have few calories and are now a major part of the food and drink industry. Artificial sweeteners are a fraction of the cost of sugar, and so offer a cheap way of making money out of often premium-priced "healthy" low-calorie or "diet" foods and drink.

Despite being declared safe first by the US Food and Drug Administration (FDA) and then the EU, artificial sweeteners have been mired in controversy for many years. Some studies show they cause cancer and neurological problems; others show that they don't (generally industry-funded research). At this stage there is **no conclusive proof** either way, and anyway it is difficult to test the cumulative effects of the ingestion of a wide range of foods and drinks containing a combination of artificial sweeteners. Early sweeteners (1960s cyclamates and saccharin) were banned by the FDA after research showed they caused bladder cancer in rats and mice. But saccharin (discov-

// Some studies have linked the chemically derived sweeteners to cancer in laboratory rats, and others claimed that such sweeteners, by 'tricking' the brain without satisfying the body's cravings for sweet treats, may actually promote over-eating. Whatever the scientific merit of those studies, consumers are more wary of such unnatural products than they used to be. *//*

The Economist

ered in 1869 and used in Coca-Cola's Tab and as a table sugar substitute as Sweet'N Low) was allowed back on the market after aggressive advertising and political lobbying by the Calorie Control Council (the diet drink industry association) overturned the FDA decision but conceded on the point of allowing a health warning.

What are artificial sweeteners?

Broadly speaking, there are two types of sweetener:

▶ **Nutritive**: white and brown sugar, fruit juice sugar, honey, syrups and sugar alcohols (maltitol, mannitol, sorbitol, xylitol, which can have a laxative effect). These contain about four calories per gram.

▶ **Non-nutritive**: zero-calorie artificial sweeteners such as acesulfame-K (Ace-K), aspartame, saccharin, sucralose (Splenda) and stevia.

Aspartame (sold under such brand names as Nutrasweet and Canderel) has always been tainted by controversy over claims it could cause cancer and brain tumours. Developed by the company G.D. Searle, it took a long time to be approved. This approval was controversial; critics say it was only came about after newly elected President Reagan replaced the Head of the FDA with Arthur Hull Hayes, Jr., who sanctioned aspartame's use in 1981 (Hayes later went off to a highly paid job at Searle's PR company).

Health-risk claims centre around the way in which aspartame is broken down in the body and its subsequent effects. It is made of aspartic acid (40%) and phenylaline (50%), both amino acids, and 10% methyl ester. As the body absorbs these substances, the methyl is broken down into **methanol** (a poisonous chemical used in antifreeze and present in tiny amounts in the atmosphere), and then the toxic substances formaldehyde and formic acid. Repeated formaldehyde exposure, even at low doses, has been implicated in neurological and immune system damage and headaches. High levels of formic acid in the body can damage the retina, leading to blindness.

It is now often used in combination (to conform to legal intake limits) with Ace-K (Sweet One, Sunnett) in drinks such as Coca-Cola Zero, Fruit Shoots (aimed at young children) and even children's flavoured waters. The Center for Science in the Public Interest (CSPI) considers Ace-K to be "very poorly tested and not worth any risk." The original approval in 1988 was based on research dating from the 1970s.

Sucralose (Splenda): manufactured from sugar and misleadingly labelled "natural", sucralose has been the subject of many legal challenges in the US. It is a laboratory-engineered altered molecule of sugar that replaces three hydrogen–oxygen groups on the sugar molecule with three chlorine atoms. Manufacturers like it for its stability during processing.

Is there a safe limit?

The UK government-set acceptable daily intake (ADI) of artificial sweeteners is 40mg per kilogram of body weight, meaning that an average-sized adult's limit would be about two litres of diet cola a day. With super-sized portions and the presence of these sweeteners in a wide range of foods, it could be easier than you think to reach this limit. (A 355ml soft drink contains about 180mg of aspartame.)

All diet drinks contain artificial sweeteners either singly or in combination, so if you're cautious about your health then the best advice is to avoid them, unless your doctor has recommended them to you in order to try to lose weight. Stick to natural sugars but lower the quantities and try to retrain your taste buds to enjoy other drinks (tea, fizzy water with a slice of lemon or fruit juice). Don't give diet or "juice drinks" to children. Offering these very sweet-tasting products to young children will increase their chances of rejecting nutritionally superior milk and plain unadulterated fruit juice as not sweet enough (see p.192).

Stevia: the healthy solution?

With consumers' health concerns over sweeteners increasing, the food industry is pinning its hopes on Stevia, a "natural" artificial sweetener extracted from the leaves of this member of the chrysanthemum family native to Paraguay. Because it has no calories, Cargill says it "allows consumers to satisfy their taste for sweetness without increasing the calories in their diet". It's already approved as a foodstuff in China (where most commercially grown Stevia comes from), Australia, Brazil and Japan.

Other governments are not yet convinced by the mixed research findings concerning its potential toxicity: these focus on whether metabolic processes could produce a mutagen in animals. Two companies are working on its development: Cargill (in tandem with Coca-Cola on the Truvia™ brand) and Whole Earth Sweetener Company (on PureVia™ in partnership with Pepsi). Both have filed requests for it to be approved for use under the FDA **Generally Regarded As Safe** (GRAS) regulations for natural substances in use prior to 1958 with no reported adverse effects.

What's good about artificial sweeteners?

▶ **Diabetics** need to avoid and reduce sugars. Sweeteners provide an alternative, but they're not essential for a diabetic diet.

▶ If you are **overweight** and cannot kick the habit of sweet-tasting foods and drinks, then switching to a brand which replaces high-calorie sugars (a standard 330ml can of Coke contains almost seven teaspoons of sugar) with artificial sweeteners is a realistic way to prevent further weight gain. Doctors say the benefits of sweeteners outweigh the potential negatives: but that is rather a qualified recommendation.

Find out more

What to Eat Marion Nestle (North Point Press, 2006) Contains a carefully considered summary of the situation regarding artificial sweeteners.

Sweet Misery: A poisoned world Janet Starr Hull (New Horizon Press, 1998) A sufferer's investigation into the possible dangers of aspartame. There is also a documentary.

Sweet Deception: Why Splenda, Nutrasweet, and the FDA may be hazardous to your health Joseph Mercola and Kendra Degen Pearsall (Nelson Books, 2006) Written by doctors, this combines the history of sugar with the rise of artificial sweeteners and a critique of the FDA.

Wrapping it all up

You might not think too much about the packaging your food comes in, apart from reflecting on the fact that there seems to be an awful lot of it. Across the EU as a whole, food packaging makes up 16% of household waste. But to think of packaging as a just a wrapper is to overlook its sophistication. Often as much thought and attention has gone into the packaging as the product. True, the main function of a package may be to stop what's inside getting out or what's outside getting in. But packaging is getting smart now:

▶ **Modified atmosphere packaging** (MAP) – this replaces the air within a bag of, for example, salad leaves with either carbon dioxide or nitrogen. This also acts as a bulking material, giving the bag its familiar "pillowy" feel. The shelf-life of bakery products can also be significantly extended by MAP. It's also used for nuts and crisps.

▶ **"Active packaging"** is packaging which has additives in the film or container which acts – in industry speak – as a "freshness enhancer". Cooked and cured meats can have "**oxygen scavenging**" labels, which modify the oxygen that reaches the product in order to slow down deterioration.

▶ **"Intelligent packaging"** takes all this one stage further and provides information about the quality and integrity of the product and is able to respond to changes in the environment and the product; "packaging which senses and informs", as an industry source puts it. Intelligent ink senses when food is no longer safe to eat and changes colour to warn the consumer. There are also packaging components which can track your movements round the supermarket and prevent theft (see pp.214–215).

Read the label to avoid the processed "nasties"

Manufacturers would much rather you made your buying decision based on what they put on the front of their packets rather than the small print they are obliged to put on the back. When the EU proposed in 2008 that legal information about ingredients should feature in type no smaller than 3mm, manufacturers complained that compliance would cost them millions and would necessitate all sorts of additional labelling. (Though they never seem to have trouble accommodating their marketing messages on the packs.) Here's how not to be taken in:

▶ **Turn the pack over and look at what's in it** Remember that by law ingredients have to appear in order of size, biggest first. So if sugar or water come near the top of the list, that's largely what you are paying for, plus the chemicals to bind the water content in.

▶ **Look out for sugars in disguise** Remember that sugar can take many forms – anything ending with -ose is a sugar. So are syrups. "Fruit concentrates" are a euphemism for sugar, too. Maltodextrins are moderately sweet starch derivatives found in baby food and sports drinks. Avoid HFCS.

▶ **Ignore the health claims** They are usually based on some additive put in at the end of the process. Look at the ingredients. Avoid the ones with long lists, especially if they are mainly unfamiliar chemicals.

Processing the future

Rising oil and other commodity prices are severely challenging the food industry. Long used to good rates of profit and growth, share prices and profits have lately begun to falter. Food processors are fossil-fuel hungry all the way down the production chain, from the fields spread with chemical fertilizers, to the manufacturing equipment that pumps food round factories, to the distribution systems that truck it across countries and continents. They also face a growing backlash from consumers against products increasingly recognized as unhealthy. The carbonated drinks market, for example, is in long-term decline.

However, it would be naïve to expect the manufacturing giants to switch to healthier, more natural alternatives to their products when it is so much cheaper simply to create an aura of health with marketing claims and neutraceutical products that blur the boundary between food and medicines.

// It would be cheaper to give your kids a big old bowl of white sugar and a shovel. //

Almost Vegetarian blog

// Fat and sugar are what get produced, fat and sugar are cheap, fat and sugar are therefore what get used, and fat and sugar are what we end up eating. //

Felicity Lawrence, *Eat Your Heart Out*, 2008

Every bit as much as their customers, the food processors are truly dependent on fats, sugars and salt. But their business model, based on selling ever-greater volumes of processed food and obtaining economies of scale by buying up smaller players, won't be sustainable indefinitely. The Earth's resources are finite and so are our stomachs. Of course, if everyone switched tomorrow from processed foods to a healthy diet rich in fruit and veg, there wouldn't be enough to go around. Meanwhile, if you're concerned about health, authenticity and value for money, the advice is very simple: eat as little as you can from the processed foods aisles.

Organic
food

We are spending around £2 billion a year in the UK on organic produce. The retail market for organic food has grown by an average of 25% a year over the last decade. Millions of us buy organic food at least some of the time, motivated by a desire to protect our health, or concern for animal welfare or the environment. Some people think that it just tastes better or seems more "natural". Advocates argue that organic food, not being reliant on toxic pesticides, is better for us and the only truly sustainable form of agriculture. Critics say this is nonsense, that organic food is overpriced and over-hyped, and that there is no evidence that it is better in any way than "conventional". Despite the media attention given to organic food, it only represents 4% of total UK food consumption and it usually costs more than conventional. So why do we buy it? And why is it so heavily promoted by its supporters?

Organic food is at the centre of some major debates about our food, but with continuing disagreements over scientific claims, the picture remains confusing for most consumers. Despite mounting evidence and increasing EU support for organic farming, the UK government remains steadfastly sceptical, and if research funding is anything to go by, then the £50 million recently allocated to biotech agricultural research makes the £1.6 million spent on organic research look paltry.

What is organic food?

Organic food developed as an alternative to the intensive form of chemical-dependent agriculture created during the "Green Revolution" in farming (see p.113). Some see it as a return to traditional farming methods of the pre-chemical era, but organic farmers today are interested in using new technology to work in harmony with nature and actively improve crops through traditional plant breeding (using non-GM technology) in order to adapt to changing climatic conditions and increase disease resistance and yields. To qualify as organic, farm land has to have been **free from agrichemicals**, sewage sludge and non-organic manure for at least two years (see certification standards on p.25). The FSA calls organic "a **holistic approach** to food production, making use of crop rotation, environmental management and good animal husbandry to control pests and diseases", and the EU and Defra define organic as food produced:

▶ without artificial pesticides, fertilizers or GMOs

▶ with exemplary crop and animal husbandry standards

▶ with a remit to protect the environment and encourage wildlife.

The organic movement
Where did it come from?

The term "organic" was used in its modern sense to describe a method of cultivation without pesticides by the American publisher J.I. Rodale in 1942 when he started a new *Organic Gardening* magazine. This was taken up and expanded upon by the new Soil Association four years later. In the 1970s, when interest in organic food was growing fast, Rodale and Lady Balfour formed the international group IFOAM (International Federation of Organic Agriculture Movements) to bring together the many separate international bodies to develop a set of standards.

By the 1990s, amid a series of serious health problems linked to intensive agriculture such as BSE and salmonella (see p.40) and press revelations about agricultural pollution of our water supply, pesticide residues on our food and animal maltreatment, the public started to distrust the complacency of government and the marketing-speak of the food industry and

> **//** Making a commitment to buy local and organic produce is one of the most important actions we can take to build a more secure and climate friendly food future against a background of fossil fuel depletion and climate change. **//**
>
> Patrick Holden, Soil Association

look for alternative methods of food production. This led to the burgeoning of demand for organic food.

With demand in the UK now outstripping supply, there are many opportunities for producers and their number is growing. In January 2007, there were 4639 organic producers in the UK, up 7% on the previous year and showing substantial growth from 2500 in 2001.

Ethical principles

Organic principles are about more than just farming methods; they also embody ethical principles in all areas of business. IFOAM has declared that "those involved in organic agriculture should conduct human relationships in a manner that ensures fairness to ... farmers, workers, processors, distributors, traders and consumers." The Soil Association's plans to **restrict labelling of organic air-freighted produce** to that which is Fairtrade or Soil Association certified came in for criticism for straying into non-farming territory. But this was not a new development, merely an attempt at a compromise between environmental needs and social needs in developing countries.

Conventional or organic? Naturally produced muddy carrots or their intensively produced cousins? Without the organic movement you would have no choice.

The Soil Association

One of the best-known and most respected organic bodies, the **Soil Association**, was set up in 1946 by a group of farmers, nutritionists and scientists to challenge chemical-based, intensive agriculture and champion sustainable organic production. In the 1960s it published its standards for organic growing and from there developed a certification and advisory role. Its aim is to research, develop and promote sustainable relationships between the soil, plants, animals, people and the biosphere, in order to produce healthy food while protecting and enhancing the environment. The association campaigns to build public awareness, and influence government on such matters as: genetic engineering, animal welfare, local food production, pesticides, antibiotics and the harmful effects of intensive farming on food quality and safety. As a charity, its activities are financed by its 25,000 members and other donations and grants.

Soil Association

Soil Association soilassociation.org

How can you tell it's organic?

The strict regulations governing organic food (and resultant bureaucracy) make life more difficult for producers, but reassures customers that we are buying unadulterated food that is produced as naturally as possible. EU countries, the US and Japan have strict regulations and certification schemes and organic produce entering these countries from abroad must comply with their regulations. There are more than three hundred **certification bodies** worldwide and many of these are accredited by the IFOAM-approved independent International Organic Accreditation Service (IOAS). All food sold as organic must be approved by government-appointed certifiers, who carry out on-site inspections and an audit of the paperwork to prove regulations have been followed.

The EU has set the legal rules and minimum standards for European organic food since 1993. As part of continued moves towards the harmonization of trade, the EU recently amended the regulations and developed a new organic logo for use on all approved foods. The Soil Association opposed these regulations, concerned about the integrity of organic food and the possible effect on its own logo. The

If we are going to move farming in a different direction and use the buying power of the consumer to drive that, then the ability to trust the products that you purchase is critical.

Patrick Holden,
Soil Association

// When you choose organics, you are voting for a planet with fewer pesticides, richer soil and cleaner water supplies. //

Marion Nestle, nutritionist and author

new rule allows an unlabelled 0.9% maximum level of GMOs, an implicit acceptance of the inevitability of GM contamination of the food chain, even in organic produce. The regulations stipulate that products have to contain at least 95% organic ingredients to carry the new logo and make clear where they were farmed.

UK organic certification

Defra follows EU regulations, producing a *Compendium of UK Organic Standards* to be followed by all producers. The government also set up an Advisory Committee on Organic Standards (ACOS) to advise ministers on all organic issues.

There are currently nine UK certifying bodies. All organic products on sale in the UK have to bear the mark of one of them:

▶ Organic Farmers and Growers Ltd (UK2)

▶ Scottish Organic Producers Association (UK3)

▶ Organic Food Federation (UK4)

▶ Soil Association Certification Ltd (UK5)

▶ Bio-Dynamic Agricultural Association (UK6)

▶ Irish Organic Farmers and Growers Association (UK7)

▶ Organic Trust Limited (UK9)

▶ Quality Welsh Food Certification Ltd (UK13)

▶ Ascisco Ltd (UK15)

The two main bodies certifying more than 90% of the UK's organic food are the Soil Association, and the smaller Organic Farmers and Growers Ltd. The Soil Association is considered by most to be the gold standard of organic, with a set of its own stringent standards which go beyond the minimum required by Defra and the EU, outlawing GMOs from its certified foods, reducing still further the amount of natural pesticides allowed and building in an ethical element. The Soil Association carries out on-the-spot inspections and follows up any complaints with a visit. Its mark is the most widely recognized organic logo and is found on 80% of the UK's organic food. Although certification protects consumers, it sometimes proves uneconomical and time-consuming for very small producers. The

What about eating out?

EU organic regulations do not yet cover restaurants or cafés, so the Soil Association offers a voluntary service either for the whole establishment or for certain ingredient, such as meat. Those supplying caterers with organic foods such as pre-packed sandwiches, meat or prepared vegetables do have to be legally certified. With higher costs and fewer suppliers to buy from, going all-out organic is a bold move for any restaurant. Here are two worth checking out:

Bordeaux Quay, Bristol Barny Haughton's carbon-neutral riverside restaurant sources all its key ingredients from organic suppliers, growers, producers and farms in the West Country and the South West of England.

The Duke of Cambridge, St Peter's Street, Islington The UK's first and only Soil Association-certified gastropub. The drinks are all organic, too.

SA make the process as straightforward and affordable as possible, with small producers (under £180,000 turnover p.a.) paying around £500 a year to cover the costs of inspection. Any profits from the scheme are put back into the campaigning fund.

Is imported organic just as good?

Any organic food on sale in the UK is required to follow the same basic EU regulations as home-produced products. The EU checks any non-European imports; Defra approves all imports to the UK from outside the EU. Where a country does not have organic legislation or IOAS approved certification, then outside bodies such as the Soil Association can provide this through their local inspectors. US legislation was introduced in 2002 through its National Organic Program (NOP) run under the United States Department of Agriculture (USDA), which also monitors US-approved certifiers. There are differences in organic standards between the UK and US, but any US producer wishing to export to the UK is expected to follow UK standards and vice versa.

Organic: arguments for

Supporters argue there are three main benefits of organic farming and food production: environmental, animal welfare and human health. Sceptics argue there's no proof that there is any difference between organic and non-organic food. Let's look at the arguments for each of them.

Environment

UK government studies found that organic farming typically uses 26% less energy than non-organic to produce the same amount of food, giving it a relatively low carbon footprint. The Sustainable Development Commission considers organic certification to be "the gold standard" for sustainable food production. UK taxpayers spend £120 million a year cleaning up the mess of pesticide pollution and nitrogen fertilizer use from conventional farming. Organic farming is supported by environmental organizations such as English Nature, the Soil Association and Friends of the Earth, who believe that that it is best in terms of minimizing damage to the environment and encouraging wildlife. A review of the scientific literature shows that organic farms have 30% more wild species, and around 50% higher numbers of those species.

Animal welfare

Organic farm animals are healthier as they are looked after with regard to their physical and behavioural needs (allowed to interact naturally) and their diet (organic cows enjoy access to grass pasture, for example). Because animals are free range there is no need for the routine use of **antibiotics** as in intensive farming (over 70% of the antibiotics administered in the US are used on farm animals), which creates overcrowded, unhealthy conditions in which animals are more likely to develop disease. The WHO has warned that "there is growing concern that antibiotic residues in meat and dairy products could result in antibiotic resistance in bacteria prevalent in humans, reducing the effectiveness of antibiotics used to treat human disease."

Some critics accuse organic farming of causing unnecessary pain to animals by denying them antibiotics (and tend to blow the occasional use

Food fraud

In 2006 an undercover TV investigation highlighted a number of butchers in south-west England who didn't have an organic licence and who were mis-selling conventionally produced meat as organic. It is the local authority Trading Standards officers' job to follow the paper trail, which should prove whether organic regulations have been followed and to prosecute if they haven't. One officer commented: "It is obvious with such a fast-growing market that some people will be anxious to cash in with fake organic meat." This is why the accreditation schemes exist and why, if you're in doubt, you can ask to see the producer's up-to-date certificate (they are supposed to have it on display) or buy from a trusted source.

of homeopathic remedies out of proportion). Organic farmers dispute this saying that the difference is that they only use antibiotics when there is a clear need. Compassion in World Farming's expert auditors of farming welfare standards say: "the Soil Association's organic standard provides the highest welfare standard in the UK." Some organic farms such as Sheepdrove in Berkshire have their own abattoir, so their animals do not have to endure the confusion and discomfort of being driven across the country for slaughter. While it is not the case that all non-organic meat is raised poorly, it is the case that without an organic assurance you would need to visit farms yourself to be sure.

Pesticides and organic farming

Pest control on organic farms is by prevention rather than cure, using natural predators such as ladybirds and lace-wings. Only seven of the 350 pesticides allowed in conventional farming are allowed in organic farming (the Soil Association limits this to just four), but only with special permission and in exceptional circumstances. Organic farmers bear the financial cost of not spraying, as the growing season is not artificially extended by chemical use. UK potatoes, carrots and onions harvested in the autumn are stored through the winter, but by spring they start to sprout. Conventional farmers spray inhibitor chemicals over potatoes to prevent this (see p.14).

The Soil Association allows pesticides which are either of natural origin (rotenone and soft soap) or simple chemical products – copper compounds and sulphur. The active ingredients in rotenone and soft soap break down rapidly when exposed to sunlight, minimizing risk to the environment. Copper and sulphur are used to combat devastating problems such as potato blight and as a natural fungicide in orchards. These can only be used with consent by the certification body where the farmer provides evidence of a threat to the crop and no available alternatives. No residues of these have been found in organic food. Despite the greatly increased risk of disease as a result of unusually wet weather in 2007, only 3% of Soil

// Drugs are not used to cure sick animals but to prevent them from getting sick, because we crowd them together under filthy circumstances. We have created the perfect environment in which to breed superbugs that are antibiotic-resistant. We've created a petri dish in our factory farms. //

Michael Pollan,
The New Yorker

The plight of the bumblebee

"Without bees there would be no jam, no honey, no fruit and very few vegetables."
British Beekeepers' Association

If a clear sign were needed that intensive farming is damaging the environment and reducing biodiversity, then look no further than the 70% decline of the ordinary UK honeybee over the last thirty years due to habitat loss and mystery deaths of colonies. The only way to revive wild bee populations is to set aside land for wild flowers, something which is common in organic farming, which encourages the growth of hedges and meadows. Even the food industry magazine *The Grocer* admits that "it is now widely accepted that modern farming methods have stripped the land of natural pollen and nectar."

There is now consensus that the situation is serious and action needs to be taken as bees are crucial to our food supply and are in decline globally. Many foods such as apples, pears, raspberries, sunflower oil, alfalfa cattle feed, tomatoes and peppers rely on bees for **pollination**.

Possible causes: it could be the pesticides sprayed in hives and antibiotics administered to control the varroa mite. In the US, some beekeepers and scientists blame a decade of GM crops disrupting the balance of nature. Others think it is the long distances bees are transported to pollinate crops. Another possible cause for Colony Collapse Disorder may be the **Israeli Acute Parasitic Virus** (IAPV) (possibly imported from Australia), which has decimated US bee populations in recent years. Colony numbers there have halved since the 1950s.

A World Without Bees Alison Benjamin and Brian McCallum (Guardian Books, 2008)

Association farmers that year used pesticides with only 2% of organic crops being sprayed.

No organic farmer wants to use artificial pesticides; they are only used as a last resort. But the continuing use of copper is considered by some organic insiders, such as Dr Hardy Vogtmann, professor of organic farming at the University of Cassell, Germany and honorary president of IFOAM, to be a weak point. In order to use copper, farmers are expected to test levels in the soil to guard against problems of toxic accumulation which kills worms; this is most likely to be a problem in orchards where there is no crop rotation. Research into alternatives like potassium bicarbonate and milk waste shows they appear to be effective in getting rid of molds and fungus. The Soil Association accepts that copper is not ideal, but argues that its use is

Ducks out of water

When you pick up a packet of duck pâté from the chill cabinet, what image comes to mind? Wild ducks at the riverside, a straggling trail of fluffy ducklings? The Jemima Puddleducks of our childhood bear no resemblance to the nineteen million factory-farmed ducks which are killed each year to provide 98% of UK duck products.

We know that ducks spend four-fifths of their time in water, but the only water available to farmed ducks is that in the drinking water dispenser. If it were not for successful lobbying by the vegetarian group Viva (viva.org.uk), most of these ducks would have had part their beaks cut off (the industry argued it was necessary to prevent them damaging each other as a result of cramped conditions; scientists say that beaks are full of nerve endings).

If proof were needed of how far we've gone from nature in the way we produce our food perhaps the dreadful undercover film footage from Viva of workers at one of the farms owned by Manor Farm Ducklings (MFD) holding ducks by the neck and punching them or kicking them around the filthy floor, will make us sit up and think. In this Brave New World of protein production, both duck and employee are brutalized by a cruel, unethical system. National TV coverage in 2006 led to outcry – not least because this was an RSPCA Freedom Food-approved farm. The RSPCA immediately withdrew their approval of the company, but it had revealed a weakness in the system.

After the scandal, the old MFD units were bought by the Suffolk-based Green Label/Gressingham Foods as part of their consolidation of the UK intensive duck industry (they now supply the majority of supermarket duck). Today only the Gressingham farms are RSPCA-assured. But only Waitrose fresh duck is from free-range birds which have access to water to swim in.

Buy well looked after, slow-grown organic ducks from the Well Hung Meat Company, who source from Higher Fingle Farm on Dartmoor where ducks are free-range and have constant access to water. (For more details, see p.244.)

extremely limited: "In 2006, copper and derris (rotenone) were used by 3% of certified producers on only 0.3% of UK organic land."

Other UK organic certifiers (along with the EU) allow the additional pesticides: pyrethroids (deltamethrin or lambdacyhalothrin only), iron (III) orthophosphate and paraffin oil, with use of the last two being very restricted. Dr Vogtmann is concerned that the growth of the organic market has led to a "conventionalization of organic agriculture": an increased pressure from some large growers and manufacturers to relax regulations to allow for greater commercial growth.

Critics claim that organic foods such as wheat and nuts (which are susceptible to insect damage) have a higher incidence of molds which produce naturally occurring poisons called **mycotoxins** than in conventional fungicide-treated crops. But recent EU-sponsored research concluded that organic farming practices "were shown repeatedly to reduce risks associated with veterinary medicine, mycotoxin residues and the development of antibiotic resistant micro-organisms in food."

Is organic really healthier?

The organic sector admits there is very little available evidence that organic food tastes better, but there is now evidence that it can be better for your health both in terms of avoiding pesticides and providing higher nutrient levels. The main health argument for organic is the **absence of the many artificial additives** used in intensive agriculture: antibiotics, growth hormones, GMOs and agrichemicals, including fertilizer, fungicides, herbicides and insecticides. Organic food does not contain the range of typical food additives that can be harmful to our health, such as artificial flavourings and colourings, hydrogenated fat and monosodium glutamate.

But it is **pesticides** which provide the focus for much discussion about organic food and health. According to government data, 44% of non-organic fruit and vegetables samples contained pesticides. There is evidence to suggest that dietary exposure to the 350 available in non-organic farming, including long-term exposure and multiple residues, are linked to human health problems. Pesticide use is increasing without the ordinary consumer realizing it: over half of all pesticides ever produced have been applied since 1984. In the UK alone, 31,000 tonnes of pesticides are applied to UK farmland each year. Soil Association organic farms account for just 10 tonnes (0.03%) of this (see p.14).

The position of the FSA, the UK government body charged with advising the public on food, on the merits of organic, has tended to be reticent and confusing for consumers. In 2000 its then director, Sir John Krebs, said "[the public are] not getting value for money in my opinion and in the opinion of the FSA if they think they're buying food with extra nutritional quality or extra safety." Three years later he had changed his mind: "organic food contains fewer residues of the pesticides used in conventional agriculture, so buying organic is one way to reduce the chances that your food contains these pesticide residues." Factually true, but hardly a ringing endorsement. The truth is that the FSA has to balance its advice with economic considerations and cannot be seen to be criticizing the majority of the country's non-organic agriculture.

The Soil Association successfully challenged the FSA about its reluctance to reflect positive research into organic food and farming in its public statements. In 2004 the FSA's own review admitted that "the vast majority" of people consulted felt the Agency had "deviated from its normal stance of making statements based solely on scientific evidence" when "speaking against organic food and for GM food."

> **//** Based on the evidence available, organic food is not significantly different from conventionally produced food, in terms of food safety or nutrition. **//**
>
> FSA, 2007

> **//** There is enough evidence now that the level of good things is higher in organics. **//**
>
> Professor Carlo Leifert, Newcastle University, 2007

It's official: organic really is better

After years of conflicting advice, the findings of a recent £12-million EU project could help settle the long-running debate over the health benefits of organic food. The Newcastle University study was part of the first major research project into organic food and farming funded by the EU. The four-year European research project involved researchers and universities in 31 countries and offers well-researched evidence of the nutritional benefits of organic food. It found that:

▶ **Organic fruit and vegetables contain more nutrients** and 40% more antioxidants – substances which scientists believe can cut the risk of cancer and heart disease, Britain's biggest killers.

▶ **Organic foods have higher levels of iron and zinc** the vital nutrients lacking in many people's diets.

▶ **Organic milk contains up to 80% more antioxidants** than non-organic milk and higher levels of vitamins A and E.

What's lurking in your fridge?

"The evidence is very convincing that – as you'd expect – there are fewer residues by far in organically grown foods." *Food Additives and Contaminants* journal, 2002

Organic food is usually more expensive than conventional, so if you want to reduce your exposure and are on a budget, then choose organic versions of the fruits and vegetables most likely to retain residues, and the ones you eat most frequently. The FSA has found that apples receive about twenty applications of agrichemicals, leaving residues on over 60%; the organophosphate, chlorpyrifos, is the most frequently found.. You can reduce (but not eliminate) residue levels in conventional foods by washing or peeling, but the downside of this is that nutrients contained in the skins will be lost.

The US charity Environmental Working Group (EWG) compiled a list based on the results of nearly 51,000 tests for pesticides on food collected by the USDA (US Department of Agriculture) and the US Food and Drug Administration between 2000 and 2005. Produce was washed and peeled in the usual way and given scores out of 100 according to the level of contamination. The higher the score, the more contamination found.

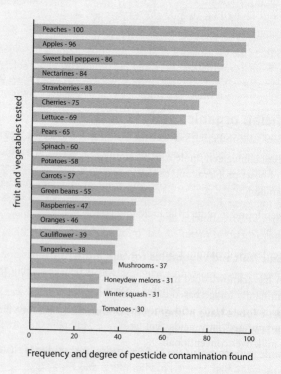

Frequency and degree of pesticide contamination found

▶ **Organic cheese can have up to twice as many nutrients** as conventional varieties.

▶ **Organic wheat, tomatoes, potatoes, cabbage, onions and lettuce** had between 20 and 40% more nutrients.

Other recent EU research also highlighted the higher nutritional quality of organic apples, peaches and tomatoes. Organic apple purée was found to contain "more bio-active substances – total phenols, flavonoids [antioxidants] and vitamin C – in comparison to conventional apple preserves". Organic peaches "have a higher polyphenol [antioxidant] content at harvest". Research found that organic methods have "positive effects ... on nutritional quality and taste". Recent US research backs up these findings.

Why is organic milk good for you?

Milk is the organic food most thoroughly researched by scientists. Price comparisons show that despite the extra cost of the animal feed and higher welfare, a pint of organic milk costs only a few pence more than conventional. A 2006 study by Liverpool and Glasgow universities compared a range of UK dairy farms over a year and discovered that organically reared cows, which eat high levels of fresh grass and clover, produce nutritionally superior milk. The findings were consistent with four earlier studies. It found:

▶ 68% more omega-3 fatty acids than non-organic milk.

▶ Levels of conjugated linoleic acid (a fatty acid credited with lowering the risk of heart problems and cancer) can be up to 60% higher in organic milk.

▶ It's been found to reduce the incidence of eczema, suffered by 10% of children, by over one-third.

▶ Higher levels of vitamin E and beta-carotene.

The FSA has acknowledged that beef produced from organic animals fed a predominantly forage-based diets rather than grain, has lower levels of unhealthy saturated fatty acid concentrations and higher levels of **omega-3** polyunsaturated fatty acids, but they are still reluctant to promote organic milk over conventional.

Organic in the marketplace

What was once dismissed as a hippy fad is now a firmly established as part of the mainstream grocery market. In summer 2008 the effects of the credit crunch were finally reflected in a drop in sales of 20% against the previous year with many customers downgrading to free-range meat and eggs while times were hard, but this may be a temporary setback when set against rapidly increasing sales over many years. Europe is the largest market by value for organic foods in the world, followed by the US, but neither produces enough to supply demand, making imports essential, which doesn't sit comfortably with the organic ideal.

Why is it so expensive?

Surveys show that organic shoppers across a range of income brackets are willing to pay more for organic because they feel sure they are getting better quality, healthier, ethically produced food. But in hard times food quality is seen by many people as something that can be cut back on. Buying direct is the cheapest way of buying organic fruit and vegetables; in the supermarket it is priced as a premium product 30–40% more than conventional. It is also more likely to be imported. Organic is struggling to keep prices down while costs rise. Non-GM organic feed now costs 80% more than non-organic feed and Nicholas Saphir (Organic Milk Suppliers Co-operative) is worried about shortages of UK-produced organic milk as farmers give up. "The extra cost of producing organically now outweighs the farm gate premium, which is clearly unsustainable."

Organic processed food

Of the three hundred food additives permitted in conventional food, only thirty are allowed under Soil Association standards (and 37 under EU law). Of these, some are required by law in certain foods, such as iron, thiamine (vitamin B) and nicotinic acid (vitamin B3) in white flour and various vitamins in some baby foods. All artificial colourings, GMOs and sweeteners are banned in organic food.

All the big food companies such as Heinz, Nestlé, Kraft and PepsiCo now have organic ranges so that you can now buy organic versions of your favourite processed foods: ketchup, cereals and ready meals. There was even, for a brief time, an organic version of Pot Noodle. What started out as a method of producing healthy and nutritious food is now turning out highly industrialized multi-ingredient (albeit organic) products. Frustrated

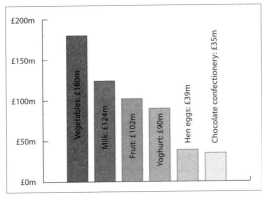

UK organic bestsellers 2006–7 (Source: TNS, for the 52 weeks to 2/12/07)

by the limitations of strict organic regulations, mainstream manufacturers have put pressure on legislators to make concessions so that they can satisfy the supermarket system's desire for products with long shelf-lives.

Is supermarket organic the real deal?

By 2000 the organic consumer market had shifted towards the health-conscious foodie looking for guaranteed provenance and top-quality ingredients. The style of organic food packaging changed accordingly to reinforce those associations of high quality. Consumer trends pointed to shoppers looking for healthier, better-quality food across income types; 77% of British households bought organic food at least once in 2005.

Spotting a lucrative market happy to pay a bit more, the supermarkets stepped in, as Michael Pollan puts it in *The Omnivore's Dilemma*, "transforming organic from a reform movement into an industry – another

Tomato ketchup can be good for you

The pigment which makes tomatoes red is called **lycopene**, and in general, the darker the tomato, the more lycopene it contains. It has been shown to help protect against breast, pancreatic, prostate and intestinal cancer. It may also be able to reduce the risk of heart attacks. After a twelve-year research study in California comparing lycopene levels and antioxidants in organic and non-organic ketchup, organic came out on top. One organic brand contained three times as much lycopene as a fast-food sample.

Whole Foods Market: the organic supermarket

Whole Foods Market opened its first US shop in 1980, expanding quickly to 250 shops across the US, often through acquisitions and at the expense of established small shops. In 2004 it moved to the UK and bought up the **Fresh & Wild** chain. When they opened a flagship London shop in South Kensington in 2007, they announced big plans for forty more UK stores. Shoppers were overwhelmed by the choice: thirty types of bread, countless chocolate bars and a whole roomful of cheese. Though often referred to as an organic supermarket, in fact only 40% of its product lines are organic.

Where health food shops keep prices down to attract customers, Whole Foods has a reputation of charging the highest price it thinks the market will bear, earning it the nickname the "Whole Paycheck". This, combined with the credit crunch and too-rapid expansion, led to a drop in profits and the closure of its large Bristol Fresh & Wild shop in 2008. Clio Turton of the Soil Association commented: "Fresh and Wild is much more expensive than the average supermarket. People … may be going for cheaper options such as growing their own or getting a vegetable box."

flavour in the global supermarket". It became possible to buy your favourite Whole Earth organic crunchy peanut butter or Green & Black's organic chocolate not just in your local health food shop but also in the supermarket (although it wasn't necessarily any cheaper). Today, supermarkets hold hundreds of organic items in stock in their larger stores (some of them own-label) and most offer a varied range of organic fruit and vegetables. Sainsbury's was the first to offer customers organic food in 1986. They, along with Tesco, are now the biggest retailers of organic food in the UK.

While supermarket organic has its critics, they have expanded the market for organic food and helped grow organic brands such as Yeo Valley into household names. This Somerset-based independent was the first organic food company to be listed in the Nielsen Top 100 Grocery Brands and the third-largest brand across the yoghurt sector. Not bad for an company which has followed its organic principles into the way it sources its milk, offering long-term contracts and a fair price to its hundred suppliers.

// Organic is not a revolution so much as a market niche. //

General Mills,
US food corporation

There are many contradictions in supermarket organic, not least the demand for heavily processed and packaged convenience foods. Anecdotal evidence suggests that organic producers experience the same problems of bully-boy buying tactics, no-notice delisting, fines and take-it-or-leave-it low prices as their conventional peers. But they have a distinct disadvantage: the absence of artificial chemicals and additives means that organic producers struggle to fulfil the supermarkets need for long shelf-life and cosmetic consistency.

Industrial organic: adapt or die?

Organic food has reached a crossroads in its development: modernizers argue that the time has come for it to follow the global food industry and scale up, and that some compromise of is standards is inevitable. To allow producers and processors more freedom to make a better profit, regulations would have to be slackened and the odd corner cut. But at what cost? It looks likely that in the UK and Europe, as in the US, a two- or three-tier system may develop, with large-scale "industrial organic" operations providing the bulk of organic food for sale in supermarkets, alongside a smaller specialist sector catering for a farmers' market clientele.

Some argue that organic food has become a victim of its own success. While US conventional food sales growth remains fairly constant at around 3%, organic food sales have grown at an annual average of 19% since the late 1990s and even the recent slowdown may not deflate the overall upward trend too badly. In the US, international organic standards have been compromised as a result of intense lobbying by US agribusiness and supermarkets of the government. Only the most basic legal requirements of EU regulations (such as animal feed and pesticide use)

Selling up and selling out?

Inevitably, seeing the commercial success of organic food, major food companies are on the lookout to acquire instant organic brands such as Cauldron Foods (bought by Premier Foods), and Green & Black's (acquired by Cadbury's), both sold off in 2005 (see p.136). With Craig Sams, founder of Green & Black's, still on the board and Cadbury's making much of the company retaining its ethical credentials, perhaps corporate organic can work. But critics worry about organic selling its soul and the gradual erosion of standards when ethical principles come into conflict with commercial pressures. Rachel's Dairy, a Welsh family firm and one of the first certified organic dairies in the UK, makes no mention of its new owner, Dean Foods, on its packaging. Dean Foods, known for their use of the controversial bovine growth hormone (rBGH), have moved into organic in a big way, and now control 55% of the US organic milk market with their mainly factory-produced, ultra-pasteurized "Horizon" brand, which a recent survey found to be "ethically challenged".

Meanwhile, Rachel's Dairy has launched a processed, chilled dessert yoghurt, complete with chocolate swirls, glucose syrup, soya lecithin and natural flavourings.

are followed and there is nothing to prevent semi-industrial-scale organic dairies keeping thousands of cows in confined feedlots, as the basic stipulation of animals having "access to pasture" is not spelt out. On the new large-scale US organic farms there is little visible difference between the conventional farm run next-door to the organic version – partly because they can be run by the same farmer. Organic is now being seen as a lucrative side-line, a diversification strategy more than a philosophy.

Soil Association standards guard against this, but for how long? The other main UK certifier, Organic Farmers and Growers take what some might see as the industry view: "What was a niche market is now becoming mainstream and that requires that it is run in a commercial and professional manner. I don't think that's the industrialization of organics or dumbing down. It is the realization of a fast-growing market." When criticized for the high level of imported organic in his stores, Tesco boss Sir Terry Leahy, blamed the overly strict UK organic standards and inadequate supply.

Find out more

Soil Association soilassociation.org The UK's leading campaigning and certification organization for organic food and farming. Their website is full of useful information with searchable supplier directories (The Organic Directory), the latest news about sustainable organic agriculture and policy information.

Elm Farm Research Centre efrc.com Information and news about organic farming and food.

The Henry Doubleday Research Association (HYDRA) gardenorganic.org.uk Specializes in organic gardening and food in the UK. It also has a Schools Organic Network.

Sustain sustainweb.org A campaign group advocating sustainable living, food and agriculture policies.

Part II

Global
Food

A global trade

We live in a food world that is interconnected as never before. Supermarkets stock fresh Thai curry spices flown in from Bangkok (9500km), beef from Argentina and Brazil (11,000km), and onions shipped from New Zealand (18,000km). The contents of the average supermarket trolley have travelled further to get to the store than most people do in a lifetime.

Everything connects

While our supermarkets give us a world of perpetual summer, at the same time we are becoming increasingly aware of the cost to the planet of our desire to eat strawberries at Christmas and mangetout from Zimbabwe all year round. And we're also more aware of the direct human cost of our global appetites. Campaigning charities such as Oxfam and War on Want and the Fairtrade movement have made it much harder to ignore the exploitation of people and the environment that goes on around the world in order to provide western consumers with cheap food.

Something is clearly not right with the international food system. According to the UN, an estimated 25,000 people die of hunger each day and 854 million are chronically undernourished. At the same time, around one billion are steadily eating their way to obesity and its associated health problems. But this is not a simple developed world versus developing world dichotomy; as incomes rise in the developing world, multinational food producers are happy to provide all the dubious attractions of a fat-laden, processed western diet.

Half the world's workers, many of whom work in food production of some form, live on less than **$2 a day**. Added to chronic poverty are the problems of slavery, child labour and other abuses of workers' rights.

Many in developing nations live in the knowledge that if they complain about their working conditions, they will be dismissed and instantly replaced. Indeed, in today's global economy a transnational corporation's entire production facility can be switched to another country very quicky if a host country gives its workers too many entitlements, and buying arrangements with growers can be terminated overnight. What ensues has been called the "**race to the bottom**", as governments of developing world countries vie with each other to attract international investment and jobs, regardless of the human and environmental cost. This part looks at some of the big questions surrounding global food choices – how can the world feed itself now and in the future? What will climate change mean for the world's food supply? And does GM technology hold the answer?

How we got here

The world food system today has its origins in colonial times. Colonies existed in order to provide food, minerals or slaves for the benefit of the colonial power. The aim was to extract the maximum value from the resources its overseas possessions offered. A growing population at home could be kept fed and contented with sugar and tea from Indian and Caribbean plantations, for example.

In the post-war world, as empires vanished, they left behind them familiar power relationships between the developed and developing worlds. Harry S. Truman's inaugural address on becoming US president in 1949 put it concisely: "we must carry out our plans for reducing the barriers to world trade and increasing its volume." Barriers bad, free trade good, was the mantra. By the late 1950s, US aid accounted for one-third of all wheat traded in the world, creating dependent nations that couldn't hope to compete on price. By the 1970s, Richard Nixon's agriculture secretary was telling farmers that: "Food is a tool. It is a weapon in the US negotiating kit." That remains true today.

Trade may seem to take place between equal partners, but it's a mirage: when western nations buy cocoa from the Ivory Coast or coffee from Guatemala, it's not the same as buying Italian parmesan or French champagne. The power relationship is quite different. The foods that Europeans pride themselves most

II Through our colonial policy, as soon as we acquire and develop a territory, we develop it as agents of civilization, for the growth of world trade. *II*

British Secretary of State for the Colonies, 1896

How green was the Green Revolution?

The "Green Revolution" began in post-war America as an initiative to develop new high-yielding varieties of wheat to feed the country's expanding population. It fulfilled that aim, but by the 1960s there remained severe problems of hunger in many parts of the developing world. To tackle this, the US exported its Green Revolution, thereby extending the methods of modern industrialized farming, with its pesticides and fertilizers, to the countries of Asia and Latin America. On the upside, new high-yielding "semi-dwarf" varieties of wheat and rice greatly increased harvests. The Mexican wheat harvest rose, for example, from 300,000 tonnes in 1950 to 2.6 million tonnes in 1970. By dramatically increasing food supply in this way the Green Revolution undoubtedly saved significant numbers of people from starvation.

But the gains came at a price: dependence on chemical fertilizers and pesticides became widespread in many parts of the world. It was also highly demanding in its water use, so some water-deprived areas saw no benefit at all. Indeed, three-quarters of Indian farmers were left out of the Green Revolution, which focused on the fertile Punjab. As in the west, economies of scale meant you had to get bigger to survive, which extended the western system of specialization and monocultures. And despite various attempts, the Green Revolution never worked in Africa, though opinion is divided on whether this was because it was badly implemented or ill-suited to African conditions.

Critics have also pointed to the high **ecological price** incurred and to the fact that it didn't eradicate hunger. But Norman Borlaug, called "the father of the Green Revolution" for his pioneering work on semi-dwarf wheat, told *Atlantic Monthly* that his environmentalist critics had "never experienced the physical sensation of hunger … If they lived just one month amid the misery of the developing world, as I have for fifty years, they'd be crying out for tractors and fertilizer and irrigation canals."

Now a second Green Revolution is being promoted by the same companies which helped bring about the first, with the same promises of ending starvation, this time based on biotechnology (see p.144).

on producing are created by artisanal processes: cured hams, speciality cheeses, estate-bottled wines. They come with information about their provenance, which is often protected by law. Compare this protection with Ethiopia's struggle to defend its right to trademark two speciality coffee names, Harar and Sidamo. It came up against vigorous opposition from global coffee giant Starbucks. Ethiopia eventually won in 2007, but the victory was noteworthy for its rarity.

Developing nations are largely producing agricultural goods for the **commodity market**, where prices are determined on trading floors in international financial centres, and what a grower receives depends on the price a middleman sets for a product, no matter how much care

> **❝** Control oil and you control nations; control food and you control the people. **❞**
>
> Henry Kissinger, former US Secretary of State

> **❝** Generally, great powers are willing to enter into some limited degree of free trade when they're convinced that the economic interests under their protection are going to do well. **❞**
>
> Noam Chomsky, writer and political activist

has been lavished upon it. Producers accept the price they are offered because they have no other option, and probably little inkling of how much profit the coffee or chocolate multinationals will make once their product has been processed, packaged and branded.

Developing nations face disadvantages that are built into the system from the start. Ever wondered why abundant raw materials come from the developing world, but few processed, "value added" goods do? The answer is partly that developing nations face tariffs four times as high as those from the rich north. According to the UN Food and Agriculture Organization (FAO), the more dependent a country is on food exports, the more hungry people in its population. Oxfam has described the rules under which developing countries have to operate as "**robbery against the world's poor**". They point out that the tariffs which developing countries have to pay in order to export their goods adds up to more than the aid they receive from the rich nations. In effect they are paying for the privilege of being allowed to trade with us.

There are other ways in which the odds are stacked against poor countries. Rich nations can afford to pay their farmers subsidies to the tune of $1 billion per day. There are export **subsidies** as well as production subsidies, so that North American and European farmers can afford to sell at prices that developing world farmers cannot match, safe in the knowledge that subsidy payments will make up for any shortfall. **Sugar** has been a particularly notorious example of this. The EU, the world's biggest exporter of refined sugar, sells sugar on the world market for one-quarter of what it costs to produce. Developing world farmers cannot compete. There are further knock-on effects: South Africa is able to produce sugar at less than half the cost of the EU, but without subsidy, local South African chocolate and sweet manufacturers are put out of business by cheaper imported confectionery from the transnational corporations.

Loans to developing countries come with conditions attached to ensure that they open up to **market liberalization**. Proponents claim it is bet-

Welcome to NAFTA: the Mexican experience

Mexico is where corn was first domesticated around eight thousand years ago and the corn tortilla remains a staple in the national diet today, so there is a bitter irony in the fact that the future of Mexico's corn growing is under serious threat from a free-trade pact with its northern neighbours.

In 1994 the **North American Free Trade Agreement** (NAFTA) created a free-trade zone throughout Canada, the US and Mexico. Since then, tariffs protecting Mexico from a tide of cheap subsidized corn from its rich neighbour have been coming down. Already the US is dumping the equivalent of nearly half of Mexico's annual corn production from its subsidized industry and as of 1 January 2008 tariffs ceased altogether. There were large-scale demonstrations against the effects of NAFTA in Mexico shortly after. A statement by the protestors could have been uttered in any number of developing countries pushed into rapid liberalization: "During the 14 years of NAFTA, unemployment, immigration, the destruction of our agricultural activities, the concentration of resources into a few hands, the deterioration of purchasing power and wages and extreme poverty have increased in an alarming manner."

Lucha Castro, a lawyer and women's right activist told *Workers' World*: "NAFTA and related government policies are responsible for expelling five million people from Mexico's countryside. Merely 2% of Mexico's agricultural production units benefit from the treaty, while 80% of Mexican farm exports are controlled by foreign capital. To compete with the US all these years, the forests and soils have been devastated, and our aquifers have been overexploited."

In essence, Mexican agriculture has found itself pitted against a much stronger opponent, which pumps out fifteen times more (heavily subsidized) corn each year than it can. It has been faced with the choice of becoming more like American agriculture or becoming extinct. That means more large farms, higher water use and greater chemical inputs. Some people might say this is a good thing, the painful but necessary price of modernization. But while productivity is up, wages in real terms are down and income inequality has widened. And millions of small farmers have deserted the land. All this would be bad enough, but **US biotech** companies have been pushing hard to gain access to the Mexican market, where GM seed is currently banned. Walmart meanwhile now sells more tortillas in Mexico than anyone else.

ter to have a short, sharp economic shock; that it generates more wealth all round and the poor benefit in time from a trickle-down effect; and that it removes the corruption that often accompanies protectionism. Unfortunately, the evidence suggests that the wealth and profits from free trade often end up being sent overseas (three-quarters of money invested in Africa turns out to be repatriated to its headquarters by the investing company). So the poor become entrenched in their poverty.

Who calls the shots?

The **World Trade Organization** (WTO) describes itself as "an organization for liberalizing trade, ... a forum for governments to negotiate trade agreements, ... a place for them to settle trade disputes". This international body, set up in Switzerland in 1995, grew out of lengthy negotiations over the **General Agreement on Tariffs and Trade** (GATT). (GATT itself was part of a long-running post-war attempt to regulate how countries trade with each other, and in particular to reduce import barriers.) Criticism of the WTO is so widespread and vociferous that its own website devotes many pages to countering some of the commonest accusations. For example, that it is dictatorial and bent on free trade at any cost, that it is unconcerned about health, poverty or the environment, and that it bullies small countries and sides with the rich and powerful nations. Despite its protestations, many in the developing world and those who campaign on their behalf see the odds in the WTO forum stacked against them, such is the negotiating power of the rich northern nations.

From the start, agriculture has proved the biggest sticking point for international agreement, because, in contrast to the rich North, so many in the Global South depend on it directly for their precarious livelihoods. The current round of international trade talks, the so-called **Doha Round**, which began in 2001 in Qatar, broke down in acrimony in 2003 over the US and the EU's continuing level of farm subsidies.

This led to the creation of a new, and increasingly powerful negotiating group, the **G20**, led by Brazil, a country well on the way to becoming an agricultural superpower of the twenty-first century, and India. Talks have lurched on since then. The biggest bone of contention remains farm subsidies.

These subsidies and access to new markets suit the true power players in the world food game, the **transnational corporations**. The modern food world is controlled to an astonishing degree by a small number of mega-corporations: seed, pesticide and biotech businesses Syngenta, Monsanto and Dow; grain and commodity dealers such as Cargill, ADM, Bunge and Louis Dreyfus (see p.67); food manufacturers such as Nestlé, Kraft and Unilever (see pp.68–69); and retailers such as Walmart, Tesco and Carrefour (see Chapter 13). You could quite easily spend a lifetime consuming nothing but products grown, manufactured and traded by those thirteen companies. They all share a desire to preserve the international food system from any change that would damage their interests. They are adept at lobbying politicians, whose parties benefit from their funding and who receive attractive job offers from them on leaving office. By so doing, they can affect legislation on a host of issues as diverse as employment and planning law, unionization and health and safety.

World Trade Organization wto.org

US Food aid: food with strings attached

The intention behind food aid is simple: to fill the gap between the food a population needs and what is locally available. The US is the world's biggest donor of food aid. Its programme was created in 1954 by the Eisenhower administration and has always been a mix of altruism and self-interest. It was stipulated when it was set up that aid had to be given in the form of food grown in the US. It couldn't be locally sourced. That way hungry people were fed, and the subsidized US agricultural surpluses disposed of.

For big shipping and food production companies, food aid is big business. In recent years over half of the US budget of around $2 billion has gone to just four big companies: Archer Daniels Midland, Cargill, Bunge and Cal Western Packaging. Because oil prices have forced transport costs up, 65% of the budget now goes on shipping American food around the world rather than on the food itself. There have been criticisms, too, that food aid is weighted towards countries that have future potential utility to the US, rather than the ones which need it most.

That food aid is **not simply about charity** was made very clear in 2002, when the Zambian government turned down a shipment of genetically modified corn from the US on the grounds that it might contaminate their own production. Zambia's president said: "We may be poor and experiencing severe food shortages, but we aren't ready to expose our people to ill-defined risks through the consumption of non-certified foods."

Viewed from one angle, the Zambians, with hungry mouths to feed, were hardly in a position to refuse ("beggars can't be choosers," one US official was reported to have muttered). Seen from another, shipping GM corn without offering any alternative was a cynical ploy on the US's part to "integrate GM into local food systems", one of the US Agency for International Development's stated aims. In the event, Zambia managed to obtain cassava from within the region and famine was averted, a demonstration that diversity of production and local food solutions can sometimes work.

> **/ /** The principal beneficiary of America's foreign assistance programs has always been the United States. **/ /**
>
> USAID website

Uganda: protecting rice farmers

Though one of the poorest countries in the world, with one-third of its people below the poverty line, Uganda has managed to protect itself from the recent rocketing price of rice, while the rest of sub-Saharan Africa spends around $2 billion a year on rice imports. Uganda has made its bid for self-sufficiency by engaging in **protectionism**, flying in the face of advice from the **World Bank** and the **International Monetary Fund** (IMF), which have long urged developing markets to open up to international trade.

In the past few years, Uganda's rice crop has more than doubled thanks to new upland varieties of the grain. And farmers have had the incentive of knowing that imported rice is subject to a hefty 75% import duty. This has given them the confidence to invest, with the reassurance that their country will not be flooded with cheap, subsidized imports. Shipping costs double the cost of fertilizer in Uganda, so input levels are low and human labour replaces fossil fuel. There are concerns over land clearance, but at least the home-grown rice crop is feeding local people rather than transnational corporations' profits.

Protectionism has a bad reputation as it's often kept close company with **corruption** and **inefficiency**. But according to Africa specialist, G. Pascal Zachary, it should be one of the economic tools available to African governments to help sustain local producers, feed their populations and prove that African nations needn't be "passive victims of global economic forces".

The end of cheap food

Food prices in rich industrialized nations have been falling for decades in real terms, absorbing less and less of family budgets. Most households in the West spend only between 10 and 20% of their income on food. In poor countries it can be as high as 80%. This means consumers in rich nations find it easier to absorb price rises than in the past, and don't radically change their buying habits. This further restricts poor countries' buying power, causing the pain of price rises to be felt even more acutely.

Most western consumers had become used to the idea that food would be cheap and plentiful forever. But in the course of 2007 wheat, maize and rice prices all reached record highs. By the end of the year *The Economist* declared: "The era of cheap food is over." The following year saw **food demonstrations and riots** over in countries as diverse as Cambodia, Cameroon, Ethiopia, Honduras, Indonesia, Madagascar, Peru, the Phillipines, Senegal, Thailand and Uzbekistan. In Haiti, where the price of staple foods rose by 50% in a year, protestors took to the streets chanting "We're hungry!" A week of food riots eventually brought down the government. In Egypt, the army was drafted in to start baking bread to quell popular unrest, while in Cameroon 24 people died in food riots. Ration cards were introduced in Pakistan for subsidized wheat.

There's not just one reason, of course, for rising food prices and circumstances vary in different parts of the world, but, in general, demand is on the rise and supply is being disrupted by a number of factors. These have come into play in a period when supply and demand are much more finely balanced than in the past, since policy in recent years has been to reduce the world's stocks of food, as though the world were a supermarket run on a just-in-time basis. Food has also become a **commodity for speculators** and traders in the derivatives market, where billions of dollars worth of food futures can change hands, as though food were an entirely abstract concept.

As the economies of countries such as Brazil, Russia, India and China grow, there is increasing **demand for higher-value foodstuffs** such as meat and dairy produce. Whereas steadily growing population numbers in poor countries have relatively little impact on the overall demand for food, since abundant staple grains form the bulk of their diet, increases in affluence shifts the *kinds* of food that people are able to buy. The higher up the food chain they aspire to be, the greater the resources needed to feed them. Last but not least, as China's affluence grows, its power as an international purchaser of food is growing, too, sending ripples through the world food system that could in time become waves.

A woman in Haiti preparing "mud cakes" made from clay plus a little margarine and sugar. These are eaten to stave off hunger pangs.

Climate change and food miles

"Global warming will bring a big opportunity for UK farmers," ran the headline above a story in *Farmers Weekly* in December 2007. The opinion was that of Wales's Chief Scientific Adviser, Chris Pollock, who had told a farming conference that global warming presented British farmers with the chance to grow new crops and reach new markets. This may be true, but it does risk missing the main point: the overall stability of the global food supply looks precarious as average temperatures around the world are rising at a rate unprecedented in historical times.

Our over-heating planet
What it means for our food

The **Intergovernmental Panel on Climate Change** (IPCC), the leading body for assessing scientific research in the field, picked out some **food-related threats** in its 2007 report. The main ones are an increase in the number of undernourished people in the world, the disruption of food stability and greater dependence on food imports in the poorest parts of the world. In other words, the effects of climate change won't be felt equally by all of the world's population; those who pollute least are likely to pay the highest price.

Already an increasingly volatile climate is having an impact on agriculture. In many parts of the world, especially the southern hemisphere, water is becoming scarcer. **Drought** reduced the size of the Australian wheat harvest by a half in 2007. In the same year, dry, hot weather caused the wheat crop in Romania to fall by 46% and in Morocco by 76% year on year. Meanwhile, **flooding** in England destroyed the pea and onion crop and severely reduced potato and salad yields. And in 2008 flooding in Iowa caused crop damage estimated at $3 billion.

According to the IPCC's report, which is based on its assessment of a vast array of scientific research, some parts of the world are likely to suffer particular problems:

▶ **Africa** By 2020, between 75 and 250 million people will suffer from increased **water shortages** and in some countries crop yields could be down by as much as 50%. This will affect food security and exacerbate malnutrition.

▶ **Australasia** By 2030, agricultural and forestry production will decline over much of southern and eastern Australia and parts of eastern New Zealand due to increased drought and fire.

▶ **Southern Europe** Climate change will increase **high temperatures and drought** in a region already vulnerable to climate variability.

▶ **Latin America** By mid-century, productivity of some important crops will decrease and livestock productivity decline. Overall, the number of people at risk of hunger is projected to increase.

Crops under threat

Most of our staple crops are essentially **grasses**, which are sensitive to changes in average temperature. There's been comparatively little variation in those average temperatures during the ten thousand years in which humans have been farming. But in many tropical and subtropical regions, crops are already being grown close to the **maximum temperatures** they will tolerate. For most crops, ideal growing temperatures are in the 20°–35°C range. Averages above 35°C in many plants' growing season cause growth rates to drop by about 10% for every 1°C. Above 40°C – the sort of heatwave temperatures that are becoming increasingly common – plants suffer **heat stress** and photosynthesis can cease altogether. Other malign effects of rising temperatures include greater risk of **animal and foodborne diseases**; threats to the **marine environment** and fish stocks; and greater **pest resistance** to pesticides.

▶ **North America** In the early decades of this century, moderate climate change is projected to **increase agricultural yields** but with major regional variation. Severe challenges for crops that are sensitive to high temperatures or are particularly water-dependent are expected.

Agriculture is, of course, not an innocent victim of global warming. It's also one of its major causes. Around **one-third of all greenhouse gas** emissions caused by human activity come from agriculture: **thirteen to fifteen billion tonnes a year**. The typical UK family of four is responsible for around four tonnes of CO_2 emissions from their car and the same from running their home each year, and a further eight tonnes from the production, processing, packaging and transportation of all the food they consume. On a global scale, the big contributors to agriculture's carbon footprint are **deforestation** of land for growing crops, **cattle** rearing (a big producer of methane) and **fertilizer** use (the biggest single source of nitrous oxide, a potent greenhouse gas).

What can we do?

Obviously, with a problem of this magnitude there's no quick fix, but cessation of the biofuels programme would be a step in the right direction (see box opposite), as would the reduction of the consumption of beef and other livestock, which use a high proportion of the world's grain production, and reduction of agricultural methods heavily dependent on fossil fuel, such as chemical fertilizer use. Beyond that, experts agree there is going to have to be a great deal of **adaptation** to different and changing environmental situations round the world. We are going to have to change our habits; business as usual isn't going to work. Find out more:

Intergovernmental Report on Climate Change ipcc.ch/ipccreports

The biofuel dilemma: filling stomachs or petrol tanks?

Not so long ago, biofuels (from "bios", the Greek for "life") were held up as the answer to our looming energy crisis. They would, we were told, help reduce our dependence on dwindling oil resources by offering a fuel source that could be grown in the fields rather than drilled out of the ground. They would reduce greenhouse gas emissions without forcing motorists to change their ways and even help deal with the corn surpluses piled up by US agriculture. The EU established a **target of 10%** for the

Biofuel facts

▶ Bio-energy is produced from plant sources. Biodiesel is typically made from palm oil or oilseed rape. Ethanol is derived from sugar cane or maize.

▶ Biofuels took an estimated 100 million tonnes of grain out of the food supply in 2007.

▶ The world's leading biofuel producers are the US and Brazil. The US supports its biofuels industries with hefty subsidies, effectively pricing foreign competitors out of the market.

▶ Companies such as Tesco have made major investments in biofuels. Tesco has a 25% stake in biofuel refiner Greenergy.

▶ It would take a person a year to eat the amount of grain needed to fill the 25-gallon tank of an SUV just once.

▶ Thirst for biofuel has created numerous cases of human rights abuses in South America, as small farmers are thrown off their land to make way for biofuel crops. See waronwant.org for more.

Biofuelwatch biofuelwatch.org.uk campaigns against the use of bio-energy from unsustainable sources and in favour of positive climate change action.

percentage of biofuel in our petrol tanks by 2020. George W. Bush set a goal of 24% biofuel in US gas tanks by 2017.

Why then did Jean Ziegler, the UN's special rapporteur with responsibility for "the right to food", describe biofuels in 2007 as "a **crime against humanity**"? First, using land for biofuel crops either means taking it out of food production, which pushes prices up, hurting the world's poorest disproportionately, or else it brings further environmental damage through the clearance of carbon-absorbing tropical forests. In Borneo and Sumatra the orang-utan has been pushed to the brink of extinction as its home has been given over to palm oil. Many other species face a similar fate.

It gets worse. Nobel laureate for chemistry Paul Crutzen found that the greenhouse gas nitrous oxide from fertilizers cancels out any ecological benefit from biofuel, which may even require *more* fossil fuel to make it than drilling oil. All in all, biofuels turn out to be much less green than their proponents claim. Dutch consultancy Delft Hydraulics worked out that a tonne of palm oil, for example, produces **ten times as much greenhouse gas as petrol**.

As a fall-back position, biofuel enthusiasts claim second-generation biofuels will be much more efficient, as they'll use agricultural waste such as straw. But that really won't wash either: such "waste" has in fact a role to play in nourishing the soil. Without it, more fertilizers will be needed, giving rise to more need for oil.

Food miles
Keeping on trucking?

Research suggests that two-thirds of us would prefer to use products with a low carbon footprint. The food chain creates 18% of UK greenhouse gas emissions. Farming and fishing contribute around 7% of total emissions. Food manufacturers and supermarkets have been told by the government that they've got to reduce their emissions substantially in the coming years. As consumers we can make it clear to supermarkets, through our shopping choices, that we care about this and that it's worth them making more effort. But in order to make meaningful choices we need to know how climate-friendly (or not) a product is. This requires a standardized, rigorously measured carbon emissions labelling system of all the emissions generated throughout the entire lifecycle of a product, be it an organic carrot or chill-cabinet ready meal, from soil to landfill site.

Measuring the environmental impact of food is relatively new, fiendishly complicated and highly controversial. Professor Tim Lang of City University, London, coined the phrase "food miles" (the distance food travels from field to plate), which helped raise awareness about the origin of our food and the effect of transport on the environment. But after a few years of debate about its value as an indicator for carbon emissions there is general consensus that the concept is too blunt an instrument to

// There is only one way of being sure that you cut down on your carbon emissions when buying food: stop eating meat, milk, butter and cheese ... sheep and cattle produce a great deal of harmful methane. In other words, it is not the source of the food that matters but the kind of food you eat. //

Tara Garnett,
Food Climate
Research Network

The great green bean dilemma

Air-freighted green beans from Kenya have become the arch-villains of the food miles debate. With global temperatures rising, it's crazy, say the carbon-counters, to buy a product that has been flown 7000km. But those who defend Africa's right to economic development argue that it's immoral to punish African farm-workers, who contribute almost nothing to global warming and to whom these exports offer a vital way out of poverty.

In fact, simply counting food miles is not a good way to calculate food's total carbon footprint. Many of Kenya's green beans are grown on the country's half a million small-holdings with manual labour and no agrichemicals. European produce, by contrast, will most likely have been grown with the aid of chemical fertilizers and energy-hungry tractors. Out of season European produce will also have needed heated greenhouses.

That said, the **carbon impact of air-freighting** can't be ignored: it is fifty times greater than that of shipping, and the effects of climate change in the course of this century are going to hit Africa more severely than Europe. It's also true that the global food system grows by consolidation, so the tide is not running in favour of the smaller Kenyan producers.

Consolidation can leave Kenyan growers vulnerable to buyers deciding to source their supply elsewhere. And with oil prices rising, the pressure will be on the growers to lower their costs or face deselection. There's no easy answer to the green bean question, but the following facts may help you to make up your mind the next time you debate whether to buy them:

▶ Encouraged by the supermarkets, our appetite for air-freighted produce is on the up. This sector in the UK more than **tripled** in size between 1992 and 2006.

▶ **Pre-prepared fruit and vegetables** are more delicate than whole ones, so they require more refrigeration, which creates more CO_2.

▶ Avoid food grown in **greenhouses out of season**. The taste is never as good and the carbon price is high.

▶ The International Institute for Environment and Development (IIED) calculated that a boycott of all air-freighted produce from Africa would reduce the UK's total emission by **less that 0.1%**.

▶ Over half of the CO_2 associated with food comes from the **meat and dairy** sectors, since animal feed and waste create a great deal of greenhouse gases. So putting a tub of mascarpone cheese back on the shelf will do more to limit your carbon footprint than refusing to buy Kenyan beans.

▶ Oxfam argues that if we all replaced a 100W light bulb with a low-energy equivalent this would "pay for" any African air-freight emissions on UK-bought produce **nearly five times over**.

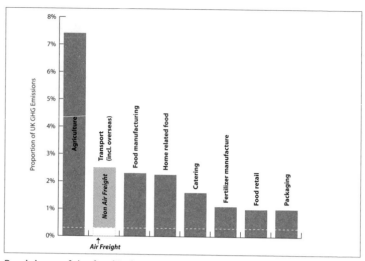

Breakdown of the food industry's greenhouse gas emissions
(Sources: Oxfam 2008, T. Garnett 2007, Defra 2005)

tackle so complex a problem. Now it is widely accepted that all aspects of a food's production, processing, packaging, refrigeration, distribution, selling and finally waste disposal need to be taken into account when calculating carbon footprints.

Local or imported?

The mass transportation of food accounts for 25% of all heavy goods vehicle traffic on UK roads. According to a Defra report on food transport in 2005, this amounted to just under **twenty billion vehicle miles** a year. But how produce travels is as important as how far it travels.

We import a great deal of food into this country by sea, air and road. Supermarkets like to be able to provide year-round supply of fresh produce, and we've developed a taste for exotic foreign fruit and veg, too. But a Tesco Argentine beef joint is responsible for eight times the emissions of its Welsh equivalent. Chicken from Thailand is imported for ready meals and the catering trade, though this can be easily produced in the UK.

But local is not always greener in carbon terms: UK apples are refrigerated from September when they are picked (and sold fresh) until the next harvest is due. This means that by July the carbon cost of those UK apples is higher than those shipped from New Zealand. Then again, if we replaced the UK orchards lost over the last thirty years (see pp.28–29) and didn't sell predominantly imported apples during the UK season, that would represent a benefit in carbon (and taste terms, too).

Researchers at Exeter University investigating food transport for Riverford Farm weighed up against the mode of production in an attempt to get a better sense of how to lower carbon emissions. Their results confirmed that food grown and transported from warmer countries had lower carbon emissions than those grown in heated greenhouses in the UK.

Carbon-footprint labelling

The government-funded **Carbon Trust** has been given the task of helping to convert the UK to a low-carbon economy by 2050, something it says is technically possible but also a tall order given the shifts in business and personal behaviour required. The Government's 2003 Energy White Paper specified the aim of a 60% reduction in carbon emissions by 2050 in response to the Kyoto agreement. This was increased to an 80% reduction in 2008 by the new Department for Energy and Climate Change. The aim of the EU and the UK in the short term is to reduce emissions to 20% below the 1990 level by 2010. The Carbon Trust, working with British Standards, Defra and food companies is responsible for the development of a single authoritative national standard which can be used to create **carbon-footprint ratings** for food items (see carbontrust.co.uk).

Tesco, Innocent Smoothies and Walker's crisps were part of a new labelling scheme trial. Initial ratings showed that a bag of Walker's Ready Salted crisps carried a $75g/CO_2$ rating: 44% from growing the potatoes, 30% from the production stage, 15% for packaging, 9% for delivery and 2% for disposing of the bag. The energy-hungry infrastructure of supermarkets doesn't help, either (Waitrose found that 60% of its energy use is refrigeration, for example).

As Sir Terry Leahy of Tesco says, it's nice to be able to make informed choices about food. But for that to happen, the figures need to transparent and easily comparable and any portion sizes use need to be accurate and realistic (manufacturers are often criticized for using unrealistically small portion sizes on nutri-

// We want to give our customers the power to make informed green choices for their weekly shop. //

Sir Terry Leahy of Tesco on the launch of carbon-footprint food labelling

How carbon-hungry are you?

A carbon footprint is a measure of your impact on the climate through releasing CO_2 and other greenhouse gases into the environment. It's only when you start to compare figures that the message sinks in. Where you do your shopping and how you get there counts too: each year Britons drive about **nine billion miles** to buy food, making around 117 separate journeys each. Supermarket online deliveries (see p.217) are better than us all visiting the supermarket separately in our cars, but because of the vast amounts of energy that the industrial system of food uses it is far better environmentally to buy direct from organic farmers through box schemes (see p.239) or walk to local shops.

Given that the world average total yearly footprint is currently four tonnes of CO_2 and needs to be halved, it is sobering to make comparisons between the average Briton (9.8 tonnes), American (19.8) and then, Chinese (3.4), Indian (1.2) and African (0.9). Online **carbon footprint calculators** help you identify your own impact and areas where you could reduce it. George Marshall, carbon lifestyle specialist at the Climate Outreach and Information Network came up with variable carbon ratings for certain lifestyles.

How carbon-hungry are you?

▶ "I buy the latest items, love shopping, eat mostly packaged convenience food": add three tonnes to your total annual carbon footprint.

▶ "I'm fairly careful with money, buy new things when I need them and get most food from the supermarket": add two tonnes.

▶ "I grow most of my own organic food, shop locally, reuse and recycle, never buy out-of-season fruit and veg": add 600kg.

(Source: Mark Lynas, *Carbon Counter* (Collins Gem, 2007))

Carbon-offsetting is seen by some as a cop-out, one rule for big business and the rich and one for the poor. If you have money, you can buy your way out of having to reduce your footprint in real terms. You pay to have a few trees planted in the developing world and carry on driving your high-carbon-emitting 4x4. Replanting forests and wind power schemes will help reduce climate change and someone has to pay for it, so this could be the only realistic option for a western world used to its luxuries. Alternatively we could keep a few carbon-hungry pleasures and cut out or reduce others: eating meat rarely, reducing supermarket visits, fewer foreign holidays. For advice on carbon offsetting and a carbon calculator, see:

Climate Care climatecare.org

The footprint above left represents the average Briton's annual contribution to CO_2 emissions (9.8 tonnes CO_2). The footprint on the right represents the targeted maximum level for all the Earth's inhabitants (2 tonnes CO_2).

tional labels to make foods look less salty, sugary and fatty). The Tesco potatoes figures (see below) are disconcerting, as the prepared potatoes (packed in a typical two-person serving at 225g each) were rated at an unrealistically low portion size; a quick recalculation shows that a standard half portion would create a carbon rating nearly double that of the unprocessed potatoes:

Product and pack weight	Serving measurement used	Carbon footprint CO_2 equivalent
Organic baby new potatoes (750g)	250g	140g
Freshly prepared new potatoes with butter (450g)	150g portion (a third of the pack)	200g
Prepared potatoes at normal portion size (½ pack)	225g portion	299g

Find out more

Carbon Counter Mark Lynas (Collins Gem, 2007) Very useable concise guide to reducing your carbon footprint. Also read his book about what will happen as the Earth hots up, **Six Degrees** (Harper Collins, 2007) to find out why we all need to start carbon reducing now.

The Rough Guide to Climate Change Robert Henson (Penguin, 2nd edition, 2008) Covers all aspects of this complicated and wide-ranging problem from causes to effects.

Riverford Sustainable Development Project riverfordenvironment.co.uk reveals the often surprising results of a two-year research project in conjunction with the University of Exeter. A useful site that covers carbon footprints, food miles, growing and packaging.

Carbon Footprint carbonfootprint.com An independent company which advises on reducing carbon usage levels. The website has a handy personal carbon calculator.

Free trade or Fairtrade?

This chapter looks at the international food system in action and the relationship between developing world producers and the western food industry, first by considering how three products which are on almost everyone's shopping list are produced and traded: bananas, coffee and chocolate. All three are (reasonably) cheap and plentiful in our shops, but who is paying the price? And for the growing number of consumers who believe that the ethical price of cut-price food is too high, does Fairtrade offer a straightforward solution?

A world gone bananas
The cost of our favourite fruit

No industry illustrates the nature of the modern global food system better than that of the world's most popular fruit, the banana. Banana-producing nations, situated in tropical southern countries, include some of the poorest on Earth. Most of the profits in this multi-billion-dollar industry go to a handful of all-powerful transnational corporations in the US: Chiquita controls 25% of the world bananas trade, Dole (the world's leading producer of fresh fruit and vegetables) 25% and Del Monte 15%. Those who grow the bananas have no power, but in a host of ways they pay the price of transnationals delivering a cheap product to consumers and dividends to their shareholders.

The banana trade has its roots in the old **colonial and neo-colonial links** of powerful trading nations. It began as a small-scale business between US ships and Caribbean small-holders. But as the public developed a taste for the new fruit, the trade became fiercely competitive and banana growing was scaled up. 1899 was a decisive year: that was when the **United Fruit Company** was set up. This company, which later rebranded itself Chiquita, became known throughout Latin America as "el polpo" (the octopus) for the grip that it exerted on banana-producing nations. It grew to have control of over half of the US banana market.

United Fruits' influence was not just economic but also political; it's with good reason that undemocratic, unstable, corrupt regimes became known as "**banana republics**". United Fruit's interference in other countries affairs was seen nowhere more clearly than in Guatemala in 1954. United Fruit had its headquarters there and wielded an extraordinary degree of control over the country's infrastructure, including its transport and ports. When the country's first democratic government made plans for a land reform that favoured the poor, United Fruit, which grew a quarter of its output in Guatemala, used its highly placed connections in Eisenhower's administration to encourage fears that the country was about to become communist. This led to a CIA-orchestrated invasion which resulted in four decades of instability, civil war and the loss of more than 200,000 lives.

Bananas can be bad for your health

These are just some of the charges laid at the door of the big banana companies:

▶ **Exposure of workers to serious health hazards** Large banana plantations are frequently sprayed with pesticides from the air. In 2007 a Los Angeles court awarded over $3 million in punitive damages against Dole, for example, for exposing Nicaraguan banana workers to a banned pesticide which made them sterile.

▶ **Abuse of workers' rights** Banana plantation workers work long hours in dangerous conditions for low wages. A 2002 Human Rights Watch report found that **child labour** is widespread in Ecuador, the biggest banana supplier to the US and the EU. In 2002 Ecuador's biggest banana company deployed hundreds of armed men against striking

Women in Ecuador weighing bananas which have been washed to reduce traces of pesticide.

workers who had formed a union to defend their rights.

▶ **Links to terrorism** In March 2007 Chiquita pleaded guilty to paying money the AUC, a brutal right-wing Colombian militia whose methods include extortion, kidnapping and rape, in return for its protection of the company's plantations. It was fined $25 million.

▶ **Environmental damage** After a few years, bananas significantly deplete the soil, leading to increased use of fertilizers and pesticides or else the clearance of forests to make way for more plantations. A Costa Rican institute estimated that for every tonne of bananas shipped, two tonnes of waste were left behind.

▶ **Tax avoidance** A 2007 investigation by the *Guardian* discovered that Dole, Chiquita and Del Monte have elaborate systems for avoiding paying tax in both banana-growing and consuming countries.

▶ **Monoculture** There are over 300 different types of edible banana, but almost all of the commercially grown ones belong to just one type, the Cavendish variety. Besides depriving us of delights such as the giant Red Makabu and the tiny Lady Finger, this makes bananas much more vulnerable to disease, since whole regions are planted with genetically identical stock.

The banana split and banana wars

The big banana-exporting nations of South America belong to the so-called "dollar banana" system of transnational plantation-owning corporations, but not all bananas are grown on vast plantations. The African Caribbean Pacific (APC) system, which has long supplied the European market, tends to be made up of small, family-run farms in former European colonies. Its small-scale structure means it has been less dependent on pesticides and therefore has been easier to convert to organic. It has also been better able to meet Fairtrade requirements.

The dollar banana companies have long wanted to achieve the sort of dominance in the lucrative European market which they enjoy in North America, and in order to do this they have waged a long-running battle through the World Trade Organization (WTO) to dismantle the system of tariffs and quotas which South American bananas are subject to in the EU. Ecuador and a number of other South American countries allege that the tariffs the EU imposes discriminates against their fruit, and the WTO keeps finding in their favour. It remains to be seen whether European consumers will stick to their principles if cheap dollar bananas begin flooding the market. For more on the international banana trade, see:

Banana Link bananalink.org.uk

Coffee
Selling black gold

Every day the world drains an estimated **two billion cups of coffee**. Britons drink an average of three to four cups a day, some of them bought from one of the 3000 high street coffee shops in the UK. The value of coffee is second only to oil as an internationally traded commodity and is a hugely important to producer countries. One-quarter of Ugandans, for example, depend on it for their livelihood, and well over half of Ethiopia's total export revenue is derived from coffee. Three-quarters of the world's supply of coffee still comes from small farmers, so downturns in the coffee price hurt some of the poorest in society.

Coffee beans are produced by 25 million growers throughout the tropics. A Mexican farmer said "the coffee-producing zones coincide exactly with a map of extreme poverty", and control of the market is in the hands of a tiny number of transnational corporations: Nestlé, Kraft, Proctor and Gamble and Sara Lee. International coffee prices are determined in New York (for the smoother, higher quality arabica beans) and London (for bitter, higher-caffeine robusta, used in most instant coffees).

Until 1989, when the US withdrew, the **International Coffee Agreement** (ICO) managed quotas and kept prices within a band acceptable to the coffee-producing and drinking nations. In the 1990s, **Vietnam**, which was not a traditional coffee-growing nation, heeded World Bank and IMF advice and got into coffee planting in a big way, in part supported by the

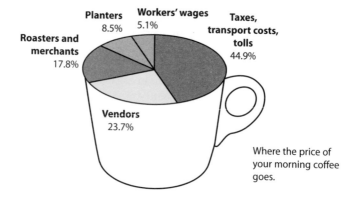

Planters 8.5%

Workers' wages 5.1%

Taxes, transport costs, tolls 44.9%

Roasters and merchants 17.8%

Vendors 23.7%

Where the price of your morning coffee goes.

big four coffee roasters. Before long it had upped its output from one million to fourteen million bags per annum and was producing more coffee – albeit mainly of a low quality – than any other nation except Brazil. The green coffee beans flooding the international market combined with the end of the ICO to cause the price of coffee to tumble to its lowest level in a century.

Since then, prices have crept up, but not enough to move millions of small farmers out of poverty. Vietnam is currently the world's biggest producer of robusta coffee, ensuring a buyer's market for the big roasters, who use steam-washing techniques and flavourings such as vanilla and hazelnut to disguise the taste of low-quality beans, which has been compared to burning rubber. This, plus the rapid global expansion of coffee chains (Starbucks has over 7000 coffee shops, for example) has helped coffee retailing worldwide go from a $30 billion a year business to an $80 billion one.

For some coffee growers, the Fairtrade Foundation has brought new hope of making a sustainable living. There are now over half a million certified Fairtrade coffee producers, who operate small farms with low chemical inputs and receive a guaranteed minimum price for their coffee. For some, Fairtrade came as too little too late; they'd already grubbed up their coffee plants in favour of coca to produce cocaine.

For more on the international coffee trade, see:

Mugged: Poverty in your coffee cup (Oxfam, 2002) You'll find this report on the injustices of the coffee system and proposals for change at oxfam.org.uk.

Black Gold blackgoldmovie.com The 2007 documentary about the coffee trade.

Bitter chocolate
The industry where slavery lives on

More than two-thirds of the world's cocoa crop comes from west Africa, in particular the nations of Ivory Coast and Ghana. A 2002 investigation by the **International Institute of Tropical Agriculture**, which looked at labour practices on cocoa plantations in those countries (and in Nigeria and Cameroon), revealed that around 284,000 children were working in cocoa production. These children were often performing dangerous tasks such as clearing virgin forest and harvesting cocoa pods using machetes or applying pesticides without any protection. Some were working on family farms, but others were victims of trafficking. In other words, much of the world's chocolate supply bore the taint of child slave labour.

"Big Chocolate" is big business (worth $13 billion in the US alone), but you wouldn't guess that from the way the cocoa growers live. Cocoa comes from some of the world's poorest, most indebted countries. The growers of **west Africa** may get as little as $1.35 per kilo for their crop, and most of the under-age workers have never even tasted chocolate. Enforced deregulation of the markets left small growers at the mercy of middlemen. Cocoa is one of the most unstable of all international commodities in terms of price, which is set far from west Africa in the futures markets of London and New York. **The Ivory Coast**, the world's biggest producer, agreed to remove guaranteed prices for its growers in return for partial debt relief, which was followed by an inevitable drop in price.

Small plantation owners, who extract the beans from the cocoa pods and dry them, sell them on to middlemen, who in turn sell them on to transnational corporations such as Cargill, ADM and the world's largest chocolate producer, Barry Callebaut. This Swiss-based giant produces a quarter of all chocolate eaten worldwide and supplies liquid chocolate to the likes of Nestlé, Cadbury's, Marks & Spencer and Thornton's, who shape and flavour it.

When news about the treatment of plantation workers became publicized in the West earlier this decade, there were calls for legislation, which the industry strenuously resisted, with a mixture of and protestations of innocence and denials of responsibility. Instead, they proposed a voluntary code of conduct to clean up the

> **//** They enjoy something I suffered to make. I worked hard for them but saw no benefit. They are eating my flesh. **//**
>
> Enslaved worker freed from an Ivory Coast cocoa plantation

Green and Black's: selling out?

When Green & Black's chocolate was sold to Cadbury Schweppes in 2005, ethical shoppers let out a collective gasp. This trailblazing organic and Fairtrade company led by ethical food lifer Craig Sams and his partner, the writer Jo Fairley, has been one of the major success stories of the ethical food movement. Their signature Maya Gold chocolate, influenced by the tastes of the Rainforest area which produces their cocoa beans, was launched in 1994. By 2003 they were so successful that they were able to support hard-pressed cocoa farmers through their Belize Project.

For Cadbury's, this was an easy and relatively cheap way to buy in some instant (and market-leading) ethical credentials, but to its fans it seemed as though Green & Black's had sold out. An advertising campaign was launched to convince people that the company would retain some independence and retain its Fairtrade and organic credentials. Given that these are the cornerstones of the brand's identity, it seems unlikely that Cadbury's would risk alienating customers. Perhaps in being part of a major company Green & Black's producers are more protected than they would have been if left as an independent? Or maybe their values would be under threat in a takeover? In 2006 they had 8% of the UK chocolate bar market and were growing at 70% a year. Recent forays into nut and cereal bars have involved another Cadbury brand, Burton's Foods of Maryland Cookie fame. All eyes remain on Cadbury's for signs of change for the worse, and they know it.

industry, the so-called Harkin–Engel Protocol, which would aim to eliminate the worst child labour abuses by 2005. When this target was not met, the deadline was extended to 2008. But the protocol had been adulterated – rather like cheap chocolate – so that it is now an expression of intent to monitor than a blueprint for change. So third world children are continuing to miss out on education and risk their health to harvest a crop that makes first world children obese.

What can you do?

▶ **Buy Fairtrade or organic chocolate** Both are grown on plantations which do not use slave labour. Fairtrade is still only around 1% of global chocolate supply. Currently Fairtrade cocoa comes from Belize, Bolivia, Cameroon, Costa Rica, the Dominican Republic, Ecuador, Ghana, Nicaragua and Peru.

▶ **Contact chocolate companies** Ask about their policy on sourcing.

▶ **Avoid slavery chocolate** Watch Kate Blewett and Brian Woods'
shocking 2002 film, *Slavery*, which investigates the cocoa plantations
of the Ivory Coast and discovers that a slave can be bought for as little
as £20, about the same price as an upmarket box of chocolates. You can
find it here:

Free documentaries freedocumentaries.org/film.php?id=192

Fairtrade
Answer to the ethical shopper's prayer?

Fairtrade is an **ethical certification scheme** which rejects
the big business approach of screwing prices down and
dropping suppliers without notice, and instead offers
producers a fair, sustainable price and long-term contracts. The Fairtrade movement has directly benefited
700,000 individual farmers, producers and their families

over the last decade enabling income to be translated into the provision
of clean water, schools and medical care in some of the world's poorest
countries.

Only a decade ago few people had heard of Fairtrade, let alone bought
any of its products. Now one in four bananas bought in the UK is Fairtrade,
70% of us recognize the distinctive logo and in 2007 we spent over half a
billion pounds on Fairtrade products. Globally, consumers spent £1.6 billion on Fairtrade products in 2007, up 47% on the previous year.

Trade not aid

This alternative trade movement has its origins in grassroots activity in
the 1980s and has now hit the mainstream. It's everywhere in the form
of coffee and tea, in our office canteens and
in café chains. There are even 350 Fairtrade
towns including Garstang in Lancashire (the
world's first), Manchester and Brighton, which
requires local councils and businesses to make
a commitment to selling Fairtrade products.
Harnessing consumer power to create change
is not new; William Wilberforce's eighteenth-

> **❚❚You can trust
> the Fairtrade mark
> because we trust
> no one. ❚❚**
>
> Harriet Lamb,
> Executive Director,
> Fairtrade Foundation

century anti-slave trade supporters bought sugar only from plantations with free labour or went without. Today, the focus is on helping developing world producers to develop business practices and distribution streams so that they can lift themselves out of poverty through independent long-term trade rather than short-term aid. Fairtrade is good for sustainability, too, giving growers the confidence to invest in new techniques and crops, and go organic.

Who's behind it?

The UK Fairtrade Foundation is an independent non-profit organization set up in 1992 by the Catholic Agency for Overseas Development (CAFOD), Christian Aid, Oxfam, Traidcraft and the World Development Movement (the National Federation of Women's Institutes joined later).

Why wouldn't you buy Fairtrade?

▶ "It's not local" You can't buy UK-grown sugar, tea, bananas or coffee.

▶ "It's airfreighted" If you feel yourself getting hysterical about a packet of green beans, remember who's responsible for global warming. It's not the developing world producers, but they have to live with the resulting droughts and tidal waves. Consider also the disparity between your carbon footprints and an African's (see p.128). Oxfam's view is that "Fairtrade products make an overwhelmingly positive contribution to poor producers' livelihoods and make a negligible contribution to climate change."

▶ "I only buy British" Take a look in your shopping basket and you'll probably find onions from New Zealand, apples from the US, prawns from Thailand. These are only imported because the cheap prices and industrial quantities suit UK supermarkets' centralized buying and distribution systems.

▶ "It's too expensive" The retail price is set by the retailer. *Which?* magazine found that Fairtrade products were 9–16% more expensive than their non-Fairtrade equivalents. However, research shows that many UK shoppers are willing to pay more for products they value highly.

▶ "It distorts the market" The argument goes that setting a higher price encourages over-production, saturates the market and lowers a commodity's value. While much of the western world is propped up with agricultural subsidies, it's a bit rich to complain about a small helping hand to developing countries (see p.114).

▶ "It only benefits its members, leaving other producers behind" The Fairtrade Foundation plans to expand the producer base. Community benefits derived from the premium aren't limited to the producers and the rise in awareness has encouraged companies to address ethical concerns in their buying policies.

Fairtrade is governed by a set of standards and processes established by the international Fairtrade Labelling Organization (FLO). It accredits 21 Fairtrade-certifying schemes worldwide through an independent body, FLO-CERT. To ensure transparency, a rigorous system of audited paper trails and inspections was set up to ensure that all involved in the chain from producer to retailer follow FLO's detailed standards.

The first UK products, Green & Black's Maya Gold chocolate, Cafédirect coffee and Clipper tea (which now accounts for about 10% of tea sold in the UK), were launched in 1994. Cafédirect's sales of coffee, tea and hot chocolate have already improved the lives of around 265,000 farmers in thirteen countries and invested over £3.3 million of its profits in the growers' businesses and communities.

▶ **"It's a con"** The Fairtrade Foundation checks traders and retailers to ensure that they are buying Fairtrade products only from Fairtrade-certified producer groups and that a fair price is received by the producer.

▶ **"It's just an opportunity for greenwash"** Some have accused Tate & Lyle of a PR stunt in switching their retail cane sugar range to Fairtrade in 2008. While it is true that their far larger non-retail business remains conventional, the effects of this change will be dramatic for the six thousand small-scale growers in Belize who will now receive Fairtrade premiums worth around £2 million.

▶ **"I prefer the taste of my regular brand"** The days of enduring nasty-tasting coffee while feeling good about yourself are long gone. Now the emphasis is on quality and taste. Cafédirect's Machu Picchu gourmet coffee beans won a Gold award in the Guild of Fine Food Retailers Great Taste Awards (2007), for example.

How does Fairtrade work?

▶ **Direct long-term relationships** These are established between producer organizations and buyers.

▶ **Minimum prices** These are set by FLO, allowing for sustainable production (however, it goes up when the market price rises).

▶ **A fixed Fairtrade premium** Set by FLO, this is paid by the trading partner to the producers for community projects.

The protection Fairtrade gives producers from sudden prices drops is not dissimilar to the peace of mind homeowners get with a fixed-rate mortgage. The difference is, of course, that we live in a country with free medical care and education, amenities not available to poorer developing world workers, who struggle to buy food let along vital medicines.

But it's not just about price. Fairtrade is a holistic approach to improving all aspects of life, with stringent rules to ensure that environmental and social welfare standards are protected: child-labour is not used, and fair pay is given to both men and women.

Sleeping with the enemy?: Fairtrade and the supermarkets

Seventeen years of effort have paid off as supermarket after supermarket, seeing that their customers want ethical products, came round to the Fairtrade way of doing business (at least for part of their range). Bananas are the best-selling grocery item of all and also the best-selling UK Fairtrade product with sales at £150m in 2007, up by 130% as a result of supermarket support. The Co-op, which bills itself as the ethical supermarket, was an early supporter of Fairtrade and sold the first Fairtrade bananas in 2000. Sainsbury's sell 20% of all supermarket bananas, so when they decided to stock only Fairtrade bananas in 2006, this almost tripled the value of its Fairtrade sales overnight. Waitrose swiftly followed and switched all its bananas to Fairtrade. Tesco started stocking them in 2002 and were soon shifting eight thousand boxes a week, though they still sell conventionally traded bananas.

> **//We are not doing this for altruistic reasons – we know that our customers support the objectives of Fairtrade.//**
>
> Justin King, CEO Sainsbury's

Ethical trading

"The rise of Fairtrade is also having a wider impact upon public expectations of how companies should trade with their partners in developing countries – it is no longer acceptable for companies to turn a blind eye to poor practice." *The Grocer*, 2006

UK consumer spending on ethical foods has risen sharply in the last five years and is now worth around £4.8 billion a year. Ethical credentials, and the certification marks which go with them, enable companies to show their customers that they understand their concerns and make ethical choices on their behalf, known as "choice-editing". Pret A Manger distinguishes itself from the competition by providing only Fairtrade and Rainforest Alliance coffee. AMT coffee commuter kiosks, set up by the McCallum brothers from Seattle in 1992, were the first national take-away coffee company to sell only Fairtrade-certified coffee.

As Fairtrade took off, big business wanted its share. Only they didn't want to have someone with a clipboard watching them; they just wanted to be able to make a few concessions to farmers and suppliers to allow their advertising copy to create a warm feeling amongst their customers. Fairtrade is too restrictively pro-supplier for most big corporations, so companies such as Unilever-owned PG Tips and Kraft-owned Kenco and McDonald's (UK and Ireland) chose another ethical mark, the **Rainforest Alliance** (rainforest-alliance.org). (McDonald's, Kraft and Nestlé are all rated as "very poor" on UK-based Ethical Consumer Research Organization's ethiscore scale.)

The US Rainforest Alliance mark is primarily concerned with **environmental conservation** and **sustainable agriculture**. It does not negotiate and set minimum prices and does not encourage independent worker co-ops. It works with farms to encourage good practice but their claims are not as convincing as Fairtrade's as regards the treatment and pay of farmers and suppliers. Their main concern is the environment and so they do not carry out the kind of rigorous checks which are the norm for Fairtrade.

"No other certification system but Fairtrade guarantees that small producers get a decent return for their hard work". Raúl del Águila, President of the Latin American Fairtrade Producers' Network and a Peruvian coffee farmer

The independent Fairtrade Foundation logo is the only thorough assurance that the products you buy are genuinely fairly traded. You can check **ethiscore** (see p.143) to make sure the products you buy meet high ethical standards.

What about processed foods?

Ingredients available as Fairtrade must not be replaced by non-Fairtrade items, and products can only carry Fairtrade logo if over 50% of total ingredients (by dry weight) are sourced from Fairtrade-certified producer organizations. (The exception is juice in which the main ingredient is water and the rest is 20% Fairtrade-certified fruit juice.)

What can I do?

▶ **Vote with your shopping trolley** Fairtrade, like organic and local food, offers positive product selection rather than boycotts. With over two thousand Fairtrade food and drink products now available, from avocados and lemons to biscuits and ice-cream, it's just a matter of getting into the habit of choosing Fairtrade. This will benefit producers directly and encourage supermarkets to stock these products.

▶ **Support independent companies** Buy from Equal Exchange, Cafédirect and Clipper, whose whole business is Fairtrade. Ask for Fairtrade when buying your morning cappuccino.

Baobab: African success story in the making?

The baobab tree is an African icon. The trees can live for hundreds of years and have spiritual significance for rural communities. They bear a pendulous furry fruit with an exceptionally high vitamin C content, which is also rich in antioxidants, natural fibre, calcium and iron. These qualities have won it a place in the southern African diet, where its sherbetty pulp is made into a refreshing lemonade-type drink and also used to flavour porridge.

Until recently the fruit was virtually unknown in Europe, where so-called "novel foods" are subject to a stringent approval procedure by the EU. But in 2008, thanks to the efforts of PhytoTrade Africa (phytotradeafrica.com), the baobab won EU approval, and products such as drinks and health bars are now appearing on European supermarket shelves.

Phytotrade Africa deals with around sixty producers in eight southern African countries, which include some of the world's poorest. Lucy Welford of PhytoTrade told Rough Guides that the baobab had been carefully selected for its potential for delivering economic benefit to poor rural communities. Baobab fruit is processed locally as far as possible and transported to Europe by ship, cutting down its carbon

footprint. PhytoTrade is very involved with sustainability, too, and supervises monitoring programmes to ensure that new trees are planted.

Is Welford worried that the lion's share of the profits are still likely to go to western manufacturers, who can capitalize on the baobab's health claims? She's pragmatic and feels that what is important is that the people all the way along the chain get a fair price and that sales take off to the extent that they make a real impact on a large number of rural producers. The cash from crops such as the baobab can enable the rural poor to afford school fees or hospital visits for the first time.

▶ **mysupermarket.co.uk** This site allows you to search "Fairtrade" (and "organic") to compare prices at Asda, Ocado, Sainsbury's and Tesco on branded and own-label products.

Find out more

Fighting the Banana Wars Harriet Lamb (Rider, 2008) This book tells the story of the UK Fairtrade organization and its battle to win over supermarkets.

Fairtrade Foundation fairtrade.org.uk This website has general information about Fairtrade and the Foundation, recent news, and a complete list of approved products.

Action Aid actionaid.org Download their report "Power Hungry" about the way in which a handful of transnational agrifood companies are squeezing out small producers in developing-world countries.

Oxfam oxfam.org.uk A leading charity balancing the needs of developing-world countries with international trade and development.

Ethical Consumer Research Association ethiscore.co.uk This is an excellent website which examines all aspects of a product's ethical credentials from the treatment of farmers, animal testing and the environment. Run by a not-for-profit co-op to "to promote the ethical use of consumer power".

Fairtrade specialists Fairtrade products are available from health-food shops, Oxfam and Traidcraft shops and most supermarkets. They are also available online from ethicalsuperstore.com and Abel & Cole.

Equal Exchange equalexchange.co.uk They have been fair-trading since 1981 and now sell a wide range of products from all over the world such as honey from Peru, peanut butter from Nicaragua and olive oil from Palestine.

Traidcraft traidcraftshop.co.uk Operating since 1979 to develop fair trading practices for developing countries. Wide range, from chocolate snack bars to nuts and rice.

Ethical Superstore ethicalsuperstore.com Stock up on organic and Fairtrade cereals, chocolate, tea and coffee, and snacks. Bulk buy for excellent discounts.

> **What I hear as I talk to people is this phenomenal sense of despair about their inability to do anything about climate change, or the disparity between rich and poor... But when they go into a grocery store they can do something – they can make decisions about what they are buying and send a very clear message.**
>
> Marion Nestle, What to Eat, 2006

GM and the future of food

10

After some thirty years (and billions of dollars) in development, the only people eating substantial amounts of food containing ingredients from genetically modified (GM) crops is America, although GM crops have been extensively planted in Argentina, Brazil, South Africa, India and China. Attempts to launch GM foods in the UK in the 1990s proved a PR disaster for what the media called "frankenfoods". The public's concerns about health, safety and maintaining the integrity of organic farming solidified European opposition to GM imports. Today, food shortages and price rises have brought GM foods back into the headlines, and have won them support among farmers and governments. Genetic engineering is a technology in relative infancy and although, on the one hand, it may have the potential to revolutionize global food production for the better, many critics feel we should proceed with more caution than has been shown so far, and that we cannot yet know what impact GM food may have upon farming and farmers, human health, or the ecosystem.

What is GM food?

As a generation crowded round the first television sets to watch the coronation of Queen Elizabeth in 1953, Francis Crick and James D. Watson had just unlocked the "secret of life" carried in a DNA molecule. Decades later this discovery would develop into the new field of genetic engineering.

Genetic modification involves altering the genes of a plant, animal or micro-organism (such as bacteria). It can also involve inserting one or more genes from other organisms. Genes contain the instructions (DNA) for the characteristics that an organism or living thing will inherit.

//Biotechnology has an immense potential for improving human welfare but ... it could also pose risks to biodiversity and human health.//

Klaus Töpfer, Executive Director, UN Environment Programme

By 2007, 282 million acres had been planted with GM crops, 142 million acres of these in the US. The main GM crops currently being grown (soya beans, corn, wheat and canola or oilseed rape) are widely used as ingredients in processed foods (such as soya milk, glucose syrups, biscuits and cooking oils). Processing can, in the case of soya oil, break up the DNA, making it impossible to identify the GM variety from the non-GM one.

The first GM crops were sown in the US during the early 1990s. By 1999, 25% of America's corn and 38% of soya bean fields were GM. In 2008 this had risen to 80% and 92% respectively. GM bacteria now produce the chymosin enzyme used as a processing aid in cheese-making, replacing the majority of the US's animal-derived rennet (which, incidentally, makes it a vegetarian option for GM-friendly vegetarians) and GM rice is sold in some countries. However, before being sold in the EU, all foods with GM ingredients have to pass a rigorous safety assessment (for its toxicological, nutritional and allergenic potential) by the European Food Safety Authority (EFSA).

Greenpeace protestors uprooting a GM crop in Norfolk in 1999 during GM field trials. Greenpeace believe that GM crops "increase the stranglehold multinational biotech companies already have on food production".

GM food labelling

In the US, 70% of processed foods contain GM ingredients, but these aren't mentioned on food labels – a result of the government acquiescing to industry demands. In the EU, foods containing over 0.9% GM products (with the exception of meat, eggs and milk produced from GM grain-fed animals) have to be labelled, something the US government and food industry has tried to prevent. South Africa also decided to label GM foods in 2008 despite pressure from the US food industry.

According to the Soil Association, a recent survey found that over 50% of Americans did not want to eat GM foods and 87% thought it should be labelled, so clearly there's a lot of confusion about what Americans are eating. A backlash has begun, headed by a group of natural food companies (backed by Whole Foods and Seeds of Change) to develop a "non-GMO" verification scheme (to be launched in October 2009) and an ingredient supplier database to help manufacturers find uncontaminated ingredients.

Get off our land: GM and the UK

The UK government's response to GM crops was to examine the new technology through field research. The three-year Farm-Scale Evaluations (FSEs) found in 2003 that GM fields had lower levels of bees, butterflies and birds, leading to concerns among environmentalists about the risks to biodiversity GM fields could pose. The government "found no scientific case for ruling out all GM crops" but at the same time they could not "give them blanket approval", emphasizing that they needed to be assessed "on a case-by-case" basis before being grown in this country. A recent, renewed attempt to push GM crops has led to intense lobbying from biotech companies of hard-pressed UK farmers and the UK government. The latter appears to be re-examining its stance on the issue, and the environment minister has held meetings with the Agricultural Biotechnology Council, an industry lobby group representing companies such as BASF and Monsanto.

The FSA's *Consumer Views of GM Foods* (2003, food.gov.uk/gmfoods/gm/) noted "the apparent acceptance of GM products in the US was reassuring to many, not least because of the assumption that the US authorities were stricter than our own." It also found that the public had many concerns about GM foods: the irreversible nature of their release into the environment; cross contamination; the right to choose what they ate; and trustworthy labelling. A Eurobarometer Poll found that 71% of European consumers do not want GM food and 86% felt they should only be introduced "if it is scientifically proven that they are harmless". The EU has effectively followed the lead of its population, while the US has tried to force European countries to accept products by invoking international agreements.

GM food: friend or foe?

Supporters say GM crops could help feed the world's poor, increase crop success for farmers (by improving their drought and pest resistance), reduce herbicide use and deliver a range of nutritional and pharmaceutical benefits. The biotech companies accuse those who resist this technology and reject imported GM foods of being anti-science or protectionists restricting trade. The UK government argues that GM technology offers opportunities for UK companies and cannot be ignored.

Most opponents are not against the technology in principle, but say that at present it is flawed and requires further research, as there are indications that genetically-modified organisms (GMOs) could harm humans, wildlife and the ecosystem and could trigger an uncontrolled spread of modified genes.

The biotech big boys

The US Food and Drug Administration (FDA) maintains that "ultimately it is the food producer who is responsible for assuring safety." With such confusion over who's doing the safety checks, it's no surprise that they're virtually non-existent.

Under Ronald Reagan in the 1980s, the US government reduced industry regulation, which had existed to protect the public and the environment. Despite GMOs then being an experimental technology, critics claim that approvals for new products were rubberstamped without health or environmental testing. This was done under the rule of "substantial equivalence", whereby GM foods were not considered significantly different to conventional ones. Henry Miller, former head of biotechnology at the FDA (1979–94), told the *New York Times* that the government agencies did "exactly what big agribusiness had asked them to do".

// The early assurances from the industry and the government that a buffer zone would allow safety and choice for consumers are falling apart. It raises environmental health worries, and what we don't yet know is whether these warnings will translate into a risk to human health. //

Professor Tim Lang, City University

// Monsanto should not have to vouchsafe the safety of biotech food. Our interest is in selling as much of it as possible. Assuring its safety is the FDA's job. //

Director of Corporate Communications, Monsanto

Four multinationals now more or less control the world's GM crops: Monsanto (the biggest), Bayer CropScience, Dow and Syngenta. Between them they have the potential to wield enormous power over the world's food supplies as well as individual nations, farmers and consumers. The question is: do we really trust them? These companies have a long history of selling highly toxic and complex chemicals for use on crops, much of it implicated in environmental pollution and risks to human health. They have also proved themselves very adept at influencing government policy and regulation, possibly helped by the "revolving door" phenomenon whereby individuals switch between government and related industry roles.

Industry claims for GM crops

▶ **GM benefits humankind** The first genetically modified crops were attempts to increase yields; the second related to nutritional enhancements and weather and disease resistance; and the latest, pharma-crops, are food crops genetically modified to carry such things as vaccines against Hepatitis B, anti-sperm antibodies (for contraceptive use) and genes involved in producing human breast milk. (The latter being introduced into a rice plant.)

▶ **It's no different from traditional plant breeding** It is true that we have been adapting plants and animals through selection and cross-breeding for centuries; this is an important part of crop development in the developing world. But biotechnology goes further: altering the genetic make-up by inserting a new gene into the genome of an organism for it to be carried into all the cells and then passed down the generations. The science writer Colin Tudge has also observed that, for engineering purposes, genes are transferred without their "introns" – lengths of DNA that do not code for protein, but which regulate and modify gene function. Genes in a state of nature are shot through with introns. His point is that we are are not even at a stage where we know if this is significant or not.

▶ **GM reduces herbicide and pesticide use** Pesticide use is often lower in the first three years, but then has been shown to increase as pests and weeds become resistant. Recent US government data has shown a fifteen-fold increase in the use of Monsanto's Roundup Ready herbicide; in Brazil the increase is 80%.

Landmark case: Schmeiser vs Monsanto

After a three-year David-and-Goliath struggle, Canadian canola (oilseed rape) farmer, Percy Schmeiser won an out-of-court settlement in 2008 from Monsanto for contamination of his fields with their GM Roundup Ready canola gene. The Canadian Supreme Court told Monsanto that they would be sued for any subsequent contamination. The biotech giant was ordered to pay the clean-up costs, an important legal precedent for the reimbursement of similarly affected farmers.

In an earlier case, Monsanto had argued that Schmeiser grew their seed without a licence and accused him of patent infringement – for which they sought compensation totalling $400,000. (They had offered a lower settlement if he signed a contract agreeing to use their GM seed in future.) A Monsanto lawyer was quoted in a Canadian agriculture magazine as saying:"Whether Mr Schmeiser knew of the matter or not matters not at all."The biotech company's position was that how the GM seed got there was irrelevant – they still expected a "technology fee" of around $37 per hectare from then on. Monsanto won the first round in 2001, when the Federal Court ruled that the farmer had infringed the copyright in their patented canola. (The latter has been genetically modified to be resistant to their bestselling herbicide, Roundup, meaning more of it can be used on crops – creating more profit for the company).

Two important points made at the hearing could have wide-ranging implications for the future of agriculture. The court admitted that it would be impractical for Monsanto to be held responsible for their gene being dispersed into the environment – so short of growing crops in a bubble, every farmer could be at risk. The judge also ruled that, although farmers could generally assume ownership or free use of seeds carried by pollen, that this was not the case with GM seed.

On appeal at the Canadian Supreme Court in 2004 this ruling was altered slightly (but not on the point of Monsanto's patent) to accept that Schmeiser didn't profit from the presence of GM canola in his fields and would therefore not be liable to pay anything to Monsanto. But Schmeiser, who has spent the last forty years developing his own re-useable canola seed, never wanted to grow GM crops and has had to switch crops as his own seed is now useless – and no longer his any more.

▶ **GM increases yields** There is no irrefutable proof of long-term yield advantage; most research finds little or no difference.

▶ **GM helps farmers** Those most likely to benefit from GM crops are large monoculture farmers. Smaller farmers (such as those in the developing world) are unlikely to be able to achieve the economies of scale necessary to cover the higher cost of the seed (often three times the price of non-GM seed) and the essential chemical inputs sold by whichever company farmers sign a contract

▌▌The GMOs that are on our grocery store shelves today have never been tested for human health hazards.▐▐

Claire Cummings, former environmental lawyer, USDA

with. It prevents them from using their own seed, a traditional practice which the biotech industry has lobbied hard to outlaw in the US.

▶ **"Contamination hasn't been an issue"** That's what Monsanto's Robert Plaice claims (see box above) about Canada, where GM canola has been grown for ten years. Research has clearly shown that it is not possible to contain or control GM materials in the environment – this is a fundamental difference from medical use. The dependence on **distance barriers** between GM and non-GM crops as a means of preventing cross-contamination might be unworkable in practice, threatening the integrity of non-GM crops. **Food-chain contamination** is all too easy in our global, industrial food system. Two famous cases emphasize just how quickly GM crops can get into the food chain. The **StarLink scandal** in the US in 2000 saw GM corn (not approved for human consumption) enter the food chain to such a degree that over three hundred products had to be recalled. Exports were affected and it was even found five years later in US food aid in Central America. Bayer's uncertified **Liberty Link rice** was discovered in US rice supplies in 2006 and in 63% of US rice exports to thirty countries, from Austria to the United Arab Emirates.

▶ **No studies show that GM harms human health** There is anecdotal evidence of allergic effects of GM foods – especially of GM soya, a key component in many processed foods. Critics say that adverse effects may not be immediately obvious, especially long-term damage to the immune system. Evidence is now mounting that there is cause for concern. Newcastle University carried out the only known trials on humans in 2002 (FSA-funded), which found that GM material from soya could enter the gut bacteria.

▶ **There's no danger to the environment** We do not yet know the consequences of altering species, and nature can be unpredictable. But we do know that once released into the environment GMOs can be spread quickly by wind and wildlife, free to reproduce themselves and exchange their genes with other varieties. Once released, they are impossible to recall.

▶ **GM has nutritional benefits** The empty promises of the biotech industry are perhaps best exemplified by GM **"Golden Rice"**. Despite containing what turned out to be quite small amounts of vitamin A, it was promoted with claims of health benefits for the world's poor. Early supporters, such as the then president of the Rockefeller Foundation, felt "the public relations use of golden rice have gone too

Monsanto: ready for the big round-up

After a series of company buy-outs, Monsanto now monopolizes much of the international agrichemicals and seed business. Its aggressive policy of patenting everything from pig breeds to vegetables (they have 674 biotechnology patents) could mean that in the future we might find ourselves unable to farm freely. Monsanto's move into GM technology (it now supplies 90% of all US-grown GM seed) saw ex-Monsanto lawyer, Michael Taylor, become deputy commissioner of the FDA in 1991, at a time when GM crops and foods were being approved. He later returned as the company's vice-president for public policy.

Monsanto was founded in 1901 as a chemical company and rebranded itself as a "life sciences" company in the late 1990s. It has given the world: **Agent Orange** (a highly powerful herbicide); **PCBs** (persistent environmental toxic pollutants); and **pesticides and herbicides** such as its best-selling **Roundup Ready herbicide**. **Roundup Ready Soya**, approved in 1994, was found (six years later) to contain unexpected GM material. Its **recombinant bovine growth hormone** (rBGH) was banned in Europe and Canada after indications that rBGH milk could be harmful to human health. Monsanto sued milk producers who labelled their products "rBGH-free" and lobbied to have such labelling prohibited within individual US States.

As Americans become more aware of the silent invasion of their food by GMOs, a consumer backlash has begun. *Vanity Fair* in May 2008 raised the alarm in an investigative article detailing the history of Monsanto, its record of environmental pollution and its heavy-handed treatment of farmers, warning that "the company now profoundly influences – and one day may virtually control – what we put on our tables."

Find out more

vanityfair.com/politics/features/2008/05/monsanto200805

The World According to Monsanto, Marie-Monique Robin (New Press, 2009)
There's also a French-language film with the same title by Robin.

---

far" by giving the impression that it was being eaten worldwide, saving people from starvation and ill-health. In fact, it had not yet been grown commercially. Development experts opposed it on the grounds that it would encourage a single-food diet, leading to malnutrition, and that public funds could be better spent on helping local growing initiatives.

▶ **Consumers can choose not to eat GM** Much of the feed given to intensively produced animals is soya or corn. The main producers of these crops – and GM crops – are in the US, Canada and South America. As the availability of non-GM feed has diminished, prices have increased. As Dale Adolphe, ex-president of the Canola Council of Canada, said: "The way we win is: don't give the consumer a choice" (see p.117).

Is Europe being force-fed GM food?

A lack of appetite for GM food in Europe and Britain resulted in an EU moratorium on its use for health and safety reasons – they insisted in new product licences being subject to high levels of testing under the "precautionary principle". The American Soybean Association threatened "massive retaliation" if the EU didn't speed up its approval of GM crops, which the US government claimed was a trade restriction, penalizing its farmers and costing them lost revenue.

The only GM crop approved for use in Europe is **maize for animal feed**. Recent independent French research found signs of liver and kidney toxicity in animals eating Monsanto's MON 863 maize. Monsanto had assured the European Food Safety Authority that it was as safe as conventional maize. France, along with other EU countries, immediately banned it and called for more testing on GM crops before they are introduced.

The **UN Cartagena Protocol** on biodiversity (to which 147 nations have signed up) protects the rights of individual countries to refuse GM imports: "if there are plausible doubts about its safety for the environment, biological diversity or human health. Unlike the WTO agreement rules, no scientific evidence is required to justify a ban. The Protocol therefore allows states to impose import bans as a precaution."

Horizontal transfer between species

A three-year study by Professor Hans-Heinrich Kaatz of the University of Jena in Germany found that the gene used to modify oilseed rape, which is especially prolific at spreading and reproducing itself, had crossed the species barrier from plant pollen to bacteria living inside honey bees'

GM sceptics

"The idea that African farmers should have to buy seeds, developed from their own biological materials, from transnational corporations, because such companies have given themselves the **exclusive rights** to those seeds is outrageous." Wangari Maathai, Nobel Peace laureate

"Seeking a technological food fix for world hunger may be … the most commercially malevolent wild goose chase of the new century." Dr Richard Horton, editor, *The Lancet*

"Technological fixes alone, such as genetically modified (GM) crops, cannot solve this problem [hunger], despite the claims which have been made for them." Oxfam

stomachs, something which the bio-tech industry said couldn't happen. These GMOs were later found in subsequent generations: evidence of **horizontal gene transfer** between species, which is very rare. In the UK, honey from bees two miles away from GM oilseed rape test sites was found to contain GM materials.

"GM will feed the world"

Biotech's most recent claims to be able to feed the world are opportun-istic PR at best, or an attempt to play

a deliberately misleading trump card. As development agency Christian Aid says: "GM crops are taking us down a dangerous road, creating the classic conditions for hunger, poverty and even famine." There is no solid proof that GM crops can be used safely for human food or that they can improve yields in challenging conditions.

Two US studies at the Universities of Iowa and Michigan found that in the developing world organic farming methods were more productive than either conventional or GM. *The Independent* reported in 2008 that a three-year study by the University of Kansas "found that GM soya produces about 10% less food than conventional equivalents". In April 2008 a major study by the International Assessment of Agricultural Science and Technology for Development concluded that GM was not the answer to world hunger.

In the hands of carefully regulated international organizations and development agencies perhaps there is a chance that, in time, GM crops could help, but at present ownership of this technology is predominantly in the hands of private US corporations, whose first duty is to shareholders.

Genetically modified animals

The potential of GM animals, as with plants, tends to be overstated by the industry. The Royal Society was sufficiently worried about contamination issues to recommend a moratorium in 2001 on GM fish in pens at sea, which seems a sensible precaution given the large number of farmed fish that escape every year. It added: "Despite major improvements in the last twenty years, the techniques are still quite inefficient." At present no GM animals have been approved for use in food in the EU.

Find out more

The Future of Food thefutureoffood.com This film is an investigation of how transnational corporations have been quietly filling supermarket shelves over the past decade with patented, unlabelled, genetically engineered food. It argues their aim is to control the world's food supply.

Uncertain Peril: Genetic Engineering and the Future of Seeds, Claire Cummings (Beacon Press, 2008) Former USDA lawyer tells the story of how GM crops came to be planted in the US, detailing the early days and the later controversies.

The future of food
Feeding nine billion

The world population is around 6.7 billion. On current projections, it is likely to stand at **nine billion** by 2050. This makes finding ways to feed a much more populous world, without destroying the planet in the process, one of the biggest challenges facing humanity in the twenty-first century. There's some consolation, perhaps, in that by 2050, if the current trend of slowly declining birth rates continues (and it has been declining for decades now), demographers estimate that the world's population will peak and then gradually begin to fall. However, most of the additional two-and-a-half billion people will be born in poor countries with already stretched agricultural resources. (By mid-century India will have overtaken China as the world's most populous country.) While the proportion of people in the developing world suffering from hunger may be falling, their absolute numbers are rising as populations grow. Recent price rises have added another hundred million to the ranks of the hungry, reversing years of progress. Agriculture has stagnated in the least developed countries and currency-devouring food imports are on the rise.

The system that has fed the world for the past century is heavily dependent on oil to fuel its fertilizer plants and power its machinery. That system has grown by concentrating ownership in fewer hands and production in fewer locations. It is a system already under severe strain. The price of oil has driven up the cost of fertilizer, a prime ingredient in the system, from $100 a tonne in 1999 to $350 in 2007. Oil reserves are, in any case, finite; many experts believe that we have reached the point of **peak oil**, at which maximum output has been reached, which is then followed by a decline. Soils, too, are becoming exhausted. Water is scarcer everywhere

People power: the rise of food sovereignty

Food sovereignty is a recent concept which asserts people's right to determine their own agricultural future in the face of the steamroller of globalization. Its originators were the members of the **Via Campesina**, an international peasant movement which began in Latin American in the 1990s. The movement has now spread to over fifty countries and is backed by a wide range of NGOs. It campaigns for women's rights, human and labour rights and the preservation of biodiversity and genetic resources among many other local issues.

As writer on global food politics Raj Patel put it, it is a call for the end of a food system "defined not by the many, but by the few". What makes it different from isolated pockets of resistance is the degree to which it is organized globally. See:

Via Campesina viacampesina.org

and analysts predict future **water wars** as bitter as any fought over oil. The impacts of the global food system on our climate are also becoming more pronounced. In many significant ways, we have been drawing on the Earth's capital without putting anything aside for a rainy day.

In the second half of the twentieth century, increases in food production outstripped population growth. The world produces enough food to feed all its inhabitants, but **uneven distribution** means that hunger remains an everyday reality for a substantial proportion of the world's people. Oxfam has referred to the rising cost of food as a "**silent tsunami**" threatening every continent. A World Food Summit in 1996 set the goal of halving the number of malnourished people by 2015. But since then, progress has been too slow to meet the target. Children are particularly badly affected by malnutrition and the physical and mental development of those who survive it can be permanently impaired.

A central problem with the system is that it is set up and run by **transnational corporations**, whose priorities are growth and profitability. The way to achieve growth is to sell as much as possible at as high as price as the market will bear. When Nestlé, the world's largest food and drinks company, set out its strategy in its 2007 annual report, for example, it homed in on the increasing numbers of affluent consumers in developing and emerging countries, whom it identified as "a ten-year $70 billion opportunity". In other words, the alleviation of hunger is not a concern of those who wield most power in the food chain. Western governments, too, have all too often seen food as a way maintaining political stability overseas, gaining access to markets, or dumping their own agricultural surpluses.

In search of solutions

The corporate world has the most to lose from radical changes in the global food system and still appears to think largely in terms of **techno-fixes**: selling more food, processed in more sophisticated ways, so as to maximize profit. The cynical might point out that if that food causes ill-health, then it only goes to open up a new market for "wellness" products. But it's becoming ever clearer that tinkering with the status quo simply isn't enough.

Campaigning charities such as Oxfam, ActionAid and War on Want emphasize the need to **address the imbalances** between rich and poor and **end unfair subsidies** given to developed world producers. They favour international trade that develops in ways which protect vulnerable countries from the worst effects of deregulated markets. This means investment that is more than just a source of cheap off-shore labour, and protection of both human and natural ecosystems.

In 2008, the UN Environment Programme published research that suggested that small-scale organic farming – far from being merely a lifestyle choice for affluent nations – could hold the key to Africa meeting its own food needs. Analysts looked at over a hundred organic projects in two dozen African countries and found that, on average, yields had more than doubled from their pre-organic levels. And, most significantly, these gains had been won without having to resort to costly, oil-hungry inputs.

"Just eat less": plain-and-simple or simplistic?

Some analysts have begun to insist that the wasteful hyper-consumption of the West must change before it drags the whole world into an unsustainable nightmare diet of fatty junk food. In 2008 Professor David Pimentel of Cornell University suggested in *Human Ecology* that American consumers – and, by extension, the rest of us – could make a start by quite simply eating less.

Pimental's team estimated that the average energy consumption of a US citizen is a whopping **3747 calories per day** – up to 1500 calories more than recommended.

Part III

How we eat

Food culture

Food is more than just a collection of nutrients, carbohydrates and fats. Our relationship with it, besides being physiological, is also profoundly cultural and social. Food can mark out who we are, revealing our socio-economic status, religious beliefs and our ethical concerns. Eating habits that seem perfectly natural in one time and place may appear outlandish or even be taboo in another; eating horse meat was common in northern Europe, for example, until banned by the Christian church in the eighth century.

Other religions have formulated dietary rules, too, such as the Muslim and Jewish prohibition of eating pork, and the Buddhist and the Hindu discouragement of all meat eating. At all times and in all situations, culture influences what we eat and how we eat it, but our cultural attitudes are so deeply engrained we often think the way we eat is entirely natural; only other people have bizarre food cultures. Food can also be used as a symbol of power, status or affluence. Here, too, fashions change – in Victorian times oysters were commonplace rather than the luxury they are today; the status of salmon has gone in the opposite direction. Meanwhile, foods we may eat only occasionally still form part of our cultural identities: Christmas pudding, fish and chips, roast beef, laver bread and haggis. And when immigrants come to a new country they bring their food cultures with them, often to the mutual benefit of both cultures.

Our changing food culture

As recently as the 1970s, many families sat down together to eat at the same time each night of the week, and there would have been a good chance of predicting the menu from the day of the week. Those days are long gone. Now we are confronted with choice in abundance, new styles of

// We tended for a very long time, in a very British and puritanical way, to regard food as simply utilitarian, as basic fuel. Like sex, it was seen as slightly suspect if it dared become enjoyable. **//**

Jonathan Meades,
Observer

cooking, national and regional cuisines, new ingredients and techniques, new combinations of flavour. Novelty has come to be seen as desirable in itself.

Throughout most of human history, though, shortage has been much more common than abundance. As a species we're not used to unbridled choice, so when it arrived in the last two decades, we were ill-prepared for it. The consequences of that are visible in our expanding waist-lines and our bulging kitchen bins. There are also consequences for our heads; in an international survey of attitudes to food in 2007, over half of the 9000 people questioned

Our changing food culture

1950 Elizabeth David's first book, *Mediterranean Food*, published. Her influential writing encouraged the British to discover fresh, unfussy food from southern Europe.

1954 Food rationing, introduced in 1940, finally comes to an end.

1958 The first **Chinese take-away**, the Lotus House in Queensway, London, opens.

1960s The number of Indian restaurants grows from 500 to 1200 by the end of the decade. In the mid-1960s, the **tandoori** restaurant arrives.

1960s Fridges and freezers begin to appear in homes, though the steepest rise in ownership would come in the 1970s and 80s.

1964 Britain's original TV chef, **Fanny Craddock**, predicts that the future will bring "more dehydrated, deep-frozen and pre-prepared foodstuffs" (though she also predicted "couscous parties").

1965 The **"KFC concept"** was first introduced to Britain when an outlet opened in Preston. There are now over 700 nationwide.

1970s The **microwave** oven enters both the domestic and commercial kitchen, transforming food preparation.

1973 Marks & Spencer's first **ready meal**, the chicken Kiev, is launched.

1974 The first UK branch of **McDonald's** opens in Woolwich.

1978 Delia Smith's Cookery Course, television's first systematic attempt to teach the British to cook, is broadcast.

said they ate whatever and whenever they liked. But two-thirds of them also claimed they watched what they ate and tried to be healthy. Clearly both can't be true. The competing claims of food as pleasure versus food as fuel cause us no end of confusion. We don't divide neatly into "**foodies**" and "**fuellies**"; but the notion of food as fuel is gradually being replaced by the feeling that food should be an indulgence, treat or adventure. Some of the recent big shifts in attitudes to food include:

▶ **The traditional pattern of regular meal times** has broken down. Communal meals are becoming rarer and solitary "grazing" more common. One in four UK homes no longer has a dining table.

▶ **We spend less time cooking** and replace meals with what the food industry calls "**snack occasions**". Many ovens are never turned on.

1982 The first recorded use of the term "**Balti**" in Birmingham to describe Indian dishes cooked in a small bowl-shaped frying pan.

1984 Ann Barr and Paul Levy's *The Official Foodie Handbook* published. The book was intended as a satire, but the term **foodie** caught on.

1986 The first **Pret A Manger** opens in London, offering upmarket sandwiches using "natural, preservative-free ingredients".

Mid-80s The growing popularity of **Thai food** results from an increasing numbers of Britons bringing a taste for the cuisine back from Far Eastern holidays.

1988 Edwina Curry sparks **salmonella** crisis (see p.40).

1992 The peak year of the BSE ("**mad cow disease**", see p.40) crisis in the UK, which caused many people to reappraise their attitudes to factory-farmed meat.

1997 A Gallup poll reveals that **curry** is the nation's favourite meal. Meanwhile, the first **farmers' market** in the UK is set up in Bath.

1998 23-year-old **Jamie Oliver**'s first TV series, *The Naked Chef*, introduces a new level of "pukka" informality to TV cooking.

2003 A major BBC survey claims that **spag bol** is the nation's favourite meal and chocolate its favourite comfort food.

2008 Having previously tackled school food in *Jamie's School Dinners* (see p.173), Jamie Oliver launches his **Ministry of Food** campaign to get the nation cooking.

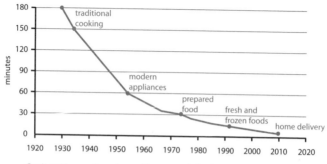

Can't cook, won't cook: appliances and the food industry have successfully persuaded us to spend less and less time in the kitchen.

▶ **Specially marketed children's food** is big business (see p.192).

▶ **We eat ever more ready meals** from the chiller cabinet (7% of all "meal occasions"), presented in ever more exotic guises as we simultaneously lose our ability to cook.

▶ **More meals are eaten outside the home** but they too are ceasing to conform to the three-course pattern.

▶ **The make-up of our diet has changed** to the point that we eat more chicken and drink more fruit juice, but eat less red meat, bread, fruit and potatoes.

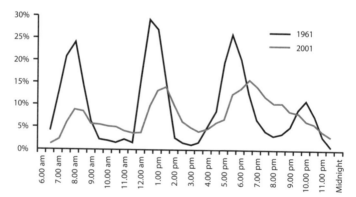

Changing meal-times: in 1961 the whole country sat down to eat its meals at more or less the same time. Forty years on, we've become a nation of round-the-clock grazers.

▶ **Our culture is saturated with food writing and images of food** in magazines, books and newspaper supplements. We're constantly exposed to exotic foreign influences, brought back from our holidays or seen on TV.

▶ **Provenance, traceability, ethical production** and other intangible attributes of food are becoming increasingly important to us, and consequently prominent in food marketing.

Fast food
"For a world that can't slow down"

Fast food is a euphemism. We're really talking about junk food. Fast food, in the sense of quickly prepared food for eating on the go, has always been around, from tacos in Mexico, noodles in the Far East and the dumplings of Chinese street food to meat pies, pasties and fish and chips closer to home. Junk food US-style applies a highly streamlined industrial approach to the challenge of feeding people quickly. This means everything is standardized, from the ingredients and cooking times to the staff's scripted questions. Food must be standardized, processes automated, stock frozen for storage and long-distance transportation and human error designed out of the system. Bright lights in the restaurant itself stop the customer lingering and reducing throughput. Better still, "drive-thru" ensures you're off the premises in a minute, clutching products designed to be easily eaten with one hand on the steering wheel.

Could you give it up?

According to Eric Schlosser, author of *Fast Food Nation*, the average American eats three hamburgers and four orders of French fries a week. But a 2007 survey of attitudes to fast food by market researchers Synovate found that of thirteen nationalities questioned, the highest percentage of positive replies to the statement "I like the taste of fast food too much to give it up" came from Britons (45%), just ahead of Americans (44%). The French were least willing to admit to a fast-food addiction (18%).

What is there to be worried about?

▶ **Your health** for starters. If you eat fast food regularly, you are pushing up your chances of **obesity** and **type-2 diabetes**. The results of a long-term study of 3000 people in the US published in *The Lancet* in 2004 showed that individuals who ate fast food at least twice a week put on an average of 10lbs more than less frequent consumers. They also had a higher incidence of insulin resistance. Fast food is high in fat, sugar and salt. In 2007 Graham MacGregor, professor of cardiovascular medicine at St George's Hospital, London, described the salt levels in many meals from the "big four" (Burger King, KFC, McDonald's and Pizza Hut) as "staggeringly high".

> **//**The executives who run the fast-food industry are not bad men. They are businessmen. They will sell free-range, organic, grass-fed hamburgers if you demand it ... The usefulness of the market cuts both ways. **//**
>
> Eric Schlosser,
> *Fast Food Nation*

▶ **Fast food on every corner** Fast food retailers say that their food should only be eaten as part of a balanced diet. But this doesn't square with their expansionist policies: McDonald's, for example, has 1200 outlets in the UK and has said its aim is to "have a site wherever people live, work, play or gather". That means fast food outlets spring up in stations, airports, shopping centres, motorway junctions, garages – even

Salt and vinegar?

Fish and chips are a British institution that had been hit hard by our love affair with curries, burgers and kebabs until the credit crunch sent sales soaring for the first time in five years. The first fried fish and chips were sold by Jewish merchants in Soho. Fish and chips were considered so central to British eating that Churchill exempted them from wartime rationing. Today there are over 11,000 fish and chip shops in the UK, providing the sole source of fish in our diet for most of us.

Harry Ramsden's in Guiseley, Yorkshire, is one of the most famous chippies and Squires Fish and Chips in Braunton, North Devon is consistently high quality and just what you need after a day's surfing at the beach. Townhead Café in Biggar in the Scottish Borders now offers sustainable fried gurnard and pollack, and The Fish Club in Clapham, London, serves freshly landed Essex coast fish. Other long-standing favourites include: Taylor's Fish & Chips in Mid-Glamorgan and Tommy's Fish & Chips in Ballykelly, Londonderry. Upmarket chains such as FishWorks and Loch Fyne restaurants often serve up this national favourite alongside simply cooked fish.

Slow Food: for a world that wants to slow down

Slow Food is a tiny snail compared to the lumbering elephant of the fast food industry. The **Slow Food Movement** began in Italy as a protest against fast food restaurants in Rome in 1986 and has grown, well, slowly since then. Its founder, Carlo Petrini, is a charismatic figure who decided to set up the movement "to counteract the potential for fast food world domination". It put down roots in the US in 1998 and opened a UK national office in Ludlow, Shropshire in 2006. It now has over 100,000 members in 153 countries, with fifty local groups in the UK (slowfood.org.uk), which run education events, market stalls and other projects.

Its three central tenets are that food should be:

▶ **Good** (in the sense of both tasty and healthy)

▶ **Clean** (sustainably produced)

▶ **Fair** (not exploitative of the producers or others in the food chain).

Slow Food opposes **globalization, GM** and **big agribusiness** and is passionately in favour of small-scale farming that is "local, seasonal, natural and traditional". The movement's brand of "**eco-gastronomy**" is not to everyone's taste. Some critics caricature it as an elitist club of smug foodies in search of rare breeds of heritage pork. (Part of the problem may be their off-putting terminology: their groups are known as "convivia" and their biodiversity programme is called the "Ark of Taste".) But they are an increasingly vocal international body speaking out for a future that includes the pleasures of food alongside concern for the environment and ethical production. To find out more, see:

Slow Food slowfood.com

Slow Food Nation Carlo Petrini (Rizzoli, 2007) sets out the Slow Food case.

some hospitals. According to the British Heart Foundation, 70% of British children no longer think of fast food as a treat. It has become the norm.

▶ **What are you actually eating** McDonald's publishes a nutrition guide to all its products, which states proudly that "our menu is based on staple foods such as meat, fish, potatoes, eggs, milk and grain". It may be technically true that it is *based* on those things, but the cheese on your cheeseburger is 55% cheese, plus water, butter, whey powder, milk proteins, natural cheese flavouring, emulsifying salts, salt, preservative and colour. And the grilled chicken is 82% chicken, but comes with added water, vegetable oil, potato starch, lactose, salt, stabilizer, flavourings, maltodextrin, yeast extract and sugar. The BSE crisis in the 1990s, which revealed that poor quality meat including **mechanically** recovered meat (MRM) and spinal cord, could find its way into burgers, caused many people to reappraise fast food. Bovine MRM has now been banned, but the high-speed throughput of meat-processing plants can lead to contamination and food poisoning. Eric Schlosser cites a study which found over three-quarters of minced beef samples taken from US processing plants contained microbial contamination from fæcal matter. Schlosser puts it more bluntly: "There is shit in the meat."

▶ **Carbon Footprint** If you're not already going off your burger, there's more: as a big purchaser of meat (McDonald's is the largest in the world) the fast food industry leaves a **gigantic footprint**. Since price is all-important, production methods have to be as cheap as possible, which pushes **animal welfare** down the list of priorities. Fast food is also a major producer of packaging **waste**, since everything has to be disposable. There are also serious concerns around the deskilling of the **workforce**, anti-union policies, low wages and long shifts.

Find out more

Fast Food Nation Eric Schlosser (Penguin Books, 2001) This best-selling book lifted the lid on the fast food industry. A more recent film version fictionalized the issues in the book (2007).

Supersize Me Documentary-maker Morgan Spurlock filmed the effects of eating nothing but junk food for a month to the increasing horror of his doctors. He gained eleven kilos and suffered liver damage, heart palpitations and sexual dysfunction.

makeupyourownmind.co.uk is a Q&A website where anyone can have their questions, however bizarre, answered by McDonald's.

Showing us the way: the cult of the celebrity chef

A Martian visiting Britain who investigated our book-buying habits would quickly form the impression that we are a nation of cooks like no other on Earth. Cook books regularly top the Christmas bestseller list. Britain can sell Jamie's cheeky style to the French and Nigella's bountiful charm to the US. TV chefs are personalities whose aura glows far beyond their studio kitchens. Their books are no longer merely collections of recipes, but offer an insight into their family lives and their travels. What the Martian would not realize, however, is that despite owning over 170

Oh Delia!

Delia Smith was for many years the culinary darling of the nation, the reliable older sister you could turn to for cooking advice before your first dinner party or Christmas lunch. She published her first cookery book in 1971 (*How to Cheat at Cooking*) and went on to present landmark TV cookery courses throughout the 1980s and 90s.

She taught us that no one should be scared of cooking and we thanked her by buying over eighteen million copies of her books. She became the first of the celebrity cooks to be known only by their first name. *The Grocer* magazine dubbed her "God's gift to grocery".

Delia came out of retirement in 2008 to revisit *How to Cheat at Cooking* in a BBC TV series in which she presented recipes which made extensive use of ready-prepared supermarket ingredients, such as frozen mashed potato and tinned minced lamb. There was a lot of talk of convenience and saving time, but nothing about the cost or healthiness of the meals. Campaign group Consensus Action on Salt and Health claimed that Delia's "Carbonara Real Quick" contained more than a whole day's salt ration, and newspapers calculated that some Delia recipes cost five times more than ready-meal equivalents. It marked a low-point in the dumbing down of cookery and earned her brickbats even from die-hard fans. Rather than encouraging the trend towards healthier eating, she seemed to be leading the charge back to processed and packaged food. All the same, the bad publicity didn't stop the book becoming a bestseller. And as the credit crunch bit deeper, she relaunched her *Frugal Food*, first published in 1976.

million cookbooks, only around one-third of them have ever been used, and many of them are only used for a very small number of recipes. Just as we overproduce food, we overproduce cookery books. Cooking has gone from being an essential activity to a hobby and is now increasingly a spectator sport.

This shift is mirrored in the style of presentation of cookery programmes. Thirty years ago, Delia had the manner of a home economics teacher instructing a class of timorous children. Contrast that with Nigella: today's emphasis is on hedonism, ease and dishes that can be put together almost casually. The style is improvisatory and presenters are eager to play down their expertise for fear of alienating their viewers. And if cooking from scratch is still too daunting, some celebrity chefs have their own ranges of ready meals, saving you more time to watch their cookery shows.

Eating out

Douglas Adams' *Restaurant at the End of the Universe* (Pan Macmillan, 1980) foresaw our modern predicament. When all questions of space, time, matter and the nature of being have been resolved, he reckoned, only one question remains: "Where shall we have dinner?" But even he couldn't have predicted the huge rise in eating out in the last two decades. As recently as the 1970s a meal out for most Britons was a treat reserved for special occasions, but now the money we spend on eating out is neck and neck with the amount we spend in food shops. Eating out has become everyday, something people do for as much for convenience and entertainment as for the quality of the food.

Since the 1980s, the long-established curry houses and Chinese restaurants have been joined by Italian-style chains such as Pizza Express and Pizza Hut, which were later joined by newcomers such as Ask and Strada. Like supermarkets and fast food outlets, their aim is consistency; your Pizza Hut pizza should taste the same whether you order it in Exeter (three branches), Norwich (five) or Aberdeen (five). Pubs, realizing that

The best restaurant in the world?

Ferran Adrià's **El Bulli** in Catalonia has won every prize going (including Best Restaurant in the World award several times) and turns away around three-quarters of a million requests for tables every year. Adrià pioneered a style of cooking which has come to be known as **"molecular gastronomy"** for its experimental, highly scientific approach to food, which includes foams and hot, savoury "ice creams". Adrià himself prefers the term "deconstructive" to describe his style of cooking, which brings together flavours in very unexpected, alchemical ways. Adria's status doesn't mean that molecular gastronomy is going to hit your local gastropub any time soon, but he can be credited with injecting a dose of creativity and showmanship into the restaurant business and breaking down the dominance of the traditional three-course meal.

Something is clearly changing in the top echelon of world gastronomy: there are now more Spanish chefs ranked in the world's top ten than any other nation, including France. Britain's **Heston Blumenthal** is one of them and his cooking has close affinities with Adrià's. At his Fat Duck restaurant in Berkshire you can sample salmon poached in liquorice gel, and enjoy "sound courses" in which food served with an iPod accompaniment. Blumenthal is also a previous winner of the best restaurant in the world accolade and, like Adrià, author of a huge tome setting out his food philosophy.

El Bulli elbulli.com Bookings at are taken in mid-October for the following year.

The Fat Duck fatduck.co.uk

drinking-only establishments didn't generate enough turnover, also got into catering as a way to broaden their appeal. The **gastropub**, serving eclectic food in unpretentious surroundings that was several notches up from the traditional pub grub of scampi and chips and a Ploughman's, was born in the early 1990s. They became ubiquitous, to the extent that "gastropub" was used by M&S as a name for one of its ready-meals ranges. Today almost everywhere that can squeeze in a few tables – from bookshops to garden centres – is eager to serve you food.

Getting the caterers in

Look around any town any morning and you'll see lorries in Brakes and 3663 liveries. They are the two biggest food distribution companies to the catering trade; 3663 (the digits spell "FOOD" on a phone keypad) has a turnover of more than £1 billion and delivers regularly to 50,000 professional kitchens in the UK (20% of the market). Not only can they supply all the raw ingredients for restaurant and pub kitchens, they can also provide **fully prepared dishes** ready for the busy chef's microwave. Brakes, for example, supplies beefburgers ready-cooked "to save you precious time" and "bar-marked for an authentic grill look". Fish cakes come "finished with a seasoned light flour dusting to give that special handmade appearance". Whites, 3663's up-market service, offers fully prepared dishes, too. Their sticky toffee puddings, for instance, can be cooked from frozen in the microwave. "Present it how you want, after all, it's your menu!" says their website breezily.

Should we care? If it tastes good, maybe it doesn't matter where it comes from. After all, Brakes' Thai curries are prepared in Thailand and their Italian pizzas come from Italy. What could be more authentic? The trouble is, a food culture in which the chef's role is reduced to reheating and garnishing without the customer's knowledge is not in robust health. If some publicans and restaurateurs are catalogue-shopping for menus, which are trucked from a distribution centre, it makes a mockery of local culinary renaissance. It's another example of the increasing homogenization of the food system and power being concentrated in fewer and fewer hands. It also raises questions about the prices restaurants charge and plays into the hands of the supermarkets, who want to convince you that their ready meals are "as good as going out".

Q: When is feta cheese not feta cheese?

A: When it's from Yorkshire. Though few consumers have heard of **PDOs**, this EU approval scheme of **Protected Designation of Origin** will be of growing importance in the years ahead, as food traceability and provenance become of greater interest. Like the *appellation d'origine contrôlée* scheme for wines, PDO gives producers legal protection from imitators outside the region. To qualify, products have to be produced, processed and prepared entirely within a designated area. So a ruling on Greek feta in 2005 meant that Yorkshire cheese-maker Shepherds Purse had to find a new name for its feta (they chose Fine Fettle).

The UK has been slower to apply for PDOs than other nations. It has three dozen, mainly dairy products, whereas Spain, Italy and France between them have over four hundred. The EU has tough decisions to make, such as whether to award the PDO **"Jersey Butter"** exclusively to that island's dairy farmers. The trouble is, there are more than ten times the number of Jersey cows in the UK than on Jersey. The name "Jersey" means their milk sells for a premium. What, farmers wonder, are they to call it if they are barred from calling it Jersey?

Current British and Irish PDOs (excluding alcoholic drinks):

▶ **Cheeses** Beacon Fell traditional Lancashire; Bonchester; Buxton Blue; Dorset Blue; Dovedale; Exmoor Blue; Single Gloucester; Staffordshire; Swaledale & Swaledale ewes' cheese; Teviotdale; West Country farmhouse Cheddar; White Stilton; Blue Stilton; Imokilly Regato.

▶ **Meat and offal** Isle of Man Manx Loaghtan lamb; Melton Mowbray pork pies; Orkney beef; Orkney lamb; Scotch beef; Scotch lamb; Shetland lamb; Welsh beef; Welsh lamb; Connemara Hill lamb; Timoleague Brown pudding

▶ **Fish and seafood** Arbroath Smokies; Scottish farmed salmon; Whitstable oysters; Clare Island salmon

▶ **Vegetables** Jersey Royal potatoes

▶ **Other** Cornish clotted cream

Who decides what we eat?

Most **food law** is made in Europe. Over 90% of all legislation affecting food safety and standards in the UK comes from Brussels. European Union members cannot restrict the use of food substances within their borders unilaterally unless they can be shown to be unsafe, since that would constitute a restriction on trade. The EU's overall aim is that consumers should know what they are eating, that it should be safe and that standards should be consistent across the Union. Thus it has to be made clear where produce comes from, whether it's graded as first or second class and so on. The EU also determines what "novel foods" are approved for import. National differences over how to define foodstuffs such as yoghurt or chocolate have led to lengthy tussles over food in the EU and produced some contorted definitions:

▶ The *cause célèbre* of EU food legislation is without doubt the **bendy banana**. It's long been believed that the EU attempted to ban bananas with too great a degree of curvature. In fact, aggrieved Eurocrats point out, their rules relate to the diameter and therefore maturity of the fruit, and are intended to ensure that producers supply only high-quality fruit.

▶ There was a thirty-year dispute over whether **British chocolate**, much of which contains vegetable fat as well as cocoa butter, was worthy of the name. Despite opposition from several nations – some of which wanted it reclassified as "chocolate substitute" – the EU eventually found in Britain's favour.

Ensuring food standards

The **Food Standards Agency** (FSA) was set up in 2000 in the wake of the BSE crisis in order to safeguard "safe food and healthy eating for all". It's a government department which acts as an independent regulator and consumer protection body. Its declared objectives are:

▶ to reduce **foodborne illness**

▶ to make it easier for all consumers to choose a **healthy diet**

▶ to enable consumers to make **informed choices**

How clean is your local?

If you want to see how pubs and restaurants scored the last time the local environmental health officer called, visit scoresonthedoors.org.uk. Establishments are awarded a food hygiene rating between zero ("major improvements required") and five ("excellent"). Some of the results, even for upmarket places, can be eye-opening.

Reading the small print: food labelling

Packaged food must under EU law carry front-of-pack information about its content. There are regulations, too, policed by trading standards officers, about what health claims can be made on the packet. But without a compulsory national system for imparting health information, weighing up what's good for your and what's not can be confusing. The Food Standards Agency backs a system which rates the fat, saturated fat, salt and sugar content of foods according to a "**traffic lights**" principle: red ("caution", or "treat" in modern parlance), amber ("moderation") and green ("go right ahead").

The trouble with this is that some foods can show two or even three different traffic lights, if they are, say, low in sugar, but moderate in salt and high in fat. So how's the busy shopper to judge? Such confusion suits the food industry, which sticks to its mantra that there is no such thing as bad food, only bad diets. Among the companies to have rejected the traffice lights are PepsiCo, Kraft, Nestlé and Kellogg's. Though some supermarkets, including Sainsbury's and Waitrose, have adopted a version of the traffic light scheme, others have devised systems of their own which lack the "red = bad" connotation. Tesco uses pastel-coloured labels, for example, which show percentages of **Guideline Daily Amounts** (GDAs), but it's up to you to judge whether the percentage is too high and whether the suggested portion size is unrealistically small.

Other systems have been devised, such as the American **NuVal** rating, which scores all foods out of one hundred, giving broccoli top marks (100) and fizzy drinks a score of just one. There is, of course, a simpler solution still: buy non-processed foods so that you don't have to worry about hidden extras in your meals.

As this makes clear, the focus is more on preventing food poisoning and providing information to consumers than getting tough with manufacturers and retailers so that they produce healthier food.

The FSA has been no stranger to controversy. Its first chairman, Sir John Krebs, angered many environmentalists with is views that anti-GM campaigners were "shrill, often ill-informed and dogma-driven". Its pro-GM position was matched by a strong scepticism over organic farming (see pp.100–101).

Defra (the department for environment, food and rural affairs) is another government department born out of a crisis, in this case Foot and Mouth. It merged the pre-existing Department of Agriculture, Fisheries and Food (MAFF) with the Department of Environment. It has a wide brief, which includes, at the top level, steering the country towards living within its environmental means, and day to day, administering subsidy payments to farmers and co-ordinating responses to outbreaks of animal disease.

Public-sector food

Hospital food: not what the doctor ordered

A 1999 NHS report revealed the shocking facts that 40% of patients were malnourished as a result of their hospital stay and one-tenth of them stayed longer than necessary simply because of poor quality hospital food. The system had been creaky for years; antiquated Victorian kitchens served up meals of grey meat, packet gravy, congealed mashed potatoes and watery soup. It was so bad that much of it went straight into the bin. The nation's diet had moved on, but the NHS kitchens were stuck in a time-warp. In the 1980s Margaret Thatcher had let market forces loose on hospital catering, introducing Compulsory Competitive Tendering, which meant that

Jamie's school dinners

Ever since Jamie Oliver took his film crew into our school canteens we have been inundated with new initiatives for healthy eating in schools. Not held back by mealy-mouthed concerns over upsetting parents or fearsome dinner ladies, he raised public and government awareness of the appalling nutritional state of our children's diets (both in school and at home) and made Bernard Matthews' Turkey Twizzlers shorthand for all that is dreadful about processed food. They are no longer served in schools, but similar products are still served up to children at home.

Over 25,000 UK schools have to provide lunch for their pupils on a tiny budget of 60p (up from 37p in 2005) per pupil for ingredients (the rest of the cost to parents goes on staff costs). Most primary schools do not have kitchens and have to serve up lukewarm food cooked at another school on plastic trays with plastic cutlery. No wonder 60% of pupils refuse to have school lunches. In Europe, by contrast, proper plates, normal food and longer lunch-breaks help prepare children for a civilized adulthood.

Jamie's School Dinners encouraged parents to work with schools and local councils to improve things, but efforts were often hampered by low budgets, inadequate facilities and complex purchasing systems. In 2006 new minimum nutrition guidelines were introduced for school food, banning crisps and soft drinks from school lunches and in vending machines. The **School's Food Trust** was set up in 2005 after Jamie Oliver's efforts and has been funded by government to advise schools. Some moves are encouraging: proper cooking lessons (rather than the depressingly named food tech) will soon be compulsory for 11–14-year-olds. Finding teachers qualified to teach them may be another matter.

the cheapest outside supplier would automatically get the contract. It was the worst of both the free-market and state-run worlds.

Then in 2001 came the **Better Hospital Food (BHF) Panel**, a government-appointed task-force charged with bringing hospital food into the twenty-first century. It was headed by TV presenter Loyd Grossman, who recruited a team of chefs to overhaul hospital catering. Not only did they rewrite the recipe book, they made recommendations for new practices such as flexible mealtimes and "snack boxes" offering patients greater choice. The press treated their initiative with some derision, ridiculing some of the more exotic menu items the panel put forward, such as navarin of lamb with couscous, though none would have been out of place in a supermarket chiller cabinet.

At its best, the panel made a bold attempt to integrate food into the healing process rather than treat it as just another financial drain on the system. But the government killed off the BHF initiative in 2006, saying its job was done, and responsibility for hospital food was devolved to NHS trusts. True, there are some beacons of excellence, such as the Cornwall Food Programme, which goes in for local, sustainable sourcing. But there remain many unreconstructed trusts where the old ways (and the gravy) are still going strong.

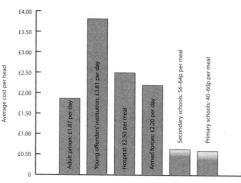

State spending on food in the UK

Porridge and prison food

The prison service is another public institution which serves tens of thousands of meals every day. Here public concern focuses less on whether too little is being spent than on whether it's too much compared to other public services. A National Audit Office report in 2006 suggested that prison food could be both cheaper and healthier. Prisoners, however, are no different from the rest of us; confronted with monotonous routine, they opt for the fatty comforts of burgers and pies, not salads and fresh fruit. In any case, a report by the chief inspector of prisons in Scotland found that even health-conscious prisoners would have trouble finding more than three portions of fruit or vegetables a day on the menu.

Prisons are the area where the **effect of diet on behaviour** has come under greatest scrutiny. Research suggests that lack of omega-3 fatty acids in prisoners' diets has a detrimental impact on concentration and self-control, which in prison can boil over into violence. In a controlled trial, multivitamins, minerals and essential fatty acids were given to a group of young offenders and the level of violent incidents decreased by one-third. John Stein, professor of physiology at Oxford University, said: "we are not saying nutrition is the only influence on behaviour, but we seem to have seriously underestimated its importance." A major three-year study is now under way. If it confirms the earlier study's findings, the implications go beyond the diet of prisoners and could have relevance for us all.

Food waste:
Waste not, want not?

Our relationship with food is full of contradictions: we want cheap food, but throw one-third of it away, all the while getting fatter and more unhealthy. Every day in the UK we throw away a staggering 4.4 million whole apples, enough to fill twelve double-decker buses. Each of us throws away our average body weight (70kg) in food every year. Forty percent of fresh fruit and vegetables is binned. The annual cost of all that wasted food, £10 billion, adds up to more than we spend on international aid.

With the rise of the ethical shopper, it seems that wasting food has been overlooked. It's not as instantly appealing as buying Fairtrade or visiting a farmers' market. It might sound a little sanctimonious, but for anyone who lived through the war years or has witnessed real hunger, the sight of a well-fed person casually leaving food on their plate, would be seen as disrespectful or even immoral. Most of us, born in a period of intensive farming and cheap pile-it-high supermarket fodder, have never really gone without. We live in a throw-away food culture where food is available everywhere and children are brought up to be fussy eaters. While we might moan about the price of organic food or "real" bread, the average British household throws away £420-worth of food each year (£610 in households with children). Judging from the results of the Waste and Resources Action Programme (WRAP) report into food waste, we would all be healthier if cut our food purchases by half. This would not only save us a fortune, but also enable us to pay more for better quality food.

What ends up in the bin?

▶ **45% of the salad** (by weight), earning it the title of the most frequently binned item of food.

▶ **31% of bread and bakery goods** (2.6 billion tonnes of bread slices per year plus 775 million bread rolls).

▶ **26% of fruit** including 4.8 million tonnes of grapes, 2.8 million whole tomatoes and 1.6 million bananas.

▶ **1.3 million unopened yoghurts** and yoghurt drinks, 1.2 million sausages, 0.7 million whole eggs, 0.3 million unopened meat-based ready meals or take-aways.

Food waste and climate change

Every tonne of food we throw away produces 4.5 tonnes of CO_2 equivalent emissions. Eighteen million tonnes of CO_2 emissions are caused by potent methane gases released from packaged foods, and the energy needed for their production, processing, refrigeration and transportation. The European Union directive on the use of landfill sites has set 2010 as the deadline for a 25% reduction (from 1995 levels) of the amount of

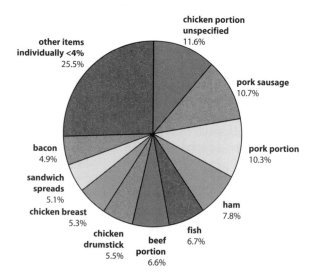

biodegradable consumer waste dumped in landfills. If we stopped wasting perfectly good food, WRAP have estimated that it would have the same effect as taking one car in five off the road.

We're not the only ones throwing away food: an enormous amount of food waste is caused by **supermarkets**, which make surprise decisions to cancel orders or refuse whole lorryloads of produce if a few items are cosmetically imperfect. They are also constantly left with food near its sell-by date which is either sent to landfill sites or given to charities, often through a national charity Fareshare. Fareshare has been redistributing supermarket food since the 1990s to community organizations for the four million Britons who cannot afford a healthy diet or have no cooking facilities. Other companies such as The New Covent Garden Soup Company, Kelloggs, Kraft, Nestlé and Pret a Manger also contribute.

What can you do?

▶ **Shop as locally and often as you can** Fresh food often doesn't last till your next weekly supermarket shop.

▶ **Plan your meals** (At least the first few.) Make a large batch of your favourite soup and have it the next day; cook extra new potatoes and use them for a warm salad a day later.

▶ **Check your fridge** while making your shopping list.

▶ **Never shop on an empty stomach** to avoid overbuying.

Why do we throw food away?

"Food takes a smaller chunk than it did of the average family budget (some 9% in 2007, down from 16% in 1984). People tend to be careless with things that don't cost them much." *The Economist*

We throw away 6.7 million tonnes of food each year, most of which is avoidable through better portion control, storing and management.

▶ **A clean plate** 1.2 million tonnes is simply left on our plates

▶ **Don't fancy it** 340,000 tonnes food is still in date when thrown away

▶ **Over-buying** 980,000 tonnes of food was either unopened or still whole

▶ **Past its use-by date** £8 billion-worth

▶ **Don't know what to do with leftovers** 1.6 million tonnes of prepared food is not used

▶ **Switch to a smaller supermarket** It's easier to stick to your list and takes less than half the time as there's less chance to dawdle.

▶ **Don't buy products you don't need** Obvious but true.

▶ **Avoid offers** Don't go for the BOGOFs (buy one, get one free). If you wanted one bag of carrots, just buy one. Statistically, a second one is likely to go off before you use it.

▶ **Don't stockpile** How many years will it take you to get through the hot spicy sauce you bought in the three-for-two offer?

▶ **Keep food fresher for longer** Put a mini thermometer in your fridge to keep the temperature at the upper end of 1–5°C; 70% of our fridges are set at too high a temperature.

▶ **Keep an eye on the contents of your fridge** Move items near their use-by date to the front where you can't miss them.

▶ **Learn how to use leftovers**

▶ **Compost your kitchen waste** Uncooked vegetable scraps, fruit peelings, teabags, coffee grounds and eggshells can go into a sealed bin.

Find out more

Waste & Resources Action Programme (WRAP) wrap.org.uk. The government-funded body set up to work with retailers, local government and the public to reduce waste across the food sector. Their Love Food Hate Waste campaign started in 2004 to research, raise awareness and reduce food waste. It published its report, *The Food We Waste*, in May 2008.

What is healthy food?

Every January, just when we're at our lowest point with post-Christmas bulge, the media rolls out new healthy eating plans. Full of good intentions, millions of us resolve to eat less and better. As most of us are pretty unclear about what food does to our bodies, we are at the mercy of those who want to tell us how to eat "properly", be it the latest celebrity, diet guru, women's magazine, the government, your mum – or even a qualified dietician.

The Anglo-American diet, full of processed foods and comparatively few fresh ingredients, has left us fat, tired and unhappy. Twenty years of low-fat foods, premium-priced diet aids, and calorie counting have not managed to stem the rising tide of obesity in the UK and US. Professor Marion Nestle, a nutritionist with decades of experience, thinks that you need to know an awful lot about nutrition and the food system to get beyond industry marketing and make good choices.

Calorie counting

Things have moved on since the first Weight Watchers meeting in the early 1960s and their calorie-related points system. Now losing weight can involve mini-meals, starvation days, carb-only or protein-only diets or more drastic intervention such as liposuction or even a gastric bypass. UK research published in *Nutrition Journal* into the four most commercially successful diets, Slim Fast, Atkins, Weight Watchers and Rosemary

Calories

Calories (sometimes known as kilocalorie or kcal) are an international energy measurement to quantify the energy made available to our bodies from food. The law of thermodynamics where more calories are burnt than are taken in, is the only scientifically proven way to lose weight. This means eating less and exercising more. If we exceed the recommended daily levels of calories (**1940 calories** per day for women and **2550** for men), we get fat. It's as simple as that.

Conley's "Eat Yourself Slim", found nothing to choose between them in terms of weight loss. The problem with diets is that they make you obsessed with food: days are planned around which foods you're allowed to eat, you experience feelings of hunger, cravings and then guilt about the inevitable binges.

What is the "right" weight?

Body Mass Index (BMI) is a way of identifying overweight and obesity, especially when used with waist circumference (which gives an idea of the level of health risk the extra weight poses).

Body Mass Index = weight (kg) ÷ height (m)²

Research indicates that fat deposited around the stomach is an early warning sign that you could be at risk of obesity. It is potentially dangerous as it indicates fatty deposits are building up around your internal organs. Men with waists of over 94cm (37″) and women over 80cm (31″) have an increased risk of heart disease and diabetes. Measure your waist (cm) at its narrowest point and then divide that by your hips (cm) at their widest part to find out your waist–hip ratio. A result of over 1.0 for men and 0.8 for women indicates potential health problems.

| Underweight | Normal Weight | Overweight | Obese | Morbidly Obese |

Calculate your BMI and work out if you fall into an at-risk category

Eyes bigger than our stomachs: portion control

It's not just what you eat, of course, but also how much you eat that affects your health. And we're eating more than ever because of round-the-clock snacking and larger portion sizes. A World Cancer Research Fund study found that, since 1980, burgers have doubled in size and pasta servings are five times larger. The low cost of manufactured ingredients in processed foods has allowed manufacturers to supersize the portions at minimal extra cost, giving the impression of good value and encouraging us to eat more.

A Government strategy unit report of 2007 found that poor diet caused 69,400 premature deaths a year from diseases such as cancer and heart disease: 42,200 deaths were linked to a lack of fruit and vegetables, 20,200 to excess salt consumption, 3500 to saturated fats and 3500 to excessive sugar consumption. Overall, treating diet-related disease costs the NHS about £6 billion each year.

Junk food: who's to blame?

There's no getting away from it: the food industry makes much more money peddling processed junk food than unadulterated real food. Research shows that the most unhealthy products (soft drinks, breakfast cereals, fast foods, confectionery and snacks) receive the most TV promotion and that this is especially true of products aimed at children. The TV advertising ban on unhealthy junk foods aimed at children was announced to uproar from the industry, despite having been given a year to get used to it, and despite web marketing being increasingly effective.

The food manufacturers and supermarkets refuse to accept any responsibility for customers' health, falling back on the "freedom of choice" and

It all adds up: five easy ways to pile on weight

▶ **Breakfast** A danish pastry (287 cals), smoked salmon and cream cheese bagel (250 cals) or a blueberry muffin (300 cals) with a cappuccino (100 cals) = c. **400 cals**

▶ **Mid-morning** Tea (10 cals) and Snickers bar (323 cals) = **333 cals**

▶ **Lunch** A bought packaged sandwich (over 500 cals), crisps (184 cals) and a fruit smoothie (50 cals) = **730 cals**

▶ **Mid-afternoon** A mug of hot chocolate (250 cals) and a single digestive biscuit (75 cals) = **325 cals**

▶ **Supper** A portion of ice-cream or pudding = **250 cals**

"personal responsibility" mantra. But if customers were really doing the choosing, why spend millions on media campaigns? When *The Grocer* magazine asked industry readers who was responsible for children eating unhealthy food, the vast majority blamed parents. Parents, of course, blame advertisers. Meanwhile, it's only when faced with devastating obesity figures and their financial implications on health budgets, that the government squares up to the industry.

The FSA have created a model to evaluate junk food which involves adding up calories, saturated fat, sugar and salt and then balancing that against whatever protein, fibre, fruit and vegetable content the item contains. It highlights how unhealthy most breakfast cereals are and recommends unprocessed foods in many cases.

Snacks and milky drinks: modern British diet disasters

On average we skip breakfast 91 times a year. For us, that means missing out on nutrients and raising the chances of bingeing on sweet snacks later, but for the food industry, as *The Grocer* reported, "that represents a lot of missed opportunities for retailers and producers." Hence the rise in convenient fruit-and-nut-based cereal bars. Check the label, though. Eat Natural, Doves Farm and Village Bakery produce bars of natural healthy ingredients plus sugar, whereas many others are half sugar and nothing else of any food value. The popular Go-Ahead "Apple and Sultana" bar's

50 cals	78 cals	91 cals	115 cals	155 cals	148 cals	418 cals
Italian cup of coffee 180ml	Starbucks Short (extra-small in the US) 236ml (half pint)	Starbucks Tall 353ml	Starbucks Grande 473ml (1 pint)	Starbucks Venti 591ml	Starbucks Latte Tall 353ml	Starbucks "Signature" hot chocolate with cream Tall 353ml

Cut the cappuccino: Italians are horrified by what passes for cappuccino in the UK. We have grown used to a supersized US-style drink in which the standard two-tablespoon shot of coffee is drowned by up to a pint of hot milk. Try switching to a lower-calorie alternative (black coffee, 5 cals; tea, 2 cals; or a macchiato doppio, a double espresso with a little foam, 14 cals).

main ingredient is glucose syrup, for example, followed by 3.5% dried apple, emulsifiers and other ingredients.

The terrible trio
Salt, sugar and fat

The amount of salt, sugar and fat that we eat has risen dramatically in the last thirty years, largely as a result of the vast quantities hidden in processed foods. Research has shown that these cause heart disease and strokes (the commonest cause of death in the UK) and contribute to other diseases, including diabetes, osteoporosis, certain cancers and obesity, and

Eating too much: the rise of obesity

The children's animation *WALL-E* showed us where we're heading – into a world where we're too fat to move and sit stupefied by TV, glugging sweet drinks from supersized, no-spill baby beakers.

Britain is the **fattest nation in Europe**, just ahead of Germany and Greece. Italy has the lowest incidence of obesity. Levels of obesity have tripled in England since 1980: around 60% of the population is overweight or obese and the trend is upwards. Some are so obese they have to be winched out of bed or confined to wheelchairs. Government forecasts estimate that by 2015, 28% of women and 36% of men (aged 21–60) will be obese. And we're raising a generation of overweight children who eat junk food and who, research shows, are likely to become obese as adults.

▶ 67% of British men are overweight (including 25% who are obese)

▶ 52% of British women are overweight (including 20% who are obese)

▶ 30% of British children (2–15 years) are either overweight or obese

▶ One-third of the US population (including children) is obese

▶ Eighteen million sick days a year in the UK are caused by obesity

▶ 30,000 deaths a year in England are caused by obesity-related illnesses

▶ 6000 gastric bypasses are carried out each year in the UK (medical experts think that obesity levels in fact warrant 60,000 a year)

▶ Being overweight increases your risk of heart disease, stroke, type-2 diabetes, high blood pressure, osteoarthritis and cancer

Read the label: compare nutritional information for a 100g serving across a range of products. Look for those with the lowest fat, sugar and salt content.

exacerbate the symptoms of conditions such as asthma. In recent years the government has encouraged voluntary reductions across the food industry through the reformulation of products and smaller portion size.

Salt

Our bodies need about 1.4g of salt a day to function properly. Too much salt is a key cause of high blood pressure (about one-third of us suffer from this in the UK). Campaigning by the FSA has reduced our intake from 9.5g a day in 2000 to 8.6g in 2007, still a long way from an ideal limit of 3g. About 75% of the salt we eat comes from processed food and it is often highest where we expect it least, in breakfast cereal and biscuits. Crisps are obviously salty (Walkers Standard 34.5g bag of ready-salted crisps contains 0.5g salt and their salt and vinegar, 2.3g), but did you realize that half a supermarket deep-pan cheese pizza contains the same amount of salt as five bags of ready-salted crisps? Here's what the Foods Standards Agency recommends as daily limits:

Adults	6g (=1 teaspoon)
Children (4–6 yrs)	3g
Children (7–10 yrs)	5g

Eating too little: anorexia nervosa

Over 1.1 million (and rising) people in the UK suffer from an eating disorder of some sort. The 14–25 age group is most at risk of developing one. **Anorexia nervosa** is the most common form and is a serious psychological disorder which has a high mortality rate. It is associated with perfectionism, obsessiveness and withdrawal, as well as psychological disorders such as anxiety and depression. Focusing on weight loss to achieve size zero provides a diversion from underlying problems that may be beyond the sufferer's control.

It is estimated that 1% of schoolgirls (some still at primary school) and young women are anorexic, meaning that body weight is maintained through self-starvation and excessive exercise at around 15% less than expected for their height. This disrupts normal hormonal function, causes hair loss and can damage bones and organs. In some cases, the disorder can be chronic and even fatal. NHS admissions (and only a small percentage find their way to hospital) for anorexia in 2006 were 620 (up from 419 in 1996). For more information and help, see:

Beat Eating Disorders b-eat.co.uk

What can you do?

Salt is also called sodium chloride, which leads to confusion over food labelling which states a product's sodium content, as it is this element which is bad for your health. Children enjoy totting up figures, so get them to work out how much salt they had for breakfast and in their packed lunch. Switch to lower salt products by checking the labels: Heinz tomato ketchup (3.1g salt per 100g) has three times the amount of salt as Tesco Organic tomato ketchup (1.0g). Try Liberation's reduced-salt nuts, which are also Fairtrade (see p.297). Crucially, bear in mind:

$$\text{salt content} = \text{sodium} \times 2.5$$

A salt content of over 1.5g per 100g (or 0.6g sodium) is high. It takes about three weeks for your taste buds to get used to a lower-salt diet. After that, what once seemed a normal level of saltiness will strike you as very salty.

Sugars

You only have to witness the end of a typical children's birthday party to see the bad effects of too much sugar. We get our sweet tooth from breast milk, which contains lactose, which in turn contains glucose. Our modern sugar habit originated in eighteenth-century imports of sugar cane. As it

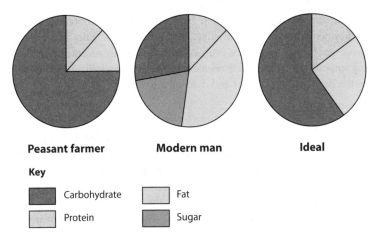

Peasant farmer   **Modern man**   **Ideal**

Key

Carbohydrate   Fat

Protein   Sugar

The ideal healthy diet is closer to a peasant farmer's than to our modern sugar and fat-rich mix.

Omega-3

"Many food manufacturers are riding the money-making omega-3 wave by adding it to all sorts of foods and failing to mention that it may not be the right sort of omega-3 – or enough of it – to be as beneficial as simply eating oily fish." *Which?* magazine, 2007

▶ **Oily fish** Salmon, trout, fresh tuna mackerel, herring, sardines, whitebait, and the like, all contain the "active" fats EPA, DPA and DHA, the commonest fat in the brain (which is composed of 60% fat).

▶ **DHA** This fat is thought to be beneficial to the heart and for brain development (especially in the embroyo in the third trimester), and in children under seven.

▶ **Seed oil** Flaxseed (a good source of another essential oil, alpha-linolenic acid), linseed and pumpkin oil can be converted by the body into active fats but only to a small degree. Research has shown that they are less beneficial than fish oils.

became increasingly cheaper we ate more of it, so that by the late-twentieth century it formed a large proportion of our diet.

▶ **Read the label** "No added sugar" means that sugar has not been added as an ingredient, but this can obscure naturally occuring sugars in fruit. Watch out for combinations of sugar, dextrose, invert sugar, fruit juice concentrate, glucose, honey, rice syrup and high-fructose corn syrup – all of which are sugars. Sugar content is also hidden on the nutrition label under carbohydrates.

Fruit sugars are found in whole fruit where they are contained within its fibrous structure to no ill effect. But when fruit is juiced or heavily processed (as in School Bars, Fruit Winders and juice concentrate, including smoothies) the sugars are released and behave much like added sugars in the body, adding calories and damaging teeth.

Fats

Eighty-two percent of us eat more than the recommended daily amounts of saturated fats. To eat healthily you need to replace bad fats (saturated) with good fats (unsaturated). Research shows up regional differences with those living in the north regularly eating twice as much saturated fat as they should, while those in London and the south-east eating one-fifth more than the daily limits: 30g a day for men and 20g for women and young children.

▶ **Good fats Monounsaturates** (avocados, olive oil) and **polyunsaturates** (nuts and seeds, oily fish, sunflower oil and spread) don't increase blood cholesterol in the same way as saturated fats. They can reduce cholesterol and provide the essential fatty acids the body needs.

► **Bad fats** **Saturated fat** (in meat and dairy products) and **trans fats** (see p.83) raise blood cholesterol levels, increasing the risk of heart disease. These are typically found in processed foods such as biscuits, cakes, deep-fried foods and pastry. The risks of trans fats have been known by researchers for thirty years, but only recently has anything been done about reducing them in our food.

Good for you?: Misleading health claims on the packaging

With the rise of the health-conscious consumer came a jumble of health claims on food packaging, many of which could easily mislead the consumer. Weight Watchers' biscuits (45 calories per biscuit) are just as calorific as normal Ginger Nuts, for example, and the packet suggests a portion size of two biscuits. A *Which?* report highlighted an example of a misleading health claim in which Tesco added small amounts of omega-3 to its "Healthy Living" pomegranate juice drink. The pack read: "DHA/EPA may be good for joint mobility and helps the normal development of brain tissue and nerve growth in unborn babies … this is a delicious way to get your recommended amount!" But omega-3 was present in such small amounts, you'd need to drink 1.5 litres a day to get the benefit.

How do you eat healthily?

Your diet should consist of a balance of proteins, carbohydrates, fibre, fats, vitamins and minerals:

► **Protein** is essential for the growth and repair of tissue, as well as hormones, enzymes, antibodies and neurotransmitters. Your body makes sixteen amino acids, but eight essential amino acids have to come from your diet. Good sources are quinoa (a South American grain) and soya (tofu), along with meat, pulses, dairy and fish.

► **Carbohydrates** are turned into energy by the body. There are two types: simple sugars and natural sugars (fast-release energy) found in milk and fruit, and the complex starches (slow-release energy) in bread, cereals, pasta, potatoes and rice.

► **Fibre** helps your digestive system process food and helps control blood sugar levels. Insoluble fibre (wholegrain bread and cereals,

Vitamins and minerals

Vitamin/mineral	Good source	Essential for
A (retinol)	Eggs, full-fat milk, cheese, oily fish (such as mackerel), red pepper	Skin, healing, immune system, strong bones, eyesight. Beta-carotene gives fruits and vegetables their dark green and orange colours and is converted into vitamin A in the body
B1 (thiamin)	Wholegrains (rice), vegetables, milk, cheese, beans, fresh and dried fruit, eggs	Nerve and muscle tissue health; with other B-vitamins it converts carbohydrates into energy
B2 (riboflavin)	Eggs, milk, rice and mushrooms, yeast	Healthy skin, eyes, nervous system and mucous membranes; creates red blood cells and can help iron absorption
B3 (niacin)	Beef, pork, chicken, wheat and maize flour, eggs	Nervous system and digestion; helps converts food into energy
B5 (pantothenic acid)	Chicken, beef, potatoes, porridge, tomatoes, kidney, eggs	Immunity and fighting infections, wound healing; converts food into energy
B6 (pyridoxine)	Pork, chicken, eggs, wholegrains (oatmeal, wheatgerm), molasses, bananas	Blood health and immunity. Hair and skin health. Converts protein into energy
B12	Meat and fish, milk, eggs and cheese, yeast extract	Blood health and nervous system. Releases energy from food; processing folic acid. The Vegetarian Society recommends taking a supplement (try Flurodix iron supplement)
Folic acid	Broccoli, Brussels sprouts, asparagus, peas and chickpeas	Works with B12 to create new red blood cells; reduces risk of neural tube defects in unborn babies (take a supplement if you're planning a baby)
C (ascorbic acid)	Fruit and vegetables (the antioxidant anthocyanin gives red and purple fruits such as berries and peppers their colour)	Keeping cells healthy and helping concentrate antioxidants and the body absorb iron from food. Good for helping the body fight infection
D	Forms under the skin in reaction to sunlight. Also from oily fish, liver and eggs or fortified breakfast cereal	Absorption of calcium in the body. Essential for healthy bones and teeth

Vitamin/ mineral	Good source	Essential for
E	Olive oil, eggs, nuts, seeds and wheatgerm	Protecting cell membranes and skin. Absorption of iron and fatty acids. Antioxidant
K	Green leafy vegetables (broccoli and spinach)	Blood clotting (and helping wounds heal properly). Helps build strong bones
Calcium	Dairy foods (milk and cheese), chickpeas, dried fruits, nuts (almonds)	Strong bones and teeth. Regulates muscles (e.g. heartbeat) and blood clotting and pressure
Iron (ferrous sulphate)	Liver, red meat, molasses, dried fruit (figs and apricots), beans, dark green leafy vegetables (watercress and curly kale), egg yolks, dark chocolate and red wine	Blood health and immune system; neurological development of foetuses
Magnesium	Green leafy vegetables (such as spinach), brown rice, peas and beans, and nuts	Cell growth and repair. Bone health
Phosphorus	Eggs, red meat, dairy foods, fish, poultry, bread, rice and oats	Strong bones and teeth; releasing energy from food
Potassium	Bananas, avocados, potatoes, lentils, nuts and seeds, milk, fish	Controlling the balance of fluids in your body. Muscle and nerve function. Lowers blood pressure
Chromium (trace)	Water, meat, wholegrains (bread, oats), egg yolk	Influences the way insulin behaves in the body
Iodine (trace)	Eggs, fish and shellfish, seaweed (try Clearspring's range from health food shops)	Helps make thyroid hormones and regulates our metabolism. Hair, skin and nail health
Selenium	Brazil nuts, wholemeal bread, sunflower and pumpkin seeds, seafood, chicken, eggs	Good for immune system, hormones and reproductive health. Can protect against depression and Alzheimer's disease
Zinc (trace)	Wheatgerm, shellfish (oysters), eggs, meat, pumpkin seeds	Bone and wound healing; fertility. Helps make new cells and enzymes, and enables our body to process carbohydrate, fat and protein. Antioxidant properties

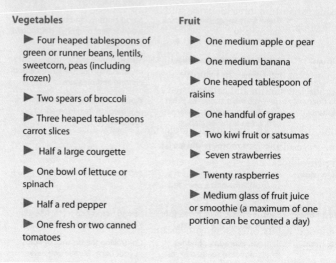

"5 A DAY": what counts?

The Department of Health launched its **5 A DAY** logo in 1994. But a decade and a half later many of us are still struggling to manage two-and-a-half portions a day (one of which is probably fruit juice). It's a confusing message, however, when soft drinks such as Coca-Cola's Appletiser are allowed to sell themselves on being one of your portions, and potatoes don't count.

Vegetables

▶ Four heaped tablespoons of green or runner beans, lentils, sweetcorn, peas (including frozen)

▶ Two spears of broccoli

▶ Three heaped tablespoons carrot slices

▶ Half a large courgette

▶ One bowl of lettuce or spinach

▶ Half a red pepper

▶ One fresh or two canned tomatoes

Fruit

▶ One medium apple or pear

▶ One medium banana

▶ One heaped tablespoon of raisins

▶ One handful of grapes

▶ Two kiwi fruit or satsumas

▶ Seven strawberries

▶ Twenty raspberries

▶ Medium glass of fruit juice or smoothie (a maximum of one portion can be counted a day)

fruit and vegetables) passes through you, taking other food and waste products along with it, keeping your gut healthy and preventing constipation. Soluble fibre (beans, oats and lentils) can be partially digested and may help to lower blood cholesterol.

▶ **Fats** help the body absorb vitamins, are a source of energy and supply the essential fatty acids that the body can't make itself. To keep our brains healthy we need essential omega-3 and -6 fats.

▶ **Acid–alkaline balance** is important for good health. Many of us have diets too high in acid (from animal protein such as meat and dairy), which cause a variety of stomach problems and increase the risk of osteoarthritis. Eating more alkaline-producing foods such as melon, green leafy vegetables, nuts and seeds helps correct this.

▶ **Vitamins and minerals** contained in food need to be eaten every day, with the exception of vitamins A, D, E and K (which are fat-soluble, so any excess is stored). Minerals build strong bones and teeth, control body fluids and turn the food we eat into energy. Calcium is essential for healthy bones (50% of your skeleton's calcium is deposited between the ages of eleven and eighteen). Full-fat milk contains more vitamins and calories than low-fat, but has the same amount of calcium.

▶ **Iron deficiency** (anaemia) is the most common nutritional deficiency, causing exhaustion, breathlessness and inability to concentrate. This essential part of haemoglobin carries oxygen in our blood to tissues and organs. Men need 8.7mg a day and women 14.8mg. Your body absorbs meat-derived haem iron more easily than iron found in plants, but if you don't eat meat you can improve absorption by avoiding caffeine. Try naturally low-tannin and caffeine-free Dragonfly Breakfast rooibos tea.

▶ **Antioxidants** such as vitamin C, flavonoids and phytochemicals inhibit free radicals, the harmful molecules that cause cell and tissue damage, resulting in ageing, higher risk of heart disease, some cancers and neurological diseases (see superfoods on p.80).

Children's food: learning bad habits?

Childhood habits often stay with us into adulthood and once the habit of drinking super-sweet soft drinks is fixed it is very difficult to switch to water, milk or real fruit juice. The UK is the only country, excluding the US, to buy such a high proportion of special "children's food" (characterized by extreme sweetness and processing, high salt and fat content and high price relative to ingredient cost). With fromage frais sales in the doldrums, Yoplait targeted the lucrative children's market with a novelty item, **Frubes**, which won them almost half of the children's chilled yoghurt and dessert market. Cartoon characters and pester power make mincemeat out of worn-out parents in the supermarket aisles and the food industry knows it. From breaded dinosaurs and Dairylea "lunchables" with reformed meat discs, novelty childhood food, laden with fat and salt, tends to morph into adult versions such as chicken Kievs and Ginster's pies. With cooking skills decreasing in line with the increase in the consumption of processed foods, we eat 50% of all the ready meals in Europe, ignoring research (and common sense) which tells us that cooking for ourselves is both healthier and cheaper.

So just how bad are children's diets? The FSA found that British children are consuming:

▶ **Fat** 58% more than recommended

▶ **Salt** 50% more than recommended

▶ **Sugar** 85% more than recommended (mostly from soft drinks)

▶ **Just two portions of fruit and vegetables a day** the lowest consumption is in low-income households

▶ **Five cans of fizzy soft drinks** each week

Children grow rapidly and have very different nutritional needs from adults; don't apply adult food needs, especially low-calorie diets (full of artificial sweeteners) to them. Children need high levels of calories relative to their size: 7–10-year-old boys need 1970 calories a day; girls 1740.

Children's lunches

For many children, lunch is the main meal of the day. While school lunches are subject to strict government nutritional guidelines, the packed lunch remains the responsibility of parents. The typical British primary school packed lunch contains lots of small items in plastic packaging: crisps, a sweetened fruit drink, chocolate and biscuits, processed cheese, novelty sweetened yoghurt or fromage frais. Manufacturers can rely on parents only scanning the fronts of packs for a few "healthy" shoutlines, which although legally admissible, are often misleading. While "no artificial colourings" or "sugar-free" get big ticks on the front of the box, artificial sweeteners can be tucked away along with preservatives and perhaps fillers in the ingredients list.

Thanks to heavy marketing, **Cheestrings** find their way into 46 million children's lunchboxes a year. At about £15 per kilo, Cheestrings are nearly twice the price of mild organic supermarket Cheddar. So ditch these rubbery orange sticks, which are so over-processed (and over-packaged) they taste of absolutely nothing. Cut a chunk of organic Cheddar for your child's lunchbox instead. See box opposite for more packed lunch ideas.

// Do not let them drink 'juice' drinks at all ... I am also reluctant to give anything with artificial sweeteners to children. These chemicals have never been tested on children ... if they do turn out to be harmful, children will be most vulnerable to their effects. Why take a chance? //

Marion Nestle, nutritionist

Healthy lunchbox guide

Pack your own: buy a few re-usable small plastic pots (for fruit or crisps) or a bento-style box with compartments. Try a mini Thermos food flask for soup, pasta or baked beans in the winter. Wrap foods in greaseproof paper to cut down on plastic packaging (and your child's carbon footprint).

▶ **Protein and starch** Sandwich with either egg, tuna, cheddar, hummus or peanut butter; falafels in a pitta; pasta or couscous salad (mix in small pieces of vegetables and cheese or ham). Avoid sausages and salami (high fat and salt content).

▶ **Fruit** Pot of strawberries, cherries or grapes; satsuma, small apple or banana.

▶ **Veg** Cherry tomatoes, cucumber slices, carrots and red pepper sticks, sprouted chickpeas and seeds.

▶ **Snack** Breadsticks, your own cheese sticks with savoury crackers, pot of seeds and nuts (some schools have a no-nut policy). If you can't avoid crisps, then buy "real" crisps (Tyrells or Burts) and dispense in small quantities (they've still got high levels of fat, but at least they still resemble a sliced potato and don't have artificial additives).

▶ **Sweet tastes** Box of plain raisins, dried fruit, an Eat Natural "lunchies" bar, which although they have similar sugar levels to other bars also have masses of healthy dried fruit. If biscuits are essential, then buy good-quality versions to wrap yourself to reduce the portion size and save money.

▶ **Yoghurt** Yeo Valley's are popular with children and easily available in supermarkets. Yoghurt, with healthy natural probiotics (to promote "good" bacteria), is a better choice than sweetened fromage frais desserts such as Frubes, which contain additives such as modified fillers.

▶ **Drink** Water (in a reusable bottle); small carton of 100% juice only, Innocent Smoothies or Ella's Kitchen Smoothie, or very diluted Ribena or other cordial (Rocks are good) without artificial additives and sweeteners. Avoid Capri Sun and Fruit Shoots. Try alternating with milk in a small reusable SIGG insulated beaker.

▶ **Friday treat** A few pieces of dark chocolate wrapped in foil, or a small (matchbox-size) piece of home-made cake or flapjack or the best you can find in the supermarket or online (see p.290).

"Thousands of children will be heading towards strokes and heart attacks if they carry on eating [packed lunches] like this."
Dr Gail Rees, dietician, Plymouth University

Food allergies and intolerances: "free-from" diets

About 7% of children and 4% of adults suffer from a food allergy, which means they develop antibodies against certain proteins which make their bodies react to a food immediately or soon after eating it. Typical reactions include itching or swelling of the mouth and throat, wheezing and skin rashes. This can be life-threatening in its most extreme form, **anaphylaxis** (anaphylaxis.org.uk). Common causes are milk (lactose), nuts, eggs, wheat, shellfish, sesame seeds, kiwi fruit and soya. In addition, some medical conditions such as Crohn's disease (inflammation of the gut), coeliac disease (a reaction of the auto-immune system to gluten) and diabetes necessitate avoiding or reducing consumption of certain foods, but be guided by your doctor on this.

Food intolerance does not involve the immune system, but can cause migraines and irritable bowel syndrome amongst other conditions. **Lactose intolerance** is most common form, followed by wheat. It's important to get a proper diagnosis from a qualified nutritionist or dietician. There are relatively few fully trained allergy specialists in Britain, but it's worth seeking them out. Beware of unproven tests such as hair analysis, kinesiology and Vega. Find out more about food allergies here:

British Society for Allergy and Clinical Immunology bsaci.org

Buying free-from foods

You can buy free-from foods (soya milk, corn pasta, dairy-free chocolate bars) from health food shops, supermarkets (Sainsbury's, Tesco and Asda have free-from ranges) and specialist online shops such as wheatand-dairyfree.com. Some companies produce specialist diabetic, dairy-free or gluten-free foods (for example, "The Stamp Collection" and Trufree), but you can also shop from normal ranges with information and guidance. Processed foods are a problem for allergy sufferers, as they contain so many ingredients. Recipes may change without warning and food labels can contain mistakes. A free texting service (alert4allergy.org) will contact you with any such problems. A good general guide for sufferers and their families, including food problems in children, is:

The Complete Guide to Food Allergy and Intolerance, Jonathan Brostoff and Linda Gamlin (Bloomsbury, 1998)

Water, water everywhere

After forking out billions of pounds for bottled mineral or spring water over the last decade, we've finally woken up to the fact it's a rip off. There's also the environmental damage to consider: all those plastic bottles and all those food miles for imported water. Almost overnight it has become acceptable to ask for tap water in restaurants (some places even used to charge you for that, too). If you still want to buy bottled, then look for "natural mineral water" on the label, which is subject to strict regulations.

Given this new awareness when we eat out, it seems ironic that we are nonetheless succumbing to the "healthy" marketing hype of new flavoured waters, which contain artificial sweeteners and preservatives. Of course, this represents a repositioning for manufacturers eager to continue making a product with one of the highest profit margins in the supermarket (just add packaging and chemicals). Never buy over-priced, artificial additive-laden Fruit Shoots H2O (the fruit content is minuscule) or Calypso's Disney-branded flavoured waters for your children.

Health advice on water is clear: adults need eight glasses of plain water a day; children six. One-third of UK children currently drink only two glasses of water or less

a day. Water is essential for our brains to function properly and for our bodies to eliminate waste. Other liquids such as squash do not have the same health benefits. Smoothies are really a food in nutritional terms; a small glass is great as one of your 5 A DAY, but not as a replacement for water.

Beat the credit crunch and buy a water filter jug (Brita's Elemaris range is excellent: brita.net). These purify the water you've already got in your kitchen tap, reducing impurities such as limescale, chlorine, aluminium, copper and lead.

Vegetarianism: not just a load of old lentils

The number of vegetarians in the UK has more than doubled over the last ten years to about four million (7% of the population), and 41% of us are now eating less meat. The UK vegetarian market is worth £700 million a year. The 150-year-old **Vegetarian Society** (vegsoc.org) found in a survey that most people gave up eating meat because they felt it was immoral to kill animals for food or because they disapproved of intensive animal rearing and slaughter methods.

▶ **Vegetarians** eat no meat (including fish) or products derived from killing animals (gelatine made from boiled animal bones, rennet from calves' stomach lining. Alternatives are respectively: agar-agar and vegetarian rennet.

▶ **Vegans** go a step further and don't eat dairy products (which exploit cows for human benefit) or eggs, nor do they wear leather.

Pros of going veggie...

▶ **Healthy** Low-fat, high-fibre, lot of fruit and vegetables.

▶ **Environmentally friendly** It helps reduce meat production and lessen the UK's carbon footprint.

▶ **Food security** Intensive meat production involves large quantities of grain in the form of feed. It takes up to ten kilos of vegetable protein to produce just one kilo of meat.

▶ **Cost** Giving up expensive meat and fish means you can afford good quality organic food.

▶ **Disease & welfare** Going veggie avoids the risks of animal diseases such as CJD and lessens animal suffering.

▶ **Lessens risk of food poisoning** Over 90% of all cases in the UK each year are related to the consumption of animal products.

... and the cons

▶ **Inconvenient** This is less an issue than it was a few years ago, as there is more choice and awareness, but it can still be awkward when abroad or eating out.

▶ **More effort** To achieve the necessary nutrients, you need to eat a very wide range of foods, some of which you might be unused to.

▶ **Iron deficiency risk** This is specially an issue for women and children. You could try **Flurodix** supplements, which are vegetarian.

▶ **Vitamin B12** The Vegetarian Society advises those not eating dairy foods to take a supplement and/or fortified breakfast cereals and soya drinks, as they have found no good alternative non-animal source.

Vegetarian diets for children

These need careful research to ensure they get all the nutrients they need (this is especially true of vegan children). That said, vegetarian children can have a far healthier diet than meat-eaters, with lower saturated fat levels, and more fruit and vegetables. It's worth giving them a daily vitamin supplement such as Higher Nature's Dinochews (gelatine-, gluten-, and dairy-free) and making sure that their soya milk has added vitamins and calcium. Nuts, lentils and foods such as hummus (high in calcium) are all good, but don't overdo the fibre in young children's diets as this can impede the absorption of nutrients.

What to eat?

We've come a long way from dried textured vegetable protein (TVP) mince and nut roast. Now cookery books, such as those by Claudia Roden and Yotam Ottolenghi, are full of exciting ideas for cooking meat-free food. Good vegetarian sources of protein include beans, lentils, nuts, seeds, grains, dairy products, eggs and **tofu** (set bean curd made from soya beans: marinade strips in tamari, garlic and lemon, then fry for a crispy addition to stir fries). Avoid the dicey-looking fake meat products (fake "bacon", sliced "meats", "fish" fingers). The level of processing is so great that you wonder whether a grilled tomato and herbs might be a better bet. Dragonfly (available from health food shops, Abel & Cole and Riverford) make excellent burger replacements (gluten-, dairy- and GM-free) from tofu, nuts, rice and vegetables.

Find out more

What to Eat, Marion Nestle (Farrar, Straus, and Giroux, 2006) A fascinating and comprehensive exposé of our food system, covering the origins of the bad food being sold today and offering expert advice from a professor of nutrition.

Optimum Nutrition Made Easy Patrick Holford with Susannah Lawson (Piatkus Books, 2008) An easy-to-use run through healthy foods. The approach promotes a balanced diet across a range of foods.

Food Standards Agency www.eatwell.gov.uk Government agency website with lots of useful information on nutrition and specialist diets.

British Nutrition Foundation www.nutrition.org.uk An educational charity whose website includes information for schools about healthy meals. There are resources and recipes for lessons or school cookery clubs.

Ten books to get you into the kitchen

Surround yourself with good-quality cookery books, learn a selection of recipes and then start to experiment, developing your own everyday favourites and special-occasion extravaganzas. This is just a small selection of the many wonderful cookery books out there to revive tired tastebuds (others are listed throughout this guide). Many of the recipes cost very little to make and taste delicious; others, especially puddings, are more indulgent, but well worth the effort.

Amaretto, Apple Cake and Artichokes Anna Del Conte (Vintage, 2006) The Italian food fan's bible: over five hundred pages of authentic, regional Italian recipes from the perfect tomato sauce for pasta to nettle risotto and more.

Arabesque: A Taste of Morocco, Turkey and Lebanon Claudia Roden (Michael Joseph, 2005) Enticing recipes including courgette and feta fritters, vegetable dips, tiny cheese pies, and the impressive "almond snake", a pastry coil of almonds, orange blossom water and cinnamon.

50 Great Curries of India Camellia Panjabi (Kyle Cathie, 1994) Authentic recipes and advice from the founder of the Bombay Brasserie restaurant: including dhals and flat breads, it's especially good for fish and vegetable dishes.

Fruits of the Sea Rick Stein (BBC Books, 1998) Great fish recipes including Mediterranean fish stew and paella and ideas for cooking mussels or squid (and sticky toffee pudding).

Garden Cookbook Sarah Raven (Bloomsbury, 2007) A treasure trove of produce-orientated recipes: Risotto Primavera (loaded with peas, broad beans, asparagus and mangetout), winter salads and blackcurrant and almond cake.

Moro Cookbook Sam and Sam Clark (Ebury, 2003) Traditional Spanish and Moroccan recipes from tortilla and baba ghanoush to exotic fish and meat stews.

Ottolenghi Yotam Ottolenghi and Sami Tamimi (Ebury, 2008) Imaginative salads and mouthwatering fruity tarts. Try their seared tuna with pistachio crust and papaya salsa, scallops with saffron potatoes and asparagus or chargrilled broccoli with chilli and garlic.

River Café Green Rose Gray and Ruth Rogers (Ebury, 2000) Recipes to help you make the most of seasonal foods: spaghetti with ginger and tomato sauce, squash risotto and a brilliant apricot tart.

Roast Chicken and Other Stories Simon Hopkinson (Ebury, 1994) Recipes using Hopkinson's favourite ingredients, from offal and pigeon, to endive and spinach, to custard and saffron. Includes his famous chocolate tart.

Sichuan Cooking Fuchsia Dunlop (Michael Joseph, 2001) Alternative Chinese cookery, introducing the fragrant and spicy Sichuan peppercorn: try dry-fried green beans, Mother Chen's beancurd, and Gong Bao Chicken with peanuts.

Part IV

Real choices

The supermarkets

How much time do you spend in a supermarket in an average week? Don't just count the weekly shop, which is fracturing into more mini trips in any case. There are also the lunchtime visits to the Tesco Metro or the Sainsbury's Local for sandwiches, and the times you nip in for a couple of things on the way home. If it adds up to an hour or so, and for most people it does, then you're on track to devote around half a year of your life to pushing a trolley up and down the aisles in search of special offers and multi-buys. Some estimates put the percentage of adult waking life spent in supermarkets at an alarming 2–3%.

Alarming though that thought may be, life without the supermarkets is almost unthinkable for the vast majority of us. A 2006 Defra report put it in a nutshell: "Supermarkets are a fact of modern economic life. Collectively, they have an immense and sophisticated influence over the grocery supply chain". Supermarkets spring up at such a rate that any calculation of how many there are in the UK is soon out of date. They are so ubiquitous that they account for **85p in every £1** that the British spend on food. And that figure increases every year.

The meteoric rise of the supermarkets in the last thirty years is the most significant change in the food system. Supermarkets have unprecedented power over every link in the food chain from farm and factory to fork. Power has long since drained away from the farmers, and now only the very biggest brand manufacturers have the muscle to stand up to these retailing giants.

The ambitions of the most successful supermarkets are unambiguously global; Tesco now dominates food retailing in Eastern Europe, for example, and is making inroads in China, the US and India. Walmart, the world's biggest retailer and Carrefour, the number two, are also pursuing aggressive overseas expansion programmes.

Despite these global ambitions, the supermarkets portray themselves as the consumer's champion, offering the best choice and value, conveniently available under one roof. They dismiss their critics as hankering after a golden age of cheery local greengrocers that never really existed and resenting a business that thrives by giving people what they want. So how did we get here and where are we heading? And how can you make the most of them without ending up a loyalty-card-holding pushover?

The relentless rise of the supermarkets

Like many things in the modern food system, supermarkets began in the United States. The **first self-service store** opened its doors in 1916 in Memphis, Tennessee. It rejoiced in the name of Piggly Wiggly (apparently in order to prompt people to ask why). To shoppers used to counter service, the idea of self-service was unheard of, but the concept caught on, no doubt helped by low prices. By the 1930s, rivals to Piggly Wiggly had sprung up and US supermarkets were firmly established, but reactions to the idea in the UK were initially sceptical. Like drive-through burger joints and giant domestic fridges, the British at first doubted they would catch on here.

Nonetheless Sainsbury's, which by then had been trading as a grocer's for the best part of a century, dipped its toe in the water with its first self-service store in Croydon in 1950, and a new era in British retailing had begun. Rationing still had several years to run and minimum prices across a range of goods were still set by manufacturers, but social changes were afoot – though the number of working married women fell immediately post-war, the long-term trend would be upwards, meaning households had more money but less time. As the decades progressed, growing affluence brought cars, fridges and freezers within the reach of more families, all of which facilitated the rise of the supermarkets.

Sainsbury's Holloway Road branch c. 1900

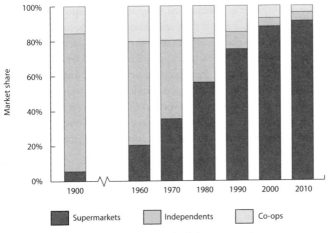

The unstoppable growth of the supermarkets

Supermarkets grew in size and number over the decades that followed, but the great leap forward came in the 1980s. Liberal planning laws and an aggressively expansionist capitalist culture under Margaret Thatcher saw the number of supermarkets grow exponentially. Until the 1980s, the big manufacturers and wholesalers had held the whip hand. But as a result of their size, the supermarkets were able to shift the balance of power, so that big retailers' brands today have much more clout than all but a few of the biggest manufacturers: in other words, New Covent Garden soups depends a lot more on Tesco than Tesco depends on it. This means that the supermarkets can call the shots over pricing, promotions and even details of packaging. While continental supermarkets pursued a no-frills, cut-price approach still favoured by the "hard discounters" today, the British supermarkets developed a model that puts quality, value for money and shopping experience ahead of rock-bottom prices.

In the past decade, supermarkets have greatly expanded what they offer, first selling non-food items such as petrol, clothes, books and electrical goods, and then picking off the services that the high street has traditionally offered one by one, turning themselves into self-sufficient retail villages. With free parking, shelter from the weather and policed by security guards and CCTV, it's a world in a bubble where you can pick up your dry-cleaning, your photos and your prescriptions, as well have an eye test, insure your car and pets and even finalize your will.

With the life-blood draining from the traditional high street, the supermarkets have moved in and bought up chains of **convenience stores**.

Tesco, for example, has gobbled up Nite and Day, One Stop, Cullens, Harts and Europa. As a result they've claimed a big share not only of the weekly shop but also the so-called "top-up occasions". A survey in 2006 found that consumers on the whole appreciated supermarket convenience stores, which had "brought fresher food, new ranges, lower prices, better store environments... [and] forced smaller players to improve". Tesco and Sainsbury's are now major players on the high street, and Asda and Waitrose plan to join them. Marks & Spencer's Simply Food outlets meanwhile have sprouted at railway and motorway service stations as well as in town centres.

This may appear like an invasion of the clones, but there's a great deal of diversity among the chains, from the up-market, pricier Waitrose and M&S to the no-frills "hard discounters" Aldi, Lidl and Netto. The broad middle ground is, of course, where the competition is fiercest for the

Invasion of the supermarkets

1863 The **Co-operative Wholesale Society** formed.

1869 **John James Sainsbury** opens his first shop in London's Drury Lane selling butter, eggs and milk.

1904 **Waite**, **Rose** and **Taylor** open their first shop in West London.

1916 Clarence Saunders opens **Piggly Wiggly**, the world's first self-service store. Over 600 Piggly Wiggly stores still operate in the US today.

1919 Jack Cohen sets up a market stall in the East End of London. A decade later he would open his first **Tesco** store in Burnt Oak, North London.

1950 **Sainsbury's** opens the first self-service supermarket in the UK in Croydon.

1955 First **Waitrose** supermarket in Streatham, London.

1961 First **Morrisons** supermarket opens (though the family firm dates from 1899).

1964 **Retail price maintenance**, which set a minimum price for a wide variety of staple goods, abolished.

1965 **Asda** (Associated Dairies) set up.

1972 First UK **Safeway** begins trading.

1973 **Marks & Spencer** launches chilled chicken Kiev and the age of the ready meal dawns.

1979 First **barcode** scanner used. They will go on to revolutionize stock control.

custom of shoppers who are neither Waitrose's ABC1s nor Netto's "time rich, cash poor" bargain hunters. And it is the battle for these customers which has driven much of the expansion and innovation in retailing over the last two decades.

Supermarkets: the case for

Even if there is a growing sense that supermarkets are bent on world domination (the biggest international ones already turn over more money in a year than the GDP of two-thirds of the world's nations), people sometimes forget that the food culture they replaced was far from perfect. When Elizabeth David first published her *Italian Food* in 1954, for example, she wrote "mozzarella is not imported [into the UK]" and suggested Primula cheese as a substitute for ricotta (though she repented of this in

1986	**Sainsbury's** takes over market leadership from Tesco.
1990	German chain, **Aldi**, becomes the first "hard discounter" in the UK.
1993	Tory minister **John Selwyn Gummer** puts a curb on the growth of out-of-town supermarkets in an attempt to stem the decline of town centres.
1994	**The Sunday Trading Act** introduced in England and Wales. Another German hard discounter, **Lidl**, arrives in the UK.
1995	Tesco launches its loyalty scheme, the **Tesco Clubcard**. Tesco overtakes Sainsbury's as the UK's biggest grocer.
1996	The first **24-hour Tesco** opens.
1999	Asda acquired by **Walmart**, the world's biggest retailer.
2000	Tesco launches **internet shopping**. It's now the world's largest on-line grocer.
2003	Morrisons buys its larger southern rival, **Safeway**, and becomes fourth-largest UK grocer.
2005	**"Make Sainsbury's great again campaign"** launched to try to recapture ground lost to rival Tesco.
2007	Marks & Spencer launches its environmental scheme, **Plan A**.
2008	Office of Fair Trading approves the Co-op's buy-out of **Somerfield**, making the Co-op the country's fifth-biggest supermarket.

a later edition). For decent olive oil, she recommended a trip to shops in Soho. Contrast this with today: most supermarkets offer a choice of several different types of parmesan cheese, from bags of ready grated to de luxe, aged organic. There will also be an array of olive oils, alongside other once-exotic products such as walnut and pumpkin seed oils, which were all but impossible to find fifty years ago. It's not just fancy imports that supermarkets have filled their shelves with: everything from tinned soup to jam and barbecue sauce is now available in an often bewildering array, since the more shoppers you entice through your doors each week, the more you can afford to segment your customer base into ever more finely targeted groups.

So the first argument on favour of the supermarkets is that they offer unprecedented **choice**. The average hypermarket can have over 40,000 different products on offer. Those lines will be constantly changing, which the supermarkets say leads to innovation and dynamism in the food industry. Managing such a big inventory has a pay-off for the supermarkets, of course: the bigger the shop and the more temptations on offer, the more time people spend in it and the more they put in their trolleys. So giant stores with vast amounts of choice make business sense.

The second argument that supermarkets put forward – and in cash-conscious times this one comes to the fore – is **price**. As the supermarkets grew, their buying-power grew, too. And though shoppers in surveys cite a whole range of things that influence their purchases, in reality, a lot of what goes in the trolley is determined by price. As Morrisons founder, Ken Morrison put it: "the poor need bargains and the rich appreciate them." The growing number of so-called "hard discounters" – Aldi, Netto and Lidl – exert a strong downward pull on prices in a market that was already fiercely price competitive.

The third plus to be chalked up in the supermarket's favour is **convenience**. Even middle-sized towns now have supermarkets where you can shop all through the night if you want to. Contrast this with most town centres where, if you hit the high street after 5.30pm, you'll find most of the butchers, greengrocers and delis closing up. The Sainsbury's Local or the Tesco Metro, though, will be ready and willing to take your money at least until 10pm. **Sunday trading**, too, has given people more flexibility over when they shop. There is pressure from the supermarkets for a further relaxation of the Sunday trading laws, which means that the prospect of genuine 24/7 shopping may not be far off. Many people are happy to trade a trip to their local high street for an hour on auto-pilot in a superstore with free parking. Now that you can self-scan your shopping at a growing number of stores, no human interaction is necessary at all. Technology may soon bring radio-emitting tags that allow the entire trolley-load to be scanned in a matter of seconds (see p.214), so you'll be able to breeze on through to the car-park with a simple swipe of your bank card.

Finally, supermarkets pride themselves on their **consistency**. They want you to be confident that the bread you buy today looks and tastes exactly like the loaf you bought last week (until it's "new and improved", that is). And that you can always find it on the shelf.

So, choice, price, convenience, consistency – and no need to go to Soho for olive oil. Sounds like an open and shut case in favour of the supermarkets. Well, it might be worth taking a closer look before reaching a conclusion. The picture isn't quite as rosy as the supermarkets would have us believe.

Tesco: a very big slice of the pie

▶ **Tesco's share of the UK grocery market stood at 31% in 2008** This was twice that of its nearest rival, Asda. In autumn 2008, the number of Tesco stores in the UK was 2184 and their UK staff numbered 280,000.

▶ **"Our market share of UK retailing is 12.5%"** Tesco boss Sir Terry Leahy told an interviewer in 2004, "that leaves 87.5% to go after." Sir Terry, not a man renowned for his sense of humour, may not have been joking.

▶ **Tesco is the third biggest grocer in the world** (after Walmart and Carrefour) with 2008 sales of £51.8 billion. Tesco first cleared the £2 billion profit mark in 2005. In 2008/09 they may breach the £3 billion barrier.

▶ **Tesco operates in thirteen countries** worldwide with over 1500 overseas stores (and counting). They have a strong presence in Malaysia and central Europe and ambitious plans for India and China. They are currently expanding their retail space at a rate of 11.5 million square feet a year. "Tesco", they say, "is about growth."

▶ **Only one postcode area** in the whole of the UK doesn't have a Tesco: Harrogate in North Yorkshire. But it can only be a matter of time...

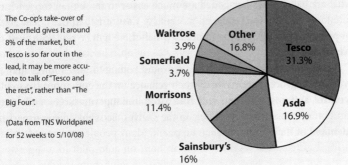

The Co-op's take-over of Somerfield gives it around 8% of the market, but Tesco is so far out in the lead, it may be more accurate to talk of "Tesco and the rest", rather than "The Big Four".

(Data from TNS Worldpanel for 52 weeks to 5/10/08)

Waitrose 3.9%
Other 16.8%
Tesco 31.3%
Somerfield 3.7%
Morrisons 11.4%
Asda 16.9%
Sainsbury's 16%

Cruising the aisles

Fresh produce

Nearly all supermarkets have a "seasonal products" aisle, where you'll find Easter eggs in January, barbecue sets in March and Christmas gifts from September. Strangely, though, the idea of celebrating seasonality is almost entirely absent from the section of the shop where you might expect it to be most prominent, fresh fruit and vegetables. Seasonality has almost entirely been banished from this section in favour of what food journalist Joanna Blythman has dubbed "**permanent global summertime**".

Fresh produce is where supermarkets' command-and-control mindset comes into conflict most acutely with the reality of food production. Supermarkets are control freaks. It's easy to achieve perfect uniformity in the processed foods section; manufacturers are dedicated to ensuring that every box of cornflakes and tin of beans looks, smells and tastes exactly like every other. Not so in fresh produce, where variety of shape and flavour are part of the pleasure of shopping. Or should be.

But that's not the supermarket way. Strawberries, for example, are stocked all year round, as is asparagus, which used to be a treat for a few weeks in early summer. Peru is now the world's largest exporter of asparagus, but the crop begins to convert its sugars into starch after it is picked, so by the time your winter asparagus reaches your kitchen, it's woody and tasteless. So quite apart from the absurd distance it has travelled, there's also a price in terms of quality to be paid. The same can be said of many globe-trotting fruits and veg.

Supermarkets do their best to iron out the irregularities that nature puts in. Apples are computer-scanned and photographed from all angles to check for blemishes before they are approved to go on sale. Products that are bagged and bar-coded are much easier to track than those which are loose. When Tesco opened its Fresh & Easy stores in the US in 2007, it pioneered a vision of the future in which there will be **no loose fruit or vegetables** at all.

Yet despite this desire for control, product quality is often lower than in your greengrocer's shop. For all their reliance on the computerized stock-control systems, you can still find tired-looking vegetables and herbs and other substandard produce on the shelves. So what do supermarkets demand of their fresh produce suppliers?

▶ **Perfect cosmetic shape and appearance** If a green bean is too short, even by a few millimetres, or a tomato the wrong diameter, it's rejected before it even gets packed. According to the Soil Association, supermarkets reject 40% of organic crops on purely cosmetic grounds.

▶ **Reliable "just-in-time" deliveries** Since suppliers live in fear of **deselection** if they are unable to supply exactly what the supermarkets want when they want it, they keep extra produce on hand just in case. This leads to waste. It also means that smaller suppliers get passed over in favour of larger ones, who can maintain a regular supply.

Keeping the shelves full: suppliers' tales

There's plenty of anecdotal evidence that the lot of a supermarket supplier is not a happy one, though worries about losing contracts mean they rarely criticize their paymasters openly. The **Competition Commission** published research in 2007 based on extensive confidential interviews with hundreds of supermarket suppliers. They learned that:

▶ Two-thirds of suppliers had been asked to enter into an **exclusive supply arrangement** with one of the "Big Four" supermarkets and one-third had complied. This puts all the supplier's eggs in one basket and makes them vulnerable to threats of **deselection**.

▶ Most suppliers felt they had **little or no control over price negotiations** with the supermarkets because they were "tough, aggressive negotiators" who could dictate terms.

▶ Two-thirds had seen their profits decrease and **competition from overseas suppliers** increase in the past five years, especially those who supplied the Big Four (Tesco, Asda, Sainsbury's and Morrisons).

▶ Being asked to **contribute to supermarkets' marketing costs** was "just the norm". One supplier who felt coerced into making payments said he did so "because we do not have a choice, it's blackmail really". Payments to keep a product on the supermarket shelves were not uncommon, nor were non-negotiable "rebates" to the retailer as compensation for unsold stock. Other unsavoury practices included being told that the price the supermarket would pay was to be reduced just as stock was delivered.

When the Competition Commission made its final report in 2008, it criticized the supermarkets for passing on **"excessive risk and unexpected costs"** to their suppliers, which was bad for investment, innovation and ultimately consumers. It remains to be seen whether their recommendation of a tightened up **code of practice** for supermarkets will have any effect on the retailers' behaviour. Read their report on supermarket strong-arm tactics here:

Competition Commission competition-commission.org.uk

This explains why so many packets of Israeli herbs are found on the supermarket shelves, even when British herbs are in season.

▶ **Varieties with a long growing season and shelf-life** The Elsanta strawberry has usurped virtually all other varieties, not on account of its flavour but because it grows faster and keeps longer. This quest for long shelf-life means produce is brought to the store chilled and unripe, often at the expense of varieties with outstanding taste.

▶ **Added value** For example in the form of prepared fruit and vegetables. There's much more money to be made by cutting a water melon into chunks than selling it whole.

▶ **The lowest prices** Above all, this is what supermarkets want from their suppliers. Fair enough – why shouldn't they? The problem comes when you compare the muscle of a global retail giant with that of a small apple grower.

Meat and fish

Managing fresh fish and meat sections presents a similar challenge to the supermarkets as fruit and vegetables. Sea-fishing in particular is an unpredictable business, which means that the supermarkets have a marked preference for frozen and farmed fish, and like to deal in consignments from big overseas suppliers. Though many supermarkets introduced fresh fish counters in the 1980s, causing the demise of many independent fishmongers, Sir Ken Morrison was being frank when he admitted that: "it's a little touch of nostalgia. You can choose the fish, the fishmonger will bone it, skin it, put a bit of parsley with it. It's activity and theatre." In many supermarkets, that theatre is decidedly lacklustre, with staff simply weighing and pricing tired-looking fish.

The same is true of meat: supermarkets have decided that bright red meat is what the public wants, so hanging and ageing, which any butcher will tell you is critical to the taste of the meat, is kept to an absolute minimum. Compare the supermarket butcher's counter, with its predictable range of expensive, pre-prepared cuts and mountain of sausages, to that of a real butcher and the poverty of choice at the former is clear.

What to avoid in the supermarket meat section

▶ **Sausages with low meat and high fat content** and low-grade processed meats of all sorts, which is full of additives, fat and water.

Some supermarket pâtés contain as little as 23% meat.

▶ **The cheap broiler chickens** which became a *cause célèbre* in 2008 when chef Hugh Fearnley-Whittingstall raised their plight on national TV. Many viewers were shocked to see the appalling conditions in which the chickens were kept for their six-week lives in order to end up with a £2 price tag on Tesco's shelves. At the time of writing, the £2 chicken remains on sale.

▶ **Check for hock burns** when buying chicken. These are the brown discolorations on the legs which indicate that the bird has been "burnt" by ammonia in the litter it stood in. One survey of three hundred supermarket chickens found that 82% had hock burns. Sometimes the burns are cut off during processing.

▶ **"Added water for extra succulence"** is simply a way of getting you to pay for water to bulk out cheap poultry, bacon and pork. Also watch out for "brine solution for grilling".

▶ **Organic meat from South America**. It's crazy to import meat produced under a so-called sustainable system from halfway across the world. The supermarkets with the best record for stocking British organic meat, according to the Soil Association's most recent survey, are Waitrose, Marks & Spencer and Sainsbury's. Tesco, Asda and Morrisons still lag a considerable distance behind them.

Eggs

Waitrose, Marks & Spencer and the Co-op no longer sell eggs from caged hens. All their eggs are free range. Morrisons and Sainsbury's are planning to phase out battery eggs by 2010 in the case of "shell eggs" (whole eggs) and Sainsbury's has pledged to remove them from its own-label products by 2012. But the two biggest retailers, Tesco and Asda, still haven't given a commitment to stop stocking them. Tesco's policy earned it the 2008 **Bad Egg Award** from Compassion in World Farming, who said: "over 80% of chicken meat sold by Tesco is from intensively reared, fast-growing breeds kept in overcrowded conditions". For the full run-down on supermarket eggs, see:

Good Egg Awards ciwf.org.uk/your_food/good_egg_awards

Fancy a sandwich?

The British are a nation of sandwich eaters, munching through over 11 billion of them every year. That's about four a week each. **Chicken salad** is by far the country's favourite filling, and variations on the chicken sandwich account for over one-third of bought sandwiches. Next on the list comes ham, followed by cheese, tuna, prawn and bacon. Around a quarter of sandwiches are bought from supermarkets and sandwich shops: a combination of convenience and the widespread belief that they represent a healthy option means the sandwich market has grown from £1 billion in 1990 to around £3.5 billion. Sandwiches are much bigger business than the burger or pizza market.

But how easy is it to find out what's in your sandwich? A loophole in the law means that sandwiches made on the premises don't have to carry any information on their contents on the pack. This means that you can end up eating a lot more salt and saturated fat that you might think. A Channel Four documentary in 2008 discovered, for example, that over half of Pret A Manger's sandwiches would receive a red traffic light for their salt content and that their Cheddar and roast tomato bloomer contained three-quarters of a woman's recommended daily saturated fat intake. They also revealed that the Marks & Spencer British Oakham chicken and pancetta Caesar sandwich was higher in fat than two double cheeseburgers from McDonald's.

New rules under review aim to make the sandwich industry come clean about what it is selling: they would prevent manufacturers from calling meats that have been branded with fake char marks being called "char-grilled" and ban the term "smoked" from artificially smoke-flavoured products. Chicken that has been deboned, rolled and then chopped would have to be described as "re-formed" rather than the more appetising if less honest "roast chicken". The British Sandwich Association claims that this would "confuse" consumers. Or it might just make them think twice about what's in their lunch. You can peek inside your Pret sandwich and check out its contents online at:

Pret A Manger pret.com/menu/sandwiches

Processed foods

Processed foods have a long shelf life, fit neatly in rows and yield high profit margins: perfect for supermarkets. Compare the floor-space devoted to breakfast cereals, confectionery, fizzy drinks and sauces in jars, and the number of them on special offer compared to apples and carrots. Environmental writer Bill McKibben has spoken of the "**mirage of choice**" in supermarkets actually concealing a "sea of high-fructose corn syrup", one of the food industry's favourite cheap ingredients found in a host of different products. The processed aisles are where the nastiest surprises lurk in terms of additives and cheap bulking agents. Even here, though, it is still possible to support the few small producers who have cleared the supermarkets' selection hurdles and made it onto the shelves. Check the labels and go for products with a small number of natural ingredients.

Bakery

Supermarket in-store bakeries are a misnomer. Reheateries would be a more accurate term for them, since most of the dough arrives part-baked and frozen. But the smell of freshly baked bread and clatter of bakers going about their work adds to the sense of theatre in supermarkets and lends much-needed glamour to the rows of so-called "plant bread", bags of wrapped, sliced bread baked by a handful of massive bakery groups which makes up over three-quarters of the UK bread market (see p.72).

The Federation of Bakers, the industry group which represents the biggest plant bakers, promotes its product on the twin virtues of long shelf life and convenience. It's less vocal about the fact that bread which has to survive in a plastic bag for many days also has to have a good dose of preservatives in it.

Supermarkets would like us to see in-store baked bread as a "treat", though in fact you are almost always paying for a fancy name – too many crimes to count have been committed in the name of "ciabatta" – and an exotic added ingredient or two rather than the quality of the bread. Supermarkets baguettes are frequently a travesty that no French person would put in their mouth: a spongy crust and dense, soggy inside. As they are often wrapped, you can with a clear conscience do a test to see if the crust has any crack to it by giving the bread a gentle squeeze. If it sags spongily, it's not worth buying. Though even this test won't tell you much about what may lie beneath the crust.

Since demand for bread is finite, the supermarkets are keen for us to eat ever more baked treats. As the Federation of Bakers sees it, "the need for indulgence and pleasure continues to be the most important consumer driver". Here again, with demand for traditional baked goods such as crumpets declining, the hunt is on for exotica to tempt our palates.

As a rule of thumb, it's worth bearing in mind that a homemade loaf or cake will keep for two or three days. If a shop-bought version lasts much longer, there is a reason for it, and it's not good.

We know where you live (and that's just for starters)

Coming soon to a supermarket near you: the RFID tag

Good shopkeepers have always prided themselves on knowing what their customers like. Forty years ago, that simply meant the shopkeeper remembering what brand of tea Mrs Jones preferred. (Waitrose has invented an imaginary Mrs Jones, who represents a typical customer: she is "knowledgeable about food, quite a keen cook… in her late thirties or early forties and is concerned about food issues". Waitrose buyers are encouraged to consider what Mrs Jones would make of any new product.)

Other supermarkets also want to get close to their customers. A plaque in Tesco's HQ espouses the core value of "creating value for customers to earn their lifetime loyalty". They took a big step towards doing that in 1995 when they launched their **Clubcard** scheme. Cardholders (of whom there were soon ten million) earn points every time they make a purchase. Those points can later be converted into vouchers to spend in-store. But crucially, the cards provide data to the supermarkets about customers' spending habits, a "portrait in data" as one commentator put it, so that special offers can be tailored to different shoppers.

When the scheme started, the early mailings to card holders came in six different versions. Within a few years, that had diversified into 60,000 mailings, which could take into account whether you were a beer drinker who liked to sample foreign lagers or an occasional organic food buyer who could be tempted to trade up more often. Loyalty cards have other advantages: they save the retailer giving away money needlessly to people who would have bought a product in any case by focusing on those who need extra persuasion.

Disconcertingly, loyalty card information has also been used to track people (wrongly) suspected of shoplifting. But there are yet more worrying developments on the horizon: **radio frequency identification** (RFID) technology allows tiny information-transmitting chips to be attached to almost any product. Once there, unlike a bar-code, each unique tag is capable of providing an almost limitless amount of information. Civil liberties campaigners discovered RFID chips had been added to in-store cards issued by Metro, a major German retail group unbeknownst to customers.

Tesco and Walmart have also been trialling RFID: Tesco customers in Cambridge who picked up packs of Gillette razors were photographed by an RFID-activated shelf camera, ostensibly to prevent theft. Both companies are enthusiastic about the prospects for stock control and crime prevention. The trouble is, it may pave the way for all sorts of other tracking and monitoring of customer behaviour. In the US, some retailers have already experimented with **biometric loyalty programmes**, which require fingerprints to access special offers. How long before the supermarkets offer us bonus points if we let them insert radio chips behind our ears? Find out more about radio tagging here:

Spychips spychips.com

New stores for hard times

With food prices on the rise and consumers more cash-conscious than ever, the spotlight has been turned on the "hard discounters". They are the true heirs to the "pile 'em high and sell 'em cheap" ethos of the early supermarkets. The German chain, **Aldi**, arrived in the UK in 1990, and, like its fellow discounters **Lidl and Netto**, has been growing steadily. They're still comparatively small; even added together they're only one-fifth the size of Tesco, but they are growing rapidly enough to make the competition sit up and take notice.

The hard discounters' European way of shopping was slow to catch on. They offer small, no-frills stores that often stock as few as a thousand different products. Even Netto's UK boss admitted their stores were "stark and barren" in the early days. Instead of twelve different makes of pasta sauce, you'll find just one. That's one way they keep prices down. Another is by stocking mainly own-brand goods purchased in huge quantities. A third is by paring staffing levels and shop-fittings to the bone. In short, if you're seeking the thrills of "retailtainment", go elsewhere. If you're after a bargain, step right up.

All three have ambitious growth plans. In the case of Aldi, they've declared their intention to quintuple the size of their network to 1500 UK stores in a decade. Tesco is worried enough to have allegedly built a mock-up of a discount store at its Cheshunt headquarters to understand the enemy better.

Are they worth it? Well, the discounters give you no-frills, imported packaged goods at knockdown prices. Netto's UK boss says his aim is to offer quality that matches the Big Four's standard ranges at a price that competes with their value range, and that's probably a fair claim. Much of their stock is processed food, so to avoid additives, read the label carefully. The relentless drive for low costs comes at a price; you're not going to find lots of ethical or organic boasts, and unlike the other supermarkets, the staff that scan your items at the checkout are not able to join a union their employer recognizes. But if you're on a very tight budget and it's a toss-up between Tesco and Aldi, then give them a try and judge for yourself.

Supermarket trick or treat?

Cruising the aisles, it's easy to glaze over and passively accept the information and claims that supermarkets bombard us with. Next time you go, here are some supermarket tricks to bear in mind:

▶ **Fake half prices** The Department of Trade and Industry's pricing rules says that a price for an item has to be charged for 28 days before it can be used to promote a price cut, except for fresh fruit and vegetables, which are perishable and fluctuate in price through the year. This loophole enables supermarkets to raise prices briefly in order to appear to offer massive reductions by bringing them down again. Strawberries, raspberries and blueberries are particularly prone to this scam. Check out your greengrocer, if you're lucky enough to have one, for the true market price of fresh produce. Chances are it will be cheaper.

▶ **Flattering price comparisons** When supermarkets display comparisons with their competitors' prices, they pick their battles carefully to convince you they're the cheapest in town. On fresh products, such as meat, fish and fruit and vegetables, local independents are often cheaper than any of the supermarkets (see p.230).

▶ **The incredible shrinking pack** A change in pack size can convince you that you're getting a bargain when in fact you're not. When commodity prices rise, some manufacturers think it's more palatable to cut the size of the pack than put the price up. Though that, in effect, is what they've done.

▶ **"Premiumization"** This is just a fancy way to say "charging more for something that's tarted up". The supermarkets would put it differently: it's adding value in the form of convenience or quality. There's nothing intrinsically wrong with a premium range, though the reality doesn't always match the hype. But now that supermarkets sell hard-boiled eggs for our busy lifestyles, things may have gone a step too far.

Point and click: the future of grocery shopping?

Online shopping makes perfect sense to supermarkets. The customer is an abstraction: a collection of data and a credit card. Online retail is a battleground that no supermarket with ambitions to be a major player can neglect. Online grocery sales in the UK reached £2.4 billion in 2007. This is only 2–3% of the total grocery market, but it's growing rapidly and some projections say that by 2012, 12% of Britons will do all their grocery shopping online and 60% will do so some of the time.

Tesco were first off the mark with online groceries in 2000 and Asda and Sainsbury's both followed suit. The player who shook things up, though, was newcomer, **Ocado**. Launched in 2002, this company, which is part-owned by Waitrose, has no bricks-and-mortar stores at all. Everything is distributed by a fleet of biofuelled vans from a purpose-built warehouse in Hertfordshire. If you live in an area Ocado serves (mostly in southern England), then their boast that you'll "never need to visit a supermarket again" could come true. In London it has captured about half of the online grocery market. An independent audit of Ocado's **carbon footprint** in 2008 came up with the astonishing finding that it was actually **greener** to use them than walk to the supermarket, since Ocado doesn't have stores to heat, light and fill with open-topped chillers, and deliveries are scheduled to minimize food miles.

Online pros

▶ Saves petrol, time and temper tantrums at the checkout

▶ Speedy reordering – you can save your favourites for next time

▶ Make price comparisons at mysupermarket.com and save money

And cons

▶ You can't examine fresh produce, meat or fish before you buy and online product information is often scanty, especially if you're trying to shop ethically

▶ There's a delivery charge. Some charge more for popular slots

▶ Substitutions – when items are out of stock you may end up with things you didn't order

Consider using the time you save by ordering the boring stuff from online supermarkets to explore your local independents for the rest of your shopping. And see the Directory (p.275) for other online retailers.

Ocado ocado.com

My Supermarket mysupermarket.co.uk

How green is your supermarket?

The greenness of the supermarkets matters because they occupy a dominant position in food retailing, and the food system plays a huge part in our carbon footprint. But it's well-nigh impossible to assess the greenness of a supermarket just by scanning the shelves, since many of the environmental impacts are invisible. That is where clear, accurate labelling comes in, an area where all the supermarkets fall well short of perfection.

Supermarkets didn't get big by being green. Their emphasis on scale, volume and centralization means there is a good deal of greenwash to penetrate to get to the truth. They all have PR machines that are skilful at putting the greenest of spins on their activities. The National Consumer Council (NCC) did an audit of the eight biggest supermarkets' green credentials in 2006 and found that **Waitrose** came out best. A year later, they produced another report card, which once again graded the chains on four criteria: **climate change measures**, including availability of seasonal produce; **sustainable fishing**; schemes to **tackle waste**; and **sustainable farming**, including organics and pesticide reduction. Clearly such assessments are highly complex and information is not always available about provenance and production methods. This time first place was shared between **Waitrose, Sainsbury's and Marks & Spencer**. When they assessed seasonal British produce, the researchers found that:

▶ **In-season UK produce** Somerfield and the Co-op stocked the highest proportion of this (both over three-quarters).

▶ **Air-freighted fruit** All the supermarkets sold produce from overseas, despite the availability of in-season UK varieties. Tesco sold the highest proportion of air-freighted fruit and the Co-op the lowest.

Booths: supermarkets with a human touch

You might think that the Preston-based Booths supermarket (booths-supermarkets. co.uk) chain is too small even to register in the world of supermarkets. It has only around thirty stores, all based in the north of England, compared to the thousands of outlets of its competitors. Yet this **family-run firm** has survived and even thrived by refusing to copy the big boys, whom it cannot match on price. Instead it uses its small size to its advantage by building long-term relationships with **local suppliers** of everything from dairy products and vegetables to local beers. This has enabled it to offer what is probably the best range of truly local produce of all the supermarkets. If more supermarkets were like Booths, there would probably be fewer anti-supermarket campaign groups.

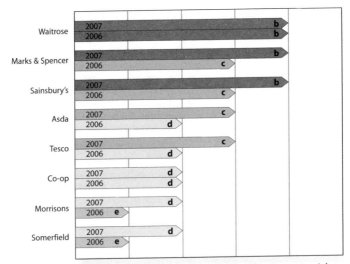

Supermarkets greenness ratings: A = excellent; B = good; C = showing potential;
D = room for improvement; E = poor

▶ **Fairtrade fruit** Sainsbury's had the highest proportion of this on its shelves, followed by the Co-op and Morrisons.

When it came to **fish**, M&S and Waitrose came out on top: they were the only retailers which "consistently provided sustainability information and method of catch on the majority of fish products that they sell". But, the report says: "We found some fish species on sale that are potentially at risk of extinction, including skate (Co-op, Morrisons and Tesco); three types of monkfish (Morrisons, Sainsbury's and Tesco); swordfish (M&S); and Dover sole (Sainsbury's and Tesco). Tesco sold the most types of potentially "at risk" species – six products in total." Asda was commended for making sustainable fish available at the value end of its range.

The **sustainable farming** rating is based on the range of organic and reduced-pesticide products on offer, and on the extent to which they were being promoted. In general, the report found that amid a general plethora of choice, there was usually only one organic option on offer (if any). Most of the supermarkets have espoused ambitious plans to grow their organic sales. But perhaps they fear that too enthusiastic promotion of organic will be seen as showing a lack of confidence in their standard ranges. Waitrose probably has least to fear from this charge and indeed

Supermarkets and animal welfare

The majority of the sixty billion animals farmed worldwide for meat, eggs and milk have miserable short lives in intensive factory-farm conditions. Tesco, as the UK's largest supermarket, could make an enormous difference to the lives of millions of animals if it improved its welfare record. **M&S** and **Waitrose** have exercised "choice editing" on their customers' behalf and have helped raise standards. Compassion in World Farming's biennial survey scores supermarkets on the standards they set their suppliers, from the treatment of pregnant and baby animals through to slaughter. It also covers fish farming. They reward the best and encourage others to improve.

As always, check the label – the beef you've just picked up has probably never seen the grass adorning the package. "Farm fresh" is usually misleading. A Soil Association organic mark will tell you that the cow was well treated. An **RSPCA Freedom Foods** logo doesn't mean that the animals haven't been factory farmed (they work within the existing system and do the best they can to maintain decent standards). If you can't buy organic, then their free-range meat is the next best thing. Red Tractor and the Lion Mark do not guarantee high animal welfare standards: they are industry marks which offer the barest of assurances based on the minimum legal requirements.

Vote with your feet: switch supermarkets for animal products. Contact your regular supermarket and ask them about where the meat they sell comes from.

Supermarket	Score out of 5	Comments
M&S	3.99	"Demonstrated a strong commitment to farm animal welfare"
Waitrose	3.98	"Strong track record on animal welfare"
Co-op	2.88	Improving
Sainsbury's	2.67	"The best of the Big Four" and most improved since 2005
Tesco	2.63	Sells battery eggs; poor record on chickens and pigs welfare
Morrisons	2.36	"Animal welfare policies do not always extend to the animals in their supply chain outside the UK"
Asda	1.86*	Refused to take part in the survey (* figures from 2005 survey)

Compassion in World Farming ciwf.org Their detailed supermarket report is on the website along with regular updates.

has the widest organic selection, but M&S and Tesco also have substantial organic product ranges.

The NCC survey isn't exhaustive, and one area it didn't cover was the supermarkets' use of **road transport**, which is huge. It has been calcu-

Step in the right direction: Sainsbury's first eco-store opened in 2008 in Dartmouth, Devon, complete with wind turbines, water recycling, a reduced number of lightbulbs, and a wood-fired boiler. In comparison to conventional stores, it should use 40% less energy.

lated that Tesco trucks, for example, cover 68 million miles in the UK every year. Any motorway trip will reveal that the majority of the lorries thundering up and down the country belong to the food system.

All their trucking gets the supermarkets bad PR, and they have sophisticated logistical systems dedicated to keeping their fuel bills down. But the fact remains that their system of centralization and distribution from regional hubs means this can only go so far. Their business is founded on transport being cheap and bulk sourcing from far away being more cost effective than having multiple regionally based small suppliers.

Supermarket attempts at local sourcing are widely trumpeted in store, to the extent that if you don't look too closely, you may get the impression that everything in the shop came from a smiling local farmer who kept happy animals. But only a tiny fraction of any supermarkets inventory is truly local; in Scotland and Wales for example, anything sourced within the country is counted as "local". Supermarket localism tends to be more

M&S: the greener grocer?

No national retailer flaunts its green credentials more than Marks & Spencer. In 2007 it launched its Plan A ("because there is no plan B"). This is a five-year, hundred-point scheme, which has among its objectives carbon neutrality by 2012, as well as health, Fairtrade and animal welfare targets. M&S has already notched up some notable successes, such as the Marine Conservation Society awards for its fish sourcing and, by switching all its eggs to free-range and beginning a similar conversion with pork, it was named "Compassionate Supermarket 2008" by Compassion in World Farming.

But in tough economic times, customers reappraise their ethical priorities and may begin to look for cheaper alternatives. M&S chairman Sir Stuart Rose knows that, in turning green, the retailer can't "get too far ahead of our customers. I think half a step is about right: any more and you can't sell to them; any less and you lose the lead."

about providing the customer with a feelgood sense that the business is rooted in the community than actually changing the way it operates. The supermarkets which have shown most commitment to sourcing local products are **Waitrose and Booths** (see box on p.218), which are themselves smaller and whose stores are concentrated in certain parts of the country. The NCC report concluded "it is yet to be seen if any retailers have gone far enough to encourage and enable consumers to change their behaviour and make greener choices".

Food packaging
The high price of convenience

With landfill sites filling up fast, the pressure is on to reduce the amount of waste dumped in them; much of it is food and packaging waste. The UK government passed legislation in 2007 requiring the food and drink industry, which creates over 50% of the UK's packaging waste, to comply with the EU's directive on reducing packaging and improving recycling. And thirteen retailers (representing 92% of the UK grocery market) signed up to the 2005 Courtauld Agreement, which agrees targets for reductions on packaging and food waste to be reached by 2010. Forty percent of our food shopping comes in **non-recyclable packaging** and many products are over-packaged. Packaging is fundamental to the way supermarkets do business: it protects and preserves food during the distribution process and while on the shelf. It also carries increasing amounts of information such as assurance marks, nutritional information, country of origin, ingredients and promotional copy. It also helps food look appealing. Alternatives do exist: in health food shops you can save money by weighing out your own loose dried ingredients (into paper or plastic bags), and you can buy direct. Some environmental campaigners have

Pocket the difference: the only winner with these over-packaged, over-priced mini broccoli and cauliflower pieces is the supermarket's profit margin. At £2.59, or 64p each, for four tiny pieces they've managed to "add value" to a cheap product, to the detriment of the shopper and the environment.

removed all packing materials at the checkout as a protest. The question is: to what extent can we, and the supermarkets do without packaging?

Global garbage patch

Vast quantities of plastic have been produced in the last fifty years, which scientists estimate will take between four hundred and one thousand years to **biodegrade**. Plastic has been accumulating in the environment to devastating effect: an average of 200,000 bags end up in landfill sites every minute of every day, only for 7% of them to fly off again as wind-borne litter. The world's oceans become the final resting place for much of our plastic. Between the west coast of the US and Japan in the North Pacific Ocean there is a spinning vortex of plastic the size of Texas known as the Garbage Patch.

What's the problem?

Around one million seabirds and 100,000 seals, sea lions, whales, dolphins and sea turtles are killed or mutilated by our discarded plastic (including many billions of tiny plastic pellets used in the plastics manufacturing industry) each year, getting caught up in it and often mistaking it for food. Birds feed plastic to their young unaware that it will kill them by filling up their stomachs so that they cannot swallow and so starve. After their bodies have decomposed the plastic goes on to kill again. Plastics absorb concentrations of toxic chemicals up to a million times greater than the surrounding seawater in which they were present and take far longer to degrade at sea leading to worries about water contamination.

Is there an answer?: reduce, reuse, recycle

We need to start using alternatives wherever possible. Using a vegbox delivery rather than the supermarket and buying loose bread and cheese from your local deli will cut your contribution to food waste. Various sorts of recyclable or biodegradable bags such as

> **[Supermarkets] have power in terms of what they buy and how it's packed... by focusing on the consumer end, they are to some extent diverting attention from what they should be doing.**
>
> Professor Chris Coggins,
> Government waste and recycling expert

compostable cornstarch carrier bags have been promoted as a green alternative, but there is much disagreement about the benefits; a recyclable item is only as good as its owner and in reality the vast majority end up in landfill via our kitchen bins. Ninety-three percent of recyclable high-density polyethylene (HDPE) milk containers are simply thrown out. The best solution is to reduce the amount of plastic created in the first place by reusing existing objects or passing on things you no longer want (for example through freecycle.org) and make sure that anything that can be recycled ends up in the right place (you'll need to find out about your local recycling system as this varies from council to council).

"I'm not a plastic bag"

"What really brought it home for me was one day filming a turtle. It had a plastic bag in its mouth and was slowly dying, there was nothing we could do."
Rebecca Hosking

In spring 2007 two women raised the public profile of the UK campaign to cut plastic bag use to such an extent that within just six months checkouts were full of shoppers piling groceries into their own cloth bags.

▶ Filmmaker Rebecca Hosking's **shocking exposé** of the results of plastics pollution in Hawaii, *Message in the Waves*, captured the public's imagination with images of seabirds and animals suffering as a result of our actions.

▶ Fashion designer, Anya Hindmarch's **iconic cotton bag** for Sainsbury's sold out immediately, spawning many copies, taking the message out onto the high street.

In 2007 Rebecca Hosking's hometown, Modbury in South Devon, became Britain's first to stop issuing plastic bags (plasticbagfree.com). Paris and San Francisco have banned them, too. Bangladesh has a "no plastic bags" policy and Ireland reduced use by 90% after a 2002 bag tax. It's conceivable they could one day become as unfashionable as fur coats.

Bags for life (if you're going to live for four hundred years)

The world uses over 1.2 trillion plastic bags a year and over one million bags are used every minute. UK consumers use thirteen billion plastic carrier bags each year for an average of twelve minutes per bag. Most come from supermarkets; three billion of them are in the red, white and blue of Tesco. Bag reduction is part of the supermarkets' way of satisfying the government's Courtauld Agreement. M&S are clear leaders in plastic bag reduction with an astonishing 80%, followed by Waitrose, who introduced the reuseable "bag for life" in 1997 (50%), and lagging behind: Asda (35%), Sainsbury's (30%) and Tesco (25%).

But with plastic bags only accounting for around **4.5% of the total plastic packaging** used by the food industry, some think that this is a convenient and cost-effective way for supermarkets to pass their responsibility on to consumers without really tackling the main offender, plastic food packaging. There has been a financial benefit to the supermarkets in focusing on bags. *The Grocer* estimates that yearly savings are significant: £9 million for M&S and £15 million for Tesco.

Find out more

Message in the Waves messageinthewaves.com The website of the film with clips and information about the effects of plastics in the environment.

Greenpeace greenpeace.com lobby to stop pollution. Read their report *Plastic Debris in the World's Oceans* (2006).

Riverford Sustainable Development riverfordenvironment.co.uk Their latest research into packaging options found that, although it seems counterintuitive, very thin plastic bags which can be reused and recycled could be the best alternative all things considered.

Are supermarkets good for your health?

Supermarkets are vocal advocates of freedom of choice for the customer. They provide the goods and then it's up to you what you eat. But this is disingenuous given the extent to which they try to influence our choices with their special offers. In spring 2008 the National Consumer Council (NCC) undertook a survey of the major supermarkets to assess the part they were playing in encouraging healthy or unhealthy eating. They looked at the types of products they chose to promote, how clearly own-brand products were labelled with nutritional information, the fat, salt and sugar content of those products and the quality of information they provided. They found:

▶ **Far more promotions on fatty and sugary foods than ever before** Especially at a time when people are feeling the pinch, supermarkets are steering them towards unhealthy food.

▶ **Sainsbury's came out as top supermarket** Assessed against a range of criteria, the chain scored well for labelling and providing information. Bottom of the league was Morrisons.

▶ **More than half the food being promoted was sugary or fatty** In Morrisons, this was almost two-thirds. Fruit and vegetables only accounted for 12% of in-store promotions.

▶ **Progress on reducing the salt content** In own-brand processed foods to comply with FSA guidelines this is going slowly, even though the recommendations were relaxed in the face of industry pressure. One-third of products failed to meet the target.

▶ **Low-cost "value" ranges tend to contain more fat** More surprisingly, so-called healthier ranges sometimes contained **more salt** than the standard item. This was the case for example with Morrison's "healthier" salt and vinegar crisps and Sainsbury's "healthier" baked beans.

▶ **Wildly inaccurate or comically unhelpful** This is how researchers described the answers often given by supermarket staff to their health questions. When the researcher asked: "The fat label says 29.7g and 42%. Is that healthy?" She was told by one employee: "the government recommends that you get 100%, so with the fat you've got 42% in the meal and that leaves you with 58%."

How to stop the supermarkets ruling the world (or at least slow them down)

Supermarket power grows by the day, and it's pretty hard for most of us to do without them completely. But that doesn't mean you need to let the supermarkets determine everything you eat. Here are some ways to stem the supermarket tide:

▶ **Spread your custom** Surviving independents have survived for a reason. Give them a try, especially if they are also producers. It needn't be hard work; it may even turn out to be pleasurable.

▶ **Think before you fill your trolley with "bargains"** Only buy in bulk when it makes sense to do so.

▶ **Look beyond the hype** Read the labels to see where things come from, what's in them and how they were produced.

▶ **Be a supermarket sceptic** "Treat yourself" or "a little bit of indulgence" invariably translates as "unhealthy, fatty and sweet". "New and improved" is rarely substantiated.

▶ **Fill in comment cards** Also, write to their head office to tell them what you think. They're sensitive about their image and keen to keep tabs on customer opinion. It was the strength of public opinion that led the supermarkets to take such a firm stand on GM food.

▶ **Don't be a loyalty card pushover** You get a bit of money off. They get a lot of data about you. Bear in mind that in the future data-mining is going to be increasingly lucrative.

▶ **Flex your muscle and exercise choice where you can** Remember that though you may feel powerless compared to a multi-billion-pound business, supermarkets operate on slender margins. As Walmart founder Sam Walton said: "There is only one boss. The customer. And he can fire everyone in the company from the chairman on down, simply by spending his money elsewhere."

Real food

When the man who ran Tesco's fruit and veg category jumps ship to open a small local grocers (see p.277), you know something's up. Peter Durose knows the modern retail trade better than most and feels it's lost its way: "Britain has so many fewer shops than France or Germany; the experience here has been sanitized; it's all about denying local choice, huge numbers and maximum profits." In the age of supermarket dominance, our access to real food has until recently been very limited. We are surrounded by the illusion of choice, but look closer and what you see is many different versions of the same processed products. If we want simple, fresh, "real" food, we need to break free of the supermarkets. Over the last thirty years we have lost what Elizabeth David called "marketing" skills for sourcing local food. But recently there have been signs of change: farmers and shoppers have started to vote with their feet, moving away from supermarkets to create more enjoyable and sustainable ways of buying and selling food.

A survey undertaken by *The Grocer* found that 50% of Tesco shoppers felt bored, stressed, frustrated or overwhelmed by the supermarket experience, feelings shared by many faced with the big weekly shop. Supermarkets are undeniably convenient, but only if you're shopping in the comfort of your car, own a large fridge-freezer and are in receipt of a decent monthly pay cheque. Those without a car have to make repeated, often time-consuming journeys on foot or irregular public transport. And as the previous chapter showed, they're not always the fantastic bargain they claim to be.

But what's the alternative? Most local high streets became food deserts after shoppers defected to the **Big Four**. For many people, their nearest "local" shop may be a large Tesco or Asda. Anyway, how would we survive without all that pre-prepared food now we seem to have lost the basic skills of cooking? Jamie's *Ministry of Food* did for home-cooking what his *School Dinners* did for children's lunches: it showed how far we'd departed from a healthy approach to food and inspired many of us to do something about it. He showed a nation feeding itself on take-aways, ready meals, crisps and chocolate bars rather than real food: here was the evidence behind the government's obesity and heart disease figures laid bare. We've ignored all the good advice so far, perhaps it will take a credit crunch to force us to learn to cook again and to discover that we actually quite enjoy it.

Local grocer's in London's Spitalfields

Recent market research shows that our shopping habits are changing from "value-for-money" to "values-for-money" (TNS, 2008) with Fairtrade, free-range, local produce and organic moving from niche to mainstream. Provenance, freshness, seasonality and the producers are all becoming important again: something the industrial-scale supermarkets struggle to accommodate.

Although it is difficult to shake off the supermarket habit, it is possible. Those who experiment with buying local and direct from farmers usually find it so satisfying that they reduce their supermarket visits, find they save money and are inspired to cook. When *Sunday Times* correspondent Matt Rudd experimented with a month-long supermarket boycott, he was converted to local food shopping so thoroughly (despite teething problems) that he got over his supermarket habit. He found that it turned out to be cheaper, less stressful and wasteful, encouraged home-cooking, was actually fun and tasted better, too: "Acting on a tip-off, we found a farmers' market in a village 10 miles from Sevenoaks. Wow. Asparagus. Wow. Kentish eggs, bread and Kentish goat's cheese ... and steak and kidney pie so good we could pretend to dinner guests that I'd made it."

// It's now frequently the case that, provided I shop seasonally, I can buy fruit and veg more cheaply in my local greengrocer, or even a farmers' market, than in a supermarket. **//**

Adam Leyland, editor of *The Grocer*

The rise of local food

The term "**locavore**", defined as someone who eats only locally grown or produced food, made it in to the *Oxford English Dictionary* in 2007, confirming this new trend is here to stay. Local is generally defined as food produced within a 35-mile radius of where it is sold.

Buying local as an ethical decision is about more than just locality (although this is obviously key); it includes a fair deal for the producer, shorter food chains and lower food miles and reconnects community and producers. It also creates more informed, independent shoppers who can judge good food and recognize real value for money. They cease to be supermarket zombies pushed and pointed towards the foods the multiples and big manufacturers want them to buy and soon learn to make their own choices. Felicity Lawrence, in her book *Not on the Label*, recom-

How to be an independent shopper

"The most political act we do on a daily basis is to eat, as our actions affect farms, landscapes and food businesses," says Jules Pretty, professor of environment and society at the University of Essex. Embrace this as an opportunity to make a positive difference:

▶ **Switch to a fortnightly supermarket visit** Time yourself and stick to your shopping list. The fewer times you visit, the less unnecessary food you'll buy (and throw out) and the more money you'll save. Keep the supermarket for non-fresh items such as tea and coffee; tinned goods; rice and pasta; loo roll and washing-up liquid; frozen peas and ice-cream – and emergency evening trips.

▶ **Use local high street shops** Bread, deli goods, cheese, meat, fruit and vegetables (and fish if you're lucky) are all best shopped for in this way.

▶ **Organic box delivery** Great for fruit, veg, dairy products and even meat once a week direct from local growers to your door. See p.239 for more on this.

▶ **Farmers' market** Find your nearest and build a trip into your weekend. Excellent for basics as well as artisan ready-made food at affordable prices, such as salmon and dill tarts, chocolate brownies, ginger cake, salads, pizza, smoked fish or meat pâtés, fruit tarts and all manner of regional delicacies from black or white pudding to honey and saffron cake.

▶ **Farm shops** Check Big Barn or Food Lovers' Britain (see p.254) for farms near you. These range from large shops with diverse foods to a wobbly table laden with just-picked tomatoes and raspberries and an honesty box. Some join community-supported agriculture schemes where you can invest in a local farms in exchange for a sustainable food supply.

▶ **Specialist online deliveries** The range of foodstuffs that can be delivered to your door is growing all the time, from organic general stores to specialist organic meat or fish, smoked fish, spices, cakes, oil and more (see Chapter 16).

mends a simple strategy: "shifting shopping patterns to follow three main principles: **local, seasonal and direct.**"

For entertaining reports from the front line of eating locally ("Is it boring?" "It can be. But so is queuing for industrial food at ASDA." "Do I have to eat turnips?" "Yes, but not all year."), read about one man's attempts to source his food from his home county in eastern Scotland and the widespread interest his project has generated here:

The Fife Diet fifediet.wordpress.com

//The local food sector is forecast to grow in value by 33% over the next five years. Following on from their foray into organic food, the big supermarkets are falling over themselves to develop 'local' sourcing policies.//

Corporate Watch, 2007

Real-food crusaders

▶ **Joanna Blythman** He exposes the horrors of how we really eat in books such as *Bad Food Britain* (Fourth Estate, 2006), providing inspiration to change our ways.

▶ **Hugh Fearnley-Whittingstall** Known for eating garden snails on TV and promoting seasonal food, grow-your-own and out-of-favour meat cuts as well as his animal welfare campaigning. Read *The River Cottage Meat Book* (Hodder & Stoughton, 2004) or visit rivercottage.net.

▶ **Matthew Fort** The *Guardian*'s food editor celebrates the best of British food and its producers in his dispatches from all around the country.

▶ **Henrietta Green** An expert and tireless promoter of Britain's small producers most recently through her invaluable FoodLoversBritain.com website.

▶ **Tim Lang** Pioneering academic food policy specialist and government adviser. A regular media commentator and much-needed voice of reason.

▶ **Felicity Lawrence** Her investigations into the way our food system *doesn't* work keeps the issue in the public eye and prevents the enemies of real food wriggling away. Read her in the *Guardian* or *Not on the Label* (Penguin, 2004).

▶ **Jamie Oliver** Cheeky-faced "Naked Chef" turned passionate social campaigner who's tried to improve school dinners and how we cook (*Jamie's Ministry of Food*). Also fronts the new restaurant chain, Jamie's Italian.

▶ **Rose Prince** Offers down-to-earth advice about how to eat better (and locally) on a budget and champions the best of British producers. Read her in the *Telegraph* and *The New English Table* (Fourth Estate, 2008).

Death of the high street?

At the end of World War II there were half a million independent shops in the UK. The figure now stands at around 30,000 and it's falling by as many as 2000 a year. As more of our spending goes through the tills of the supermarkets each year, independent food shops have almost been squeezed out of existence. The supermarkets are always telling us that they give us choice, convenience and low prices, so does it really matter?

From a nation of shopkeepers to a nation of shelf-stackers

A UK government inquiry, *High Street Britain: 2015* (2006), looked at the future of high street shopping in Britain and the picture it painted was bleak. The report reckoned that by 2015 most independent grocers and convenience stores will have gone out of business. This in turn will put the wholesalers who supply them out of business, leading, they warned, to the "virtual collapse of part of the supply chain".

Many factors can contribute to the demise of small businesses – high rents, parking charges, congestion charges – but it's clear that the biggest factor has been the rise of out-of-town and edge-of-town superstores.

Evidence from the National Retail Planning Forum suggests the overall impact on a local economy of a supermarket's arrival, even if it came with the promise of jobs, was generally negative in the long term. Immediate and nearby communities in time suffer retail and other business decline, unemployment, changes in job quality, loss of revenue and lower resources for communities.

In the 1990s Britain lost one-third of its bank branches, which had encouraged footfall in town centres, as do post offices, which have also gone through a wave of closures. Once shops begin to disappear, the downward spiral can be irreversible. And when they've gone it's very difficult for new ones to gain a foothold. Some of the detrimental effects are:

> // I put my trust in people, in consumers. Supermarkets are their creation. We prosper and grow by delivering what they want. That is our role in society. And our success is a shared success, one that benefits all. //
>
> Sir Terry Leahy, chief executive of Tesco

> // The argument that big retail is good because it provides consumers with choice is ironic, because in the end it leaves us with no choice at all. //
>
> Andrew Simms, New Economics Forum

▶ **Loss to local economies** As little as 5% of supermarket revenue stays in the community in which it is spent, unlike local shops, which have been compared to "irrigation channels" because of their ability return up to 50% of their takings to the local economy.

▶ **People on low incomes** Also those with reduced mobility can be especially hard hit. **Access to healthy foods** as well as social contact can be drastically reduced for groups such as elderly people living alone.

▶ **Loss of skills** Small retailers need knowledgeable staff in order to thrive. Pound for pound, supermarkets create many fewer jobs, and generally less satisfying ones. For supermarkets, which have begun to phase out till operators in favour of self-scan, the ideal is to limit the role of human labour (along with human error) as much as possible.

▶ **Consumer choice is reduced** Supermarkets stock what sells best to the greatest number. Producers of niche products can be dropped and ethnic communities can find their needs uncatered for.

If only the very biggest chains are able to thrive, then the prospects for the "**biodiversity**" of food retailing outside a few affluent, gastronomically favoured areas looks gloomy. Despite this, the Competition Commission's 2008 report on the UK groceries market delivered what many campaigners found a very complacent verdict on the state of UK food retailing: "competition in UK groceries is effective," it judged, and delivers "good outcomes for consumers".

Of course, it's easy to idealize local shops and forget all the surly shopkeepers you've ever met. But the independent shops which get in right – and increasingly they're the only sort which survive – can offer a quality of shopping experience that even the best supermarkets can't match.

The butcher, the baker, the crab-stick maker...

▶ **Butchers** In 2000 there were just over 9000 butchers in the UK. Seven years later, nearly one-quarter had disappeared and the number of abattoirs had shrunk dramatically, too. Concerns over a diet rich in red meat and BSE had reduced the appetite for meat. Supermarkets know that most people's shopping lists include meat and compete fiercely with each other on price to get customers through their doors. There's no way an independent butcher can match Tesco's £2 chicken. Wisely, few of them try. The demand for **organic** meat is still growing, but butchers who sell only organic are rare, partly because supplies are limited and partly because the competitive nature of the trade would make going all-organic a high-risk strategy. Organic meat is more likely to come from farm shops or direct from the producer (see p.244). Whether organic or free-range, the most successful butchers emphasize their knowledge and sourcing of their meat. If you want advice, however basic, never be afraid to ask. **National Butchers' Week** takes place in March with the aim of encouraging consumers to consider their local butcher as their first port of call for quality meat.

Cheap cuts for lean times

Many cuts of meat that were commonplace just a few decades ago fell from favour to the extent that young people are even unfamiliar with their names. These cuts were passed over for what we've come to think of think of as prime cuts: the expensive ones that cook quickly. But tougher times are making restaurants and canny shoppers alike turn back to cuts their grandparents knew.

There's lots of flavour to be had from the parts of the animal that do work (as opposed to just putting on the fat). To get the best out of most of them, slow cooking is essential, so they're something to simmer away at the weekend when you have time. All are well suited to single-pot cooking. If you want to get started with tasty, inexpensive cuts, here are three good ones to try:

▶ **Breast of lamb** Slow casserole with red wine, rosemary, tomatoes and vegetables.

▶ **Pork belly** Slow, gentle cooking over several hours, or even overnight.

▶ **Brisket of beef** Slow roasted or boiled.

Find out more

European Peasant Cookery Elizabeth Luard (Grub Street, 2007) A wonderful compendium of simple hearty food from all parts of the continent.

Nose to Tail Eating Fergus Henderson (Bloomsbury, new edition 2004) Not for the faint-hearted, this book by the chef of the St John restaurant in London will introduce you to lambs' tongues, pigs' spleen and calves' heart.

The Thrifty Cookbook Kate Colquhoun (Bloomsbury, 2009) Not just meat recipes, but plenty of ideas on how to make the food you buy go further.

Find a Butcher findabutcher.co.uk is an industry-sponsored online directory which can help you find local meat suppliers.

▶ **Greengrocers** Facing competition from the supermarkets, many greengrocers turned themselves into convenience stores, only to find in the mid-1990s that Tesco and Sainsbury's were moving in on that territory, too. Many corner-shop greengrocers have gone to the wall and the planned entry of Asda into the convenience store market won't help those that remain. Only those who can offer something really distinctive are likely to survive – be that organic, locally sourced produce or catering to a specific ethnic community's needs.

Charlie Hicks' three upmarket shops in Reigate, Hay-on-Wye and Clifton in Bristol belong to a new breed of specialist greengrocers who favour small local growers, seasonality and low environmental impact. Hicks says: "We buy as close to our shops as is practically possible. Our lemons may come from the Amalfi coast but our berries and summer salads, for example, will (weather permitting) come from within thirty miles of each shop."

▶ **Bakers** Though not immune from closures caused by the advancing supermarket juggernaut, bakers have fared better than other independents (around 8000 still exist). They have a number of distinct advantages over most other types of independent business: they are producers as well as retailers, they generally source their flour locally and they are able to innovate their range of products and match them to the tastes of their customers (see p.284).

▶ **Health food shops** These are often ethically run companies or cooperatives with knowledgeable staff. They keep prices down to allow widespread access to natural foods: good-quality oils, vegetarian and gluten-free food, healthy snacks for children, loose dried goods such as muesli, rice, pulses, nuts, spices and herbs. You can control how much you buy, from a teaspoon of spice to a three-litre can of olive oil, much cheaper than equivalent-quality bottles from the supermarket. **Essential**, one of the oldest and biggest food co-ops, supplies excellent quality foods (their muesli mixes are very fresh and full of fruit and nuts) to their own and other national health food shops.

▶ **Fishmongers** In World War II, Britain's National Federation of Fishmongers had over 9000 members. Since then their numbers have been falling; in the past twenty years alone over 6000 of them have closed down, making them almost as endangered as cod. By 2007 only 1657 remained. In the early 1990s, supermarkets set up fresh fish counters and the proportion of fish sales that went through independent fish shops, market stalls and mobile vans fell from 60 to 42% in five years. In London, Blagden's, a Marylebone fishmonger since 1892, finally ceased trading in 2005, unable to compete with a Waitrose fish counter and a FishWorks café-cum-fishshop just round the corner. Businesses that survive have to be high quality and often tend to have been passed down in families, such as Steve Hatt's shop in Islington (below). This fishmonger has been family-run since 1895 and is regularly lauded as the finest in London. They produce their own traditionally smoked fish and are fanatical about quality and freshness. Many of Britain's surviving fishmongers have diversified into supplying restaurants and pubs and generally gravitated upmarket, where their clientele is less susceptible to supermarket price promotions. Some have gone into mail order, such as the excellent Don Jones Fresh Fish (donjonesfish.co.uk) of Wellington, Somerset, Seafood Retailer of the Year in 2007. Fish is delivered in poly boxes with reusable frozen gel packs.

▶ **Village shops** Supermarkets have creamed off the custom of the more affluent rural dwellers, who are able and willing to drive miles for their food, and a good many village shops have closed. The picture is not

Artisan cheese and cheesemongers

Artisanal British cheesemaking didn't really get going until the late-twentieth century. Existing traditions of regional and fresh home-made cheese disappeared during the war years, as rationing demanded that all milk be sent to centralized factories. By the 1980s we were eating Dutch Edam, New Zealand Cheddar and Danish Blue; perhaps a slab of brie if you fancied yourself sophisticated. Meanwhile, two cheesemonger crusaders, Patrick Rance (author of *The Great British Cheese Book*, 1983) and Randolph Hodgson of the pioneering Neal's Yard Dairy, had begun a renaissance of unpasteurized cheesemaking, which took off to such an extent that today our 220 cheesemakers and 450 individually named cheeses can rival the French.

Artisan cheeses are made by hand using raw (unpasteurized) milk from cows, goats or ewes. It is the living organisms in the milk which gives the cheese a depth and breadth of flavour. Industrially made cheese can't match this as it uses pasteurized mixed milk (the high temperatures kill the organisms, reduces nutrients and the flavour). Humidity and temperature (and turning) are carefully controlled as cheese ages to develop flavour and texture. They taste best if you let them come to room temperature before eating.

▶ **Cheddars** The best Cheddars are those cut straight from the round: nutty, creamy Keens, Quickes, Daylesford, Westcombe Dairy and fruity Montgomeries are consistently good. They keep well and are great with homemade green tomato chutney or rich fruitcake.

▶ **Blue cheeses** Our traditional Stilton has been joined by the likes of creamy and mild Barkham Blue made from Guernsey milk and Roquefort-like ewe's milk Beenleigh Blue from Devon.

▶ **Great British regional cheeses** These include flaky, mineral-tasting Cheshire (Appleby's is the last in the UK to be made using unpasteurized milk and cloth binding); Kirkham's crumbly, tangy white Lancashire, which has been made by the same family for generations; and the Scottish Connage Dunlop, a cloth-bound hard cheese which is both nutty and creamy.

▶ **Goat's cheese** We've only recently discovered goat's cheese from tiny young, soft "Innes Buttons" and dry, mature French "crottins", black ash-dusted Cerney pyramids of tangy fresh cheese, cylindrical soft-rind cheeses such as Ragstone (made in Herefordshire) – perfect for slicing and grilling. Good accompaniments are fig jam and cherry tomato chilli jam.

Colston Bassett Stilton, produced at an artisan cheesemaker's in Nottinghamshire since 1920, shown here having the rind smoothed after unmoulding.

Find out more

Great British Cheeses Jenny Linford (Dorling Kindersley, 2008)

wholly bleak, though; some village shops are **community owned** and receive start-up grants. The most successful ones find ways to do things the supermarkets can't, such as making links with local small producers and becoming an active hub of village life. The number of new village shop start-ups since 2000 suggests they are far from dying species, and potentially well placed to capitalize on the growing appetite for locally produced food.

▶ **Delicatessens** The term "deli" covers a wide variety of different shops, from the most upmarket stockists of luxury and continental foods to more modest places where you can pick up a sandwich and a coffee. Many of the longest-established delis started out catering for the needs of immigrant populations, such as the Italian, Jewish or more recently Polish communities. And some of the most appealing delis are to be found among these specialists, such as Brindisa, London's Spanish specialist (brindisa.com), Austrian deli, Kipferl (kipferl.co.uk), or Polish Taste in Glasgow's Hyndland Street. That's not to say that you won't find good quality food in the generalist delis; as with all food retailing, enthusiasm, passion and knowledge are what you should look out for. Dishes made on the premises rather than bought in are also a good sign. But beware the delis that are all style and no substance, and sell tarted-up food no different from the supermarkets – but at twice the price.

Ice cream

Real ice cream is made from milk, cream (sometimes mixed with eggs in a custard) with a little sugar and natural ingredients such as espresso coffee, lavender flowers or fresh mint from the garden, which is then frozen. This is how ice cream is made in Italy, its European home. However 80% of what is sold in the UK supermarkets does not contain milk fat and is therefore not really ice cream but a pale, processed imitation made from cheap vegetable fat mixed with air and emulsifiers to create a fluffy, tasteless texture to which a variety of artificial flavourings and colourings are added. **Sorbets** are dairy free and fruity iced water. Good supermarket varieties include dairy-free Swedish Glacé and Green & Black's organic ice cream.

The real thing: make your own (an ice-cream maker is not essential but does make it smoother) or seek out proper ice cream available in delis. Good ones to try include: **Rocombe Farm** organic (Soil Association certified) ice cream in lemon meringue and hazelnut and praline flavours, and mango sorbet made from Dartmoor spring water. **Minghella's**, run by an Italian family since 1950, take their ice cream very seriously, making 150 flavours from walnut and maple syrup to Bellini sorbet. They also do a low-fat and low-sugar range for diabetics. Order online: minghella.co.uk

There are a number of new **social websites** such as tipped.co.uk and welovelocal.com (the latter supported by the Women's Institute) which aim to share information about local businesses and services. They allow you to see what other people in your area think of local shops, pubs and restaurants. Their focus so far has tended to be on eating out rather than buying groceries, but they could provide a good way of spreading word-of-mouth enthusiasm for local shops that don't have huge marketing budgets.

Back to the land
Buying direct

Organic vegetable boxes

Over 400,000 Britons order an organic vegetable box each week and these are delivered by 550 different schemes around the country whose sales now exceed £150 million a year. If you want organic, this is a good way to buy it affordably and easily, and to be sure that the farmers have been paid a decent price. The first schemes, such as **Riverford Farm Foods** and **Abel & Cole**, started in the early 1990s and at the time this was virtually the only way to buy organic food. The name has become a misnomer, given that boxes today can contain anything from herbs and cherries to milk and sausages. *Good Housekeeping*'s stringent tests declared that on convenience, value for money and quality, vegetable box delivery schemes won hands down when compared to supermarkets. Riverford, London-based Everybody Organic and Abel & Cole received top marks for the service they offered. All prices were compared over a six-week period with those on super-market shelves.

How box schemes work

Boxes offer excellent value for money as they cut out the middleman, costly outlets and the long supply chain. Setting up a box delivery from scratch is as easy as ordering from Amazon (and much quicker than supermarket online

❚❚ The straightforward vegetable box schemes were more impressive than the supermarket offerings. ❚❚

Good Housekeeping, "Tried and Tested"

ordering). Unlike the supermarkets, box schemes don't charge for delivery and use reuseable packaging.

You can order a set box of the best seasonal produce, which will mean you'll face an unfamiliar knobbly root vegetable regularly through the winter, but wonderful salads in summer. These generally come in different sizes, from extra small (starting at about £8) to one that can feed a family of four for a week (about £16). If you're ordering dairy products, extra fruit and veg items, and the odd tub of hummus and soup, you're looking at about £35 for the week for a family of four. Being fresher, the food stays good for longer.

Research has shown that 50% of those who cancelled their box did so because of receiving vegetables they don't know how to cook or found boring. The schemes have responded to this and changed their offering to suit modern diets (they also give you the option to deselect items you hate). Forget the old 1990s boxes full of turnips and kale; boxes now are fully customizable and can be changed weekly to suit your needs.

Some box schemes now an offer incredible choice of seasonal organic food: strawberries and clotted cream; apricots, jams and chutneys, cheeses, sausages, asparagus, and herbs; yoghurt, chocolate, pears, and vine tomatoes. Few sell only home-grown produce; most use additional stock from other local organic growers and from abroad for certain fruit and vegetables. Try to see unfamiliar veg as a challenge and use online recipes. Riverford's resi-

Abel & Cole

"Abel & Cole customers appreciate that not all carrots are 250mm x 45mm and straight!" *Colin Andrews, Broadward Hall Farm, box supplier*

Abel & Cole began as a London-based potato delivery service run by Keith Abel and Paul Cole. By 1993 they had started selling a range of organic food. Today it has grown to become an efficient online shop selling an incredible range of over 500 lines of food, drinks, household goods and more. They've spent years carefully sourcing from over 120 British organic farmers, bakers and producers and those abroad for Fairtrade bananas, chocolate and coffee. They'll even deliver Popina's fruit and chocolate tarts to your door (about £5 for four mixed small tarts). A good example of the high standards of customer service offered by most box schemes, they won the National Customer Service Award in 2006, 2007 and 2008.

Veg box virgin

Helen Fripp told Rough Guides: "I had been put off by the veg box I had in the 1990s – the mass of curly kale and potatoes. Then people started talking about the food they were having delivered: apricots, broad beans, melons, vine tomatoes. Suddenly it seemed more enticing." After just ten minutes on the web, her new Riverford order was set up for a regular Wednesday delivery: "It was so much quicker and easier than the supermarket deliveries I've tried in the past and I hated all those plastic bags." She found the organic meat, which she doesn't usually buy because of the high cost, particularly good value. Putting it straight in the freezer meant that was most of her meat shopping done for the next month which at £50 to feed a family of four looked like good value – and they all noticed the superior taste. Five months on, she's spending less on food and making fewer visits to the supermarket. She's also started enjoying cooking more and has even tackled her first beetroot soup.

dent chef, Jane Baxter, has put really good recipes on their website (they now have a recipe book, *The Riverford Farm Cook Book*, Fourth Estate, 2008). Check out their surprisingly delicious beetroot and chocolate brownie recipe or their squash, ricotta and pecan roulade.

Veg box deliveries are on a fixed day once a week, which can be a problem if you are out all day. Solutions could include a locked box or large plastic box with a lid for the delivery person to put it into, or asking a neighbour to take it in.

What about imports?

Box schemes keep imports to a minimum, but they are essential to provide the variety which customers want. Most box schemes do not air-freight and are involved with their overseas producers, supporting the international development of organic farming. Riverford (which in a good year can manage to supply around 90% UK-grown vegetables) together with Exeter University, have carried  out detailed research into the carbon footprint issues involved with food growing and transport. The fruit and vegetables box carried the highest CO_2 rating at about 125g CO_2/kg compared to the summer or winter box of predominantly local produce at around 40g CO_2/kg.

Vegetable box conundrums

Here's what to do with some of the less familiar contents of your veg box:

▶ **Beetroot** Much underrated. Get your Marigolds on, peel the beetroot

Organic home-delivery box schemes

This is just a selection of the many excellent schemes available. Some schemes offer local eggs, milk, bread, preserves, meat and fish, too. Search the web (boxscheme. org) for a local supplier.

National schemes using local producers: **Riverford Farm Foods** through their partner farms and producers' co-operatives can deliver to most of England and Wales. Regional partner farms of their own Riverford Farm in Devon include: River Nene, Peterborough; Stockley Farm, Cheshire; River Swale, Northallerton, Yorkshire; and Riverford at Norton, Hampshire. **Abel & Cole** predominantly deliver to the South of England, but also take in parts of the Northwest and West Midlands.

Scotland

Bellfield Organic Nursery, Fife bellfieldorganics.co.uk

Grow Wild Ltd, Bathgate, Lothian growwild.co.uk

Stair Organic Growers, Ayrshire organicgrowing.com

Vital Veg, Aberdeenshire vitalveg.co.uk

Northwest England

All Things Organic Ltd, Ramsbottom, Lancs allthingsorganic.ltd.uk

Dig, Chorlton, South Manchester digfood.co.uk

Growing with Nature, Pilling, nr Preston, Lancs growing-with-nature.co.uk

Howbarrow Organic Farm, Cartmel, Cumbria howbarroworganic.co.uk

Mansergh Hall Organics, Kirkby Lonsdale, Cumbria manserghhall.co.uk

Mossley Organic and Fine Foods, East Manchester, mossleyorganicandfine-foods.co.uk

Northern Harvest, Kenyon Hall Farm, Warrington, Cheshire northernharvest.co.uk

Riverside Organics, Northwich, Cheshire riversideorganic.com

The Farmshed, Wigan, Lancs (deliver to Liverpool, Manchester, Cumbria) farmshed.co.uk

Northeast England

Arthur Street Trading Company, Hull, E. Yorks arthursorganics.com

G&S Organics, Morpeth, Northumberland (Holy

Island mussels and oysters; meat box) gandsorganics.com

The Organic Pantry, Tadcaster, N. Yorks theorganicpantry.co.uk

Wild Star Food Co., Sheffield, S. Yorks wildstarfood.com

Teeside Organics, Stockton-on-Tees, Teeside teesideorganics.co.uk

Wales

Blaencamel Farm, Lampeter (delivers to Cardiff) blaencamelbox.com

Farmers Garden, Conwy farmers-garden.co.uk

Llangybi Organics, Pwllheli, Gwynedd llangybi-organics.co.uk

and roast, or grate with carrot and mix with lightly fried mustard seeds. Or boil, slip the skins off, add a dressing and goats' cheese.

▶ **Celeriac** Boil and mash it with potato, nutmeg and milk. Grate it raw and dress with mustard and mayonnaise for *rémoulade*.

▶ **Chard** Like other green leafy vegetables, simply steam or stir-fry it with garlic, pepper, tamari (try Clearspring's) and a squeeze of lemon.

West Midlands

Boxfresh Organics,
Shropshire
boxfreshorganics.co.uk

The Organic Mum,
Birmingham
theorganicmum.co.uk

Oxton Organics, Pershore,
Worcs oxtonorganics.co.uk

Reality Bites Organic
Market Garden, Warwick
reality-bites.co.uk

East Midlands

Eden Farms, Spilsby, Lincs
(deliver: Lincs, Notts, Leics)
edenfarms.co.uk

Red Earth Organics,
Nottinghamshire
redearthorganics.co.uk

Sound Bites, Derby
soundbitesderby.org.uk

Woodlands Farm, Boston,
Lincolnshire
woodlandsfarm.co.uk

East England

Abbey Farm, King's Lynn,
Norfolk abbeyfarm.co.uk

Desmond Duncan's, Diss,
Suffolk organicsforall.co.uk

Salle Moor Hall Farm,
Reepham, Norfolk (deliver:
Norwich to North Norfolk
and Wymondham)
salleorganics.com

Sunrise Organics, Essex
sunriseorganics.com

Waterland Organics,
Cambridgeshire
waterlandorganics.co.uk

Southwest

Cusgarne Organic Farm,
Nr. Truro, Cornwall
cusgarne.org

Duchy Home Farm,
Tetbury, Gloucestershire
duchyhomefarm.org.uk

JP Organics, Bath,
Somerset jporganics.co.uk

Rural Foods, Lower
Woolcombe Farm,
Dorchester, Dorset
ruralfoods.org.uk

Slipstream Organics,
Cheltenham
slipstreamorganics.co.uk

The Better Food Company,
Bristol betterfood.co.uk

Southeast

Ashurst Organics, Lewes,
Sussex 01273 891219

Chiltern Organics, Henley-
on-Thames, Oxfordshire
chilternorganics.co.uk

Eat Organic, Little Bottom
Farm, Oxfordshire (deliver:
Henley-on-Thames,
Reading, Wokingham)
eatorganic.co.uk

Everybody Organic,
London (delivers: London,
Home Counties)
everybodyorganic.com

Horti Halcyon, Surrey
hortihalcyon-organic.co.uk

Luddesdown Organic
Farms, Kent
luddesdownorganicfarms.
co.uk

Organically Speaking,
Hampshire
organically-speaking.co.uk

The Organic Delivery
Company, New Covent
Garden Market, London
organicdelivery.co.uk

Northern Ireland

Burrenwood Produce,
Castlewellan, County
Down burrenwood.com

Culdrum Organic Farm, Co.
Londonderry (meat and
veg boxes) 02870 868991

Orchard Organics, Armagh
(deliver throughout
Northern Ireland and
Republic of Ireland)
orchardorganics.com

North West Organic Co-
operative Society, Killaloo
nworganic.com

▶ **Fennel** There are many options including roasting, risotto, soup and salad. Slice thinly, add slivers of red chilli and a lemon dressing for a zingy salad with fish. Sauté with onions, a medium potato and a clove of garlic, simmer in stock, liquidize and add a dash of cream for a great soup for chilly British summer evenings.

▶ **Jerusalem artichokes** Roasting is the best option for these.

▶ **Kohlrabi** Add to a mixed coleslaw or curries.

▶ **Coleslaw** This is always a good veg box solution: experiment with grated root vegetables (for example, carrots, celeriac or beetroot)

The peeler is an early kitchen gadget, dating back to the eighteenth century. The Swedish "Sveico" swivel peeler (£2.50 from Amazon) is the fastest way to get through the root veg in your box (by flicking it away from you).

with courgette; or cabbage, pear or apple and a mayonnaise-based dressing topped with toasted seeds. Skye Gyngell's coleslaw recipe from *A Year In My Kitchen* combines finely sliced purple cabbage with apples, beetroot, carrots, fennel and tarragon, with a cider vinegar mayonnaise dressing.

Annie Bell's Vegetable Book (Penguin, 1999) is great for quick veg box ideas.

Organic meat boxes

These take a bit of getting used to as you'll probably have to order once a month and freeze most of it, and a minimum order is about £45 (you'll often get free delivery at that price). Ordering in bulk is necessary because of the expensive insulated packing needed to get it to you in good nick. Suppliers say they keep these costs as low as they can and often subsidize the packaging. You get top-quality, very fresh meat from well-kept animals (no growth hormones or antibiotics). Customers rave about the taste being "so different" from supermarket meat and comment that it

Well-Hung Meat Company

This multi-award-winning organic meat company delivers to your door from Devon. Based on Carswell Farm, South Devon, the company also sources meat from other small farms in Devon and Cornwall. The animals live happy lives, in stark contrast to animals destined for supermarkets, and travel just ten minutes to a local abattoir minimizing distress. They are one of the few companies to offer rosé veal – a high-welfare version of the notorious continental veal and a way of using male calves in the food chain.

Founder Geoff Sayers told Rough Guides "the meat tastes better and is high in omega-3 oils and vitamins because animals are fed a natural grass diet". Aware of the need for affordable organic meat they offer a "Thrifty" box of chicken, lamb, beef, pork, bacon and sausages for £42. It will feed a family of four for a month (eating meat every other day), especially if you make stews, pasta sauces and moussaka with it. It's delivered fresh, so keep a few things out (or split packs) and freeze the rest. The delivery charge of £7 covers the cost of high-quality packing materials and courier delivery: order more meat less often to save on delivery. They also supply geese and turkeys (and organic duck) for celebrations. Order online at wellhungmeat.com

goes further as the quality is so high. For best value, get a mixed box. You can usually select exactly what you want, from chorizo for pasta sauces to mince for home-made burgers and chicken legs or sausages for when you want something simple.) If it seems like a lot of meat to order in one go, consider splitting an order with a friend.

Guy Watson, Riverford

"For Riverford, being organic is much more than gaining an official stamp; it is about a set of business values that course through the veins of every part of the organization." Guy Watson

Guy Watson's family have always farmed South Devon land. He returned from a City job in 1986 to the family farm at Staverton, near Totnes. Three years later he was fully certified organic and started to promote organic food to the public, government and other farmers while developing his own farm-based box scheme, which would become an innovative and successful business model for other organic farmers.

Riverford is one of the country's largest independent growers through local co-operative schemes and since 2005 joint ventures with five other farms around the country. They pass on infrastructure and distribution knowledge and organize the technical side of things to help farmers in other regions contribute to box schemes, making use of their trusted brand. Guy Watson has helped develop organic farming in the UK and wants to challenge the supermarkets by providing a mainstream alternative route to market for small and medium-sized farms. Today it is a £30-million business, making it one of the most successful organic ventures in the country. Forty-five thousand vegetable boxes are delivered each week by Riverford.

The boxes can be customized online to include whatever you fancy: a brown bag of avocados here; a large bag of basil in season for pesto or a tub of Riverford's own delicious clotted cream. Newsletters let you know how the sprouts or squashes are getting on in the fields and offer recipe ideas suited to each week's contents.

Credit crunch: A recent Riverford survey found that their boxes were 22% cheaper than online supermarket deliveries and that's before you factor in the supermarkets' £5 delivery charge.

Farmers' markets

A greener way to shop

Historically, city dwellers have bought their food from street markets. Norwich's historic market, for example, bang in the centre of the city, overlooked by its Norman castle, has been feeding the city since Saxon times. The largest daily street market in Britain, it has over 190 stalls including cheesemongers, a fishmonger, stalls selling spices, wholefoods and meat dotted amongst plant, fishing tackle and shoe repair stalls. A recent survey showed that 28% of local people (including many farmers) wanted to develop a farmers' market area within the existing market.

Buying enticing food at a market doesn't have to only be a treat on foreign holidays. With over five hundred UK farmers' markets, it's likely there's one near you. These markets started in the US in the 1980s and the first to open in the UK was Bath Farmers' Market in 1997. They are not the same as Britain's 1169 street markets which *can* sell wonderful local produce – but don't always. A leisurely stroll to your regular local market is a great way to start the weekend – it's sociable and fun for children and you go home with lots of delicious food to eat.

Farmers' markets, like box schemes, make good food accessible and carry a low carbon footprint rating. They also connect farmers and producers directly with their customers. Fresh produce sold at farmers' markets is often thought to be more expensive, but as you are buying local

seasonal produce and the producer gets most of the income, prices are generally competitive and by buying only what you need, you can control what you spend more easily.

Squirrel optional: in 2007–8, 27% of people purchased red meat from a farmers' market. Research shows that ever more complicated supermarket food labelling confuses shoppers – at a farmers' market what you see is what you get and you can ask the producer about any issue you're concerned about, whether it's chicken welfare, farming methods or GM ingredients.

Find your local farmers' market

Every Friday and Saturday from 8am, **Borough Market**, London, SE1 is thronged with enthusiastic shoppers and knowledgeable producers at stall after stall of tempting food selling everything from enormous Comté cheeses, Burnt Sugar fudge and Artisan Food's roast cherry tomato tarts to Devon's Hatherleigh venison burgers and Brindisa's Iberian specialities. You'll find cakes from Soho's Maison Bertaux and breads from the City Flour Power, Rhodes and De Gustibus bakeries. It couldn't be more different from schlepping round Tesco. London has over seven million people but only around 250 farmers, so specialist produce has to be brought into the capital from further afield. Other weekly **London farmers' markets** include Blackheath, Clapham, Marylebone, Notting Hill, Queen's Park, Spitalfields and Stoke Newington.

Les (left) of Furness Fish Markets remembers the early days ten years ago, when there were just a few traders and he would drive down from Cumbria and sleep in his fish van. Today his stall of glistening whole fish, bags of shellfish and Morecambe Bay potted shrimps takes up a large corner site.

Most of the 550 markets open from 9am to 2pm, either weekly or fortnightly. Take a bag or basket with you to load up with goodies and join the fightback against the supermarkets' takeover. Here are some of the best:

Bath (Green Park Station)

Birmingham (Kings Norton and Moseley)

Brighton & Hove, Sussex

Bristol Wednesdays (also Sundays: Tobacco Factory)

Cardiff Roath Real Food Market (Saturday) and Riverside (Sunday)

Chepstow, Gwent

Edinburgh (Castle Terrace)

Glasgow (alternate Saturdays on north and south sides of the city)

Guildford, Surrey

Haverfordwest, Dyfed

Hexham, Northumberland

Huntingdon, Cambs.

Leeds (Kirkgate)

Ludlow, Shrops.

Manchester (Picadilly Gardens)

Melton Mowbray, Leics.

Stratford-upon-Avon, Warks.

Stroud, Gloucs.

Tavistock, Devon

Winchester, Hants.

Wye, Kent

York (Murton)

How to find a market near you:

FARMA Certified Farmers' Markets farmersmarkets.net for markets throughout the UK

London Farmers' Markets lfm.org.uk for markets in London

Scottish Association of Farmers' Markets scottishfarmersmarkets.co.uk for Scottish markets

What's in season?

January	February	March	April	May	June
Apples	Beetroot	Beetroot	Dandelions	Asparagus	Asparagus
Beetroot	Celeriac	Cucumber	Morel mushrooms	Dandelions	Broad beans
Cabbage	Jerusalem artichokes	Mint	Nettles	Elderflowers	Cherries
Cauliflower	Mushrooms	Parsley	Purple sprouting broccoli	Rhubarb	Currants
Celeriac	Parsnips	Purple sprouting broccoli	Rosemary	Sea kale	Dandelions
Jerusalem artichokes	Purple sprouting broccoli	Rhubarb	Sea kale	Wild garlic	Elderflowers
Kale	Rhubarb	Sorrel	Sorrel		Gooseberries
Pears	Squashes		Rhubarb		Peas
Mushrooms			Wild garlic		Peppers
Squashes					Redcurrants
					Rhubarb
					Runner beans
					Samphire
					Sorrel
					Strawberries
					Tomatoes

Although we can now buy anything we want, whenever we want, it never really tastes as good out of season. It is scientifically proven that many fruits and vegetables taste best within an hour of picking (after that, the natural sugars begin to turn to starch). When imported, taste (and nutritional value) are sacrificed for appearance and supply chain convenience as this produce is often picked before it's ripe.

Some food like squashes, beetroot and apples have a long season, whereas others such as elderflowers, samphire, wild garlic and asparagus are around only fleetingly. July and August are the feast months, so be at the ready with jam jars, freezer bags, sugar and vinegar ready to freeze, pickle and preserve. Use cookbooks that are organized seasonally (see opposite) to find recipes quickly for farmers' market impulse buys.

July	August	September	October	November	December
Beetroot	Beetroot	Apples	Apples	Apples	Apples
Blackberries	Blackberries	Beetroot	Beetroot	Beetroot	Beetroot
Blueberries	Blackcurrants	Blackberries	Brussel sprouts	Brussel sprouts	Brussel sprouts
Broad beans	Blueberries	Blackcurrants	Cauliflower	Cauliflower	Cauliflower
Courgettes	Broad beans	Cauliflower	Cavolo nero	Cavolo nero	Cavolo nero
Courgette flowers	Broccoli	Celery	Celeriac	Celeriac	Celeriac
Cucumbers	Carrots	Courgettes	Celery	Celery	Chard
Fennel	Courgettes	Cucumbers	Chestnuts	Chard	Chestnuts
French beans	Courgette Flowers	Crab apples	Elderberries	Chestnuts	Jerusalem artichokes
Gooseberries	Cucumbers	Damsons	Fennel	Fennel	Kale
Greengages	Fennel	Dandelions	Marrows	Jerusalem artichokes	Parsnips
Loganberries	French beans	Elderberries	Parsnips	Kale	Pumpkins
Peas	Globe artichokes	Gooseberries	Pears	Parsnips	Squashes
Raspberries	Greengages	Marrows	Squashes	Pears	
Red and whitecurrants	Loganberries	Parsnips	Wild mushrooms	Savoy cabbage	
Runner beans	Peas	Peas			
Sage	Peppers	Pears			
Samphire	Plums	Peppers			
Strawberries	Raspberries	Plums			
Tomatoes	Red and whitecurrants	Raspberries			
Watercress	Runner beans	Red and whitecurrants			
	Samphire	Runner beans			
	Sorrel	Sloes			
	Strawberries	Sorrel			
	Sweetcorn	Spinach			
	Tomatoes	Sweetcorn			
	Watercress	Wild mushrooms			

Cooking by the season

Chez Panisse Cookbook Paul Bertolli and Alice Waters (Random House, 1988) **A classic seasonal cookbook from a pioneering Californian restaurant.**

A Year in my Kitchen Skye Gyngell (Quadrille, 2006) **Full of enticing recipes to help you maximize the benefits of picking your own fresh food.**

The Kitchen Diaries Nigel Slater (Fourth Estate, 2007) **A diary-cum-cookbook charting his culinary responses to seasonal foods.**

Farmers' markets are all about individual producers selling their fish, cheese, jams, tarts, bread, vegetables and herbs, fruit juices and cakes. Shoppers can take advantage of the best seasonal produce and ready-made foods.

FARMA: the real thing?

The National Farmers' Retail & Markets Association has been active in one guise or another since 1979. FARMA is funded by subscriptions as a not-for-profit co-operative representing all aspects of local food retailing through farmers' markets, farm shops, pick-your-own farms and home delivery. It advises its members and also helps consumers choose by offering a benchmarking standard and certification for local foods.

> **//** Farmers' markets are successful because people want them: consumers want them; farmers want them; producers want them. They are a demonstration of people power. **//**
>
> Matthew Fort

FARMA's definition of a farmers' market requires it to meet three broad criteria. First, what's for sale must be overwhelmingly **local** – normally, it should come from within the same county, or from within a radius of 30–50 miles of the market. Second, there's a "**no middleman**" rule. Thirdly, all foods or products sold should have been grown, reared, caught, brewed, pickled, baked, smoked, cooked or prepared by the **producer**.

Farm shops

Shops selling the fresh produce of local farms on site have been around for a long time, but usually in the form of a rickety table and chalk sign board. As we've become ever keener on seeing where our food comes from (and gingham-covered jam jars and eggs with feathers on them make some of us go weak at the knees), we've started making the effort to seek out local farm shops. It's a fun way of shopping and for the farmer it can make the difference between making a living or giving up. There are over one thousand UK farm shops selling home-grown food, often alongside other local products. Those which are members of FARMA have been through a selection process to ensure they are genuinely selling mainly local foods.

A recent trend has been the expansion of fashionable farm shops, of which **Daylesford Organics** (daylesfordorganic.com), near Stow-on-the-Wold in Gloucestershire, is the leading exponent. Some rustic hardliners criticize it as the Marie-Antoinette approach to organic farming: over-designed and over-priced for Chelsea tractor drivers with sparkling clean wellies. But there's room for variety and there is no doubt that Lady Bamford's Daylesford world of tasteful pale grey-green painted woodwork, exquisite hand-made white French ceramics casually piled high with olives is one of the most beguiling shopping experiences you're

Historic estates have got in on the farm shop act, too. Chatsworth's shop in the village of Pilsey, Derbyshire, has baskets overflowing with goodies as well as a fish and meat counter.

Free food

Inspired by expert foragers Richard Mabey and Hugh Fearnley-Whittingstall, some of us have started to hunt through woods, the water's edge and hedgerows, in search of our own food. Read their books for tips on what to look for and where. Or sign up for the River Cottage mushroom foraging online course (rivercottage.net).

▶ **Blackberries** Pick in August–September for crumbles or jam.

▶ **Landcress** A wild, peppery version of watercress. Found in boggy places, you might discover some on an overgrown allotment. Excellent in soup with cream.

▶ **Mushrooms** You can find recognizable bright orange chanterelles and field mushrooms in the autumn, but seek expert guidance as many are poisonous.

▶ **Nettles** Pick the tops (wearing gloves) in the spring for soup or for tea.

▶ **Samphire** Also called "sea asparagus", this grows in marshland, especially in Norfolk and Cornwall and is ready to pick in June. Boil for a few minutes and add a squeeze of lemon and black pepper. Don't add salt – it's full of natural sea salt.

▶ **Wild garlic** You'll spot this by its unmistakable smell (May–June), when it will be growing in woodland areas. Pick the wide, tall leaves before they flower. It has a delicate fresh garlic flavour. Add it to onions, potato, stock and cream for soup.

To forage out more information, see:

Food for Free Richard Mabey (Collins, new edition 2007)

likely to have. Beyond the perfect interior design the food is good, too: delicious breads, cakes, cheeses (including the award-winning Daylesford Cheddar), jams and vegetables, heaped onto tables in understated, stylish packaging.

Riverford's farm shop at Staverton near Totnes is a good example of what you'd expect from a real country farm shop: traces of mud on the floor, a casual shop design – and lovely home-made rustic food: freshly baked pies, pizza and cakes; wonderful breads, eggs, local cheeses, smoked fish and vegetables; and an excellent meat counter. Rural farm shops near large cities can be a godsend for real-food starved townies. Customers travel from Birmingham and Worcester to visit the well-stocked **Broomsfield Farmshop**, just outside Worcester (broomfieldsfarmshop.co.uk). Fans enjoy their organic vegetables and traditional varieties of English apples from their orchard (they deliver) along with Neal's Yard yoghurt, local cheeses, meats, jams and pickles, homemade cakes every day of the week. To find a farm shop near you, see:

Farmshopping farmshopping.net

Pick Your Own

Today, there are about a thousand PYO farms, mostly on the outskirts of major cities. The concept of picking your own produce originated in the 1950s with a handful of fruit farmers keen to supplement their income. But it was the advent of the large domestic freezers in the 1970s which really led to PYO taking off in a big way. It's estimated that in the 1970s there were about 10,000 farms offering PYO. All farmers needed was a couple of fields of strawberries and a parking area: no planning permission was needed. Back then, rural children would earn pocket money in the summer holidays with a few weeks of fruit picking, blackcurrants being the fiddliest and so the least popular.

Credit crunch DIY cream teas

Scones are ridiculously easy, quick and cheap to make yourself and you can make or buy jams from a farmers' market. Add in organic or Rhodda's Cornish clotted cream and you've rediscovered the traditional British teatime.

How to make scones: Put 250g self-raising flour, half a teaspoon of baking powder, a pinch salt and 50g butter into a bowl and rub the mix between your fingers until it looks like breadcrumbs. For sweet scones, add 2 tablespoons caster sugar (and sultanas if you like) to the mix. For savoury scones (good with homemade soup), add half a teaspoon of Colman's mustard powder, a teaspoon of dried thyme and 75g grated Cheddar.

Mix to a very loose soft dough (don't pound it!) with 4–5 tablespoons milk and one egg, then drop onto a floured surface. Pat gently into a flattened 3cm-high shape and cut out six circles, dabbing them with leftover milk-and-egg mix. Cook in a very hot oven (220ºC, Gas 7) for no more than ten minutes (they need a short sharp blast of heat, so don't put them in till the oven's hot enough).

Raspberry or blackberry jam recipes can be as simple as simmering equal quantities of fruit and sugar with a squeeze of lemon and dispensing into oven-sterilized jars (fill to the top and add a waxed disc).

Preserves River Cottage Handbook No 2, Pam Corbin (Bloomsbury, 2008) A handy guide to getting the best out of seasonal fruit and veg gluts to keep you in jams and chutneys throughout the winter.

By the 1980s, the regional wholesale markets that farms had sold to were in trouble because of the collapse of the small high-street grocer, and shoppers could by now get frozen soft fruit all year round at the supermarket, so there was no longer any need to fill your freezer in the summer. These changes led to the closure of the majority of PYO farms.

But PYO has shown signs of life recently and now you can gather apples and broad beans as well as raspberries, red, white and blackcurrants. Plan your visit well so that as you arrive home with buckets of fresh fruit you've got your jam making kit all ready. Search FARMA's website (pickyourown. info) for a PYO near you: it's fun and relatively cheap, too.

Find out more

Big Barn bigbarn.co.uk The *Daily Telegraph* called it "the leading local produce website" and after eight years of trading, with over 7500 producers listed, this is the main fully searchable hub for anyone looking for local food.

LocalFood Shop localfoodshop.co.uk A new ethical not-for-profit organization which helps you research new places to shop (local butchers, bakers and more): search for a list of producers and shops near where you live. You're effectively buying direct, as 93% of the sale goes straight to the producer.

The Organic Directory edited by Clive Litchfield (Green Books, published annually) A regional directory covering a wide variety of organic suppliers from high-street shops and farm shops to online and mail order.

Food Lovers' Britain foodloversbritain.com Brilliant website run by small-producers' champion, Henrietta Green.

The New English Table: Over 200 recipes that will not cost the Earth Rose Prince (Fourth Estate, 2008) Traditional English recipes, preparation and buying advice.

Grow your own

In 2008 there were over 100,000 keen vegetable growers on allotment waiting lists across Britain and the number is growing. One in three Britons is reported to be growing their own fruit and veg to keep food bills down. After decades in the doldrums, grow your own is experiencing a revival. In 2008 seed companies sold more vegetable than flower seeds for the first time in living memory. It seems the logical next step after the rise in interest in organic and locally grown food, and with sharply rising food bills, some see self-sufficiency as a way of saving money as well as eating more healthily. TV cooks such as Nigel Slater and Jamie Oliver have urged us to rediscover the joys of growing your own whether it is in your backyard or a window-box, for the ultimate in seasonal cooking.

The allotment revival

Traditionally allotments have been popular during periods of economic difficulty and are seen as an important way of improving health and life expectancy. The 1887 Allotments Act enabled ordinary people to feed their families fresh food. Food shortages during World War I increased the demand for allotments and their number rose to 1,500,000. After a surge of growth during the Dig for Victory campaign in World War II, allotment use fell to 600,000 plots, only momentarily lifted by the late 1970s TV hit *The Good Life*, which renewed interest in self-sufficiency for a time. As supermarkets sold us the idea of convenience, we stopped growing our own, and faced with untended sites, councils sold them off to developers. During the past decade over 1500 London plots have gone, leaving thousands of would-be growers on waiting lists. But now a new breed of allotment owner is emerging: young families and women are responsible for the resurgence in allotments. In Glasgow, for the 1320 lucky plotholders, there are another 700 on waiting lists, some facing a seven-year wait; the local council is considering expanding allotment provision with private sector support. Waiting lists are long in Northern Ireland, too, where some farmers are now providing allotment plots. Across England, there are 300,000 plots, one for every 65 households.

The health benefits of working the land and eating super-fresh veg are widely acknowledged, and an invigorating contrast to our modern lives spent inside cars and offices, isolated from nature and the seasons. It's also fun and a way for children to learn that food comes from the ground not from the shop, all for about £30 rental a year. Anyone can grow their own food, but the extent to which you feed yourself will depend on how much space and time you have.

What is an allotment?

An allotment is a piece of land, rented from a local council for a small annual fee, used specifically for growing food to feed the producer and his or her family. The standard-sized plot is 250m² (usually 25×10m); more than enough growing space to feed a family. For most first-timers, this will be too much to manage in your spare time, so try to find a half- or quarter-sized starter plot.

Getting started: the tools for the job

You'll need a large digging fork and spade, solid rake to even out the top layer of soil and a hoe for weeding. Hand tools will be needed for sowing and planting out: small hand fork and trowel and a dibber for making seedling holes. You'll also need: seed trays, potting compost, a watering

// I still marvel at brown envelopes of wizened seeds becoming tiny stalks and leaves, flowers and fruits and vegetables. I get a sense of careless joy when I pick something for the kitchen that I have grown from seed – a courgette, a squash, a handful of marble-sized tomatoes. **//**

Nigel Slater

// When you buy your vegetables you are a slave – to the car that takes you to the shops; to the methods, good or bad, by which the vegetables are produced; to the market forces, and the big bosses who fix the prices; to the shelf-stacking policies that determine the freshness or otherwise, of the produce you buy. **//**

Hugh Fearnley-Whittingstall

In search of the perfect allotment

Check your local council website for information. They should have lists of sites and details of availability. Arrange to visit the nearest sites (many hold open days in mid-August during National Allotment Week). If there is a waiting list, put your name down and, if you're very keen, stress you're happy to take on a half-sized or neglected plot. Here are some other attributes to look out for in the perfect plot:

▶ **Close proximity to your home** You're more likely to manage regular visits if it's a short stroll away.

▶ **Nearby water supply** This is crucial if you don't fancy carrying full watering cans along bumpy paths.

▶ **Good location** Avoid sloping plots (especially those at the bottom of a long slope, which might have problems with frost), as you'll need to dig in terracing to grow plants efficiently.

▶ **Facilities** Such as loos, electricity, locked gates, a water standpipe.

▶ **Easy access** So that manure can be delivered straight to your plot. Ferrying it in a wheelbarrow is back-breaking work.

▶ **Also avoid** Steer clear of plots covered in brambles and thick weeds and check for problems with shade, wandering livestock and vandalism.

▶ **Ask other growers** Find out about the kind of soil you are inheriting, the access to water situation and the history of the plot.

Allotment first-timer

"Although it's hard work, coming here is a stress-reliever – from work and from being a parent. It's my sanctuary. Any talk with fellow growers is about growing and tips."

Sam Missingham comes from a long line of fruit and veg growers and has had her own allotment in Bath for two years, after being on a waiting list for 18 months. While living in East London she planted tomatoes in grow-bags on the balcony of her flat and dreamed of having more space for growing her own food.

Her first year was spent clearing weeds. Sam planted lots of potatoes as well as courgettes, mangetout and runner beans, because these were some of the most reliable crops. She has dealt with gluts by making courgette chutney (Sarah Raven's *Kitchen Garden* has a good recipe for this) and her own frozen "ready meals". On pesticides and fertilizers she says: "I'm not militant about it, but I can't see the point in spending time growing your own food and then covering it in unnatural chemicals."

Being a working single parent, time on the allotment is limited to a few hours a week, so future plans include fruit trees and bushes, such as easy-to-grow loganberries. She also wants to grow smaller quantities of a wider variety of vegetables, as that suits the way she wants to cook. Sam's daughter, Martha, has her own strawberry plants, a small apple tree and potato plant.

can, labels (a reminder about varieties and sowing times), garden twine, and bamboo canes.

Copy the experts: use big containers positioned around the plot to collect water and CDs or tinfoil trays strung up on poles deter birds. Flowers will attract bees and distract insects from your crops and a small garden shed is handy to sit in when it rains.

Once you're over the threshold, all you have to do is keep the plot properly cultivated. You can keep chickens but probably not pigs or bees (check first). Allotment officers carry out annual surveys: if your plot is weedy you'll probably get notice to quit, unless you can improve things within a set period.

The kitchen garden

Even a small back garden can provide a decent amount of home-grown food. Space is likely to be at a premium, so think carefully about what you'll want to eat regularly and work out the orientation of your garden to identify the sunniest spots. Maximizing light and warmth are essential for UK gardening (especially in small city gardens), so if you have a tree over-shadowing your growing area, thin out its branches. Large plastic pots can be useful if your sunniest spot is actually a concreted-over eating area.

Raised borders of stone or brick allow you to control drainage and soil quality, and make for a productive growing environment. Plant raspberry canes at the back and create shelter for young plants by leaning old windows against a back wall or fence. There are many space-saving plants to grow. Choose compact and trailing plants: fruit bushes or dwarf beans can be grown in pots; runner beans or mini squashes trained over an archway; garlic mixed in with your flower beds along with herbs; a living fence of espaliered fruit trees and bushes is a good space-saving technique. Remember that you'll have to carry out evening slug patrols if you want your plants to survive the night.

Windowbox growing

Even if you're limited to a balcony, conservatory, tiny patio or a single windowbox, you can still grow your own. You'll need good light, a sunny aspect and rich compost. You will also need to water regularly and sow small quantities of seed more frequently for regular crops. Many vegetables and fruits (mint, fig trees and blueberries, for example) thrive in containers and this method of growing encourages crops from plants which tend to like sun and warmth. You can even grow dwarf fruit trees and gooseberries in pots and mix plants such as tomatoes, herbs, potatoes, salad leaves and alpine strawberries in large containers.

Planning your growing layout

Just as you would spend time planning your kitchen for ease of use and to maximize storage, so too your allotment or kitchen garden need careful thought. Draw a **scale plan** and play about with the positioning of the key elements below, remembering that long-growing vegetables and perennials need to be kept in borders away from your planned spring plantings:

▶ **Shed** for shelter, tool and seed storage, planting records.

▶ **Water butt and other containers** for collecting rainwater.

▶ **Compost and manure heaps** three boxes at varying stages.

► **Paths** to prevent you compacting the growing areas. Although they cost more, **concrete paving or shingle** make a more convenient surface to walk on and unlike grass, they are not attractive homes for slugs and snails.

► **Raised beds** are simple to make with wooden planks. They are also easier to plant and weed (and do

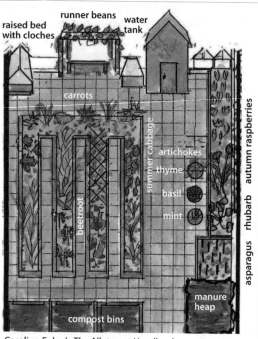

raised bed with cloches · runner beans · water tank · carrots · summer cabbage · artichokes · thyme · basil · mint · beetroot · manure heap · compost bins · asparagus · rhubarb · autumn raspberries

Caroline Foley's *The Allotment Handbook* contains illustrated layouts of a variety of plots from gourmet growers to family allotments.

not involving regular digging). Fill with topsoil and add fresh compost with every new sowing, turning over the soil lightly.

► **Cloches and cold frames** (plastic or glass) aid germination and protect seeds and young plants from bad weather.

► **Tall frames** for training fruit and vegetables such as runner beans. These can be temporary structures made out of **bamboo canes or sticks,** or fixed metal or wooden poles which make it easier to provide a net covering to keep birds out.

► **Low, slatted fence** around part of your boundary for **training fruit** such as tomatoes, rambling blackberries and raspberry canes.

// Vegetable beds are best run north to south so the vegetables don't shade each other. //

Caroline Foley

▶ **Children's grassed picnic area** with a small growing area and sandpit will help keep children occupied while you dig.

▶ **Trees** do not like being moved so don't rush planting (this usually takes place between November and January). Once established, they are easy to manage. Choose space-saving dwarf or espaliered plants.

What to grow and how to grow it

When deciding what to grow, you need to weigh up the taste and health benefits of home-grown against the space and effort needed to grow them. Organic cabbage, carrots and onions are all cheaply available from veg boxes and markets, so these could be avoided. The same is not true for potatoes as the distinct difference in taste of hours-old small potatoes makes it worthwhile and they're easy to grow.

If your only experience of growing veg is nurturing a layer of bouncy cress on a damp piece of blotting paper aged seven, then take heart: you've experienced propagation. Moving onto courgettes, French beans and ultimately globe artichokes just takes a little more time and some homework. Research likely crops to find out how much space they need. The foliage of courgettes takes up a large area; beans and tomatoes are vertical growers so take up very little. Also consider whether plants are fast- or slow-growing: purple-sprouting broccoli is delicious but takes up almost 1m² for about a year – but then it's expensive in the shops.

Soil health

Soil is your number one priority. Adding plenty of rotted manure and garden compost helps water retention, soil structure and fertility levels. Check

Ten in the bed

Make best use of the space by intercropping fast- and slow-growers in the same bed.

Fast growers...
(under four months)
French beans, runner bens, and spring-sown broad beans
Carrot (earlies)
Chard
Endive
Lettuce
Mizuna
Mustard greens
Rocket
Spinach
Summer squash

... and slow growers
(4–12 months)
Artichokes
Broad beans (autumn sown)
Brussel Sprouts
Carrots
Cauliflower
Garlic from bulb
Leeks
Onions
Parsnips
Purple sprouting broccoli

Time-poor growers

▶ **Focus on perennials (such as asparagus)** After careful initial soil preparation, are easy to maintain, and fast-growing salad crops.

▶ **Subcontract** Consider paying someone else to dig over and weed your plot.

▶ **Plant a fruit orchard** This will (after a few years) provide you with fruit and could be a relaxing place to sit. The self-pollinating Victoria plum is an all-round winner: it attracts birds and bees and you can enjoy organic plums, which are almost impossible to buy.

▶ **Order an organic vegetable box** Enjoy the fruits of others' labours, while you concentrate on producing more exotic fruit and gourmet vegetables.

your soil using a soil-testing kit (from your local garden centre) and rectify any imbalances in pH levels with either lime (for acid soil) or manure (alkaline soil). Grow "**green manure**" (such as red clover and rye) during the winter months and/or between rotations and dig it straight into the soil. Beans provide a natural source of nitrogen through their root system, making them invaluable in a crop rotation: dig their roots back into the soil. Mulch is a covering (black breathable plastic, cardboard or compost) put on top of the soil around plants (take it right up to the stems), which denies weeds the light they need to grow and prevents moisture evaporating from the soil.

Seeds and sowing

There are many different varieties of individual fruits and vegetables, all with different flavours, but we rarely get to eat any of them as supermarket varieties are limited in number and bred for shelf-life and yield, not necessarily taste. Growing your own means you can experiment with the different flavours of "heirloom varieties" (see Heritage Seed Library p.272), whose survival is threatened by the single modern F1 hybrid varieties developed for uniformity and growing ability.

Romanesco cauliflowers

▶ **How to sow** Some plants, such as members of the squash family, need to germinate under transparent cover in the warmth. Sow onto fresh compost and cover with a thin scattering of compost. As the seedlings emerge, move them away from direct sunlight but keep conditions light and warm. Before planting these outside you need to get them used to chillier conditions, known as "hardening off", by placing containers outside during the daytime for a week before planting them into the soil. Although it is tempting, do not overcrowd plants; thin them out to avoid disappointing harvests. You can choose seed or young seedlings (or plug plants) to be delivered to your door. Plug plants are more expensive, but the main benefit is that you'll have three sturdy courgette plants rather than fifty seeds to deal with. Some plants, especially roots, don't like being moved; for them, direct sowing into the ground is best.

▶ **Succession sowing** This involves sowing little and often, so that plants are ready at different times, giving you a constant supply of food.

Crop rotation

If you grow the same plant families in the same soil year after year, specific pests and disease will build up in the soil and as they survive the winter months, they will be ready to attack your new plants in the spring in greater force. However, if you plant a different crop, the bugs will be disappointed (see p.6). The vegetable families are:

▶ **Legumes** Peas, beans and clover (for green manure).

▶ **Alliums** Onions, shallots, leeks, garlic.

▶ **Brassicas** Broccoli, kale, brussel sprouts, cavolo nero, mizuna, rocket, cabbage, radishes.

▶ **Cucurbits** Cucumber, courgettes, squashes, melon, pumpkins.

▶ **Roots** Carrots, celeriac, fennel, parsnips.

▶ **Solanaceous (or deadly nightshade family)** Potatoes, tomatoes, peppers, aubergines, chillies.

A classic three-year rotation would go like this (with other vegetable families mixed in amongst these):

beans, peas and onions ▶ brassicas ▶ potatoes and roots

Fruit and veg growing

Apples	Plant: November–February (dwarf varieties in containers)
Harvest	July–January
Likes	Compatible trees for pollination; feeding in spring, mulch in April
Dislikes	Waterlogged soil, cramped branches (prune to thin these out); pests: codling moths, sawfly, earwigs and wasps
Varieties	James Grieve, Coxes Orange Pippin, Egremont Russet
Tips	Dig a very big hole, cover with mulch and keep new trees the recommended distance apart. Remove all blossom the first year
Asparagus	Plant March–April. 10 x one-year-old crowns 15–20cm deep, 30cm apart in a single well-prepared row
Harvest	Only when established after two years. From April–June
Likes	Very well drained soil, clear of weeds, seaweed fertilizer, slightly alkaline soil
Dislikes	Cold and wet conditions, slugs
Varieties	Connover's Colossal, Backlim, Gijnlim
Tips	Although slow to start, once established these perennial plants are trouble-free and last for up to twenty years. Parsley can be grown between crowns
Broad beans	Autumn: Sow seeds inside in October, then plant out small plants (10cm high) November–December. Spring: Sow seeds directly into the soil in February–April, about 20cm apart. Final height: 1m
Harvest	May–September
Likes	Fertile soil, cool conditions
Dislikes	Blackfly: Pinch out the plant's tips (which pests like) when in full flower, brush off or spray with soap mix
Varieties	Aquadulce or dwarf variety "The Sutton"
Tips	Leave a few weeks between the planting of rows to enjoy tender small beans through summer. Brown leaf marks indicates a soil potassium deficiency but won't harm the crop
Blueberries	Sow in 40cm diameter container (November–February)
Harvest	Three years after planting, July–September
Likes	Sunny, sheltered spot, acid soil (pH5 4–5.5), mulch with bark
Dislikes	Tapwater (use rainwater), birds (use nets)
Varieties	Duke (excellent all-rounder), Colville, Brigitta (late fruit), Toro (for small spaces)
Tip	Grow three varieties alongside each other for optimal cross-pollination. Fairly trouble free
Broccoli	Sow March–May (under cover for first month). Plant in 2–3 batches of 10–20 small plants, about 20–40cm apart (depends on variety) in rows
Harvest	June–October (Calabrese); January–April (purple sprouting)
Likes	Nitrogen-rich soil, sheltered site, lots of space (purple sprouting)
Dislikes	Slugs, snails, white fly – might need protecting from pests with netting

Varieties	Early Purple Sprouting Improved, Belstar (Calabrese)
Tips	Can suffer from disease "clubfoot", which remains in soil for up to twenty years
Courgettes	Sow: mid-April–May (under cover) and June into soil. Plant oval, flat seeds thin-nest edge facing up/down (or small plants) into a 30cm compost-filled hole
Harvest	July–October (ten weeks after sowing)
Likes	Lots of water, space (about 1m² per plant)
Dislikes	Frost, red spider mite and mosaic virus
Varieties	Green Bush, El Greco, Gold Rush (yellow fruits), Little Gem (small round fruits on a trailing plant)
Tips	Use mini-courgettes (about 7cm long) along with the yellow flowers (and a little onion and garlic) to make a delicate risotto; left too long courgettes swell to become marrows. About fifteen per plant. Stagger the sowing to avoid a glut or find a good chutney recipe
French beans	Sow: in 2–3 batches (for regular picking) from April (under cover) to August
Harvest	When they are the diameter of a pencil in about July-August
Likes	Sunny spot, moist, rich soil; support climbers with a wigwam structure
Dislikes	Slugs, blackfly, frost
Varieties	Dwarf (bush): Delinel, Royal Burgundy (purple); climbing: Blue Lake
Tips	Very productive and easy to grow, dwarf and climbing varieties are good for small spaces and they freeze well. Try pink and white striped Borlotti beans
Leeks	Grow small (15cm) plants from seed indoors, ready for planting out into deep, narrow holes in June; sow seeds outside in May with 10cm between plants.
Harvest	September–May
Likes	Sun, water
Varieties	Musselburgh (very hardy, dates back to 1834), Apollo
Tips	"Earth up" the emerging leek with soil to increase amount of white stem. Closer spacing of plants produces smaller leeks
Potatoes	Sow: earlies March–May; maincrop mid-late April. Planting: Earlies: Chit potato "seeds" in February. Plant 40cm apart into a 25cm deep, 30cm wide trench with dug-in manure at its base
Harvest	When flowers die down, the potatoes are ready to pick. Earlies: June–July; Maincrop: September (store over winter in a cool, dry environment)
Likes	Rich soil and potash (wood ash from stove or potash-rich comfrey); regular watering while flowering; being "earthed up"
Dislikes	Shade, frost, blight fungus
Varieties	First earlies: International Kidney (aka Jersey Royals). Second earlies: Kestrel or Wilja (high yield and good disease resistance); Charlotte (classic French salad potato). Maincrop: Belle de Fontenay (old French early maincrop); Santé (excellent for organic growers as very resistant to pests and disease)

Looking after your plants

Feeding your plants with a **slow-release fertilizer** such as organic chicken manure pellets or liquid seaweed extract helps them flourish.

Compost can be delivered to your front door or allotment, but depending on how much you need, it could be expensive. Instead use a plastic

compost bin with a lid (rats love compost as much as your soil does). You can use household waste (cardboard, junkmail, raw kitchen peelings) and garden waste.

Wild flowers provide pollen for bees, as do comfrey, red clover, vetch and the long-lasting purple scabiosa. Bees also love the flowers of runner beans, artichokes, apple and pear trees. Wildflowers also attract natural pest predators such as ladybirds and lacewings.

As your first shoots come up, you'll find an infinite **slug population** making repeated advances. It's them or your food, and even staunch vegetarians will want to get rid of them. Most start off with sunken pots full of beer to trap them, then salt them, and eventually give up and apply minimal chemical slug pellets (but note that these are poisonous to wildlife). Old-timers cut them in half; the more soft-hearted collect them up in the evening or after a wet spell and set them free elsewhere.

Companion planting: distract the pests

Given the choice, aphids would head for a row of nasturtiums rather than your precious beans, and cabbage-white butterflies prefer wild nettles to broccoli, so grow wild plants and flowers. Lacewings and ladybirds both eat aphids (white and blackfly) and can be attracted with wild flowers such as candytuft and sunflowers. Frogs love eating slugs so making a small pond could be worth the effort.

Herb growing

The great thing about herb growing is that it is pretty easy and the benefits are huge: a tiny packet of supermarket herbs will cost you around a pound, whereas your own herbs can be picked when you need them in the amounts you want and cost next to nothing. Marjoram, mint, rosemary, thyme, chives, parsley, coriander, chervil and sage grow easily in normal flowerbeds or pots with occasional trimming.

Fresh herbs make all the difference to your cooking; a handful of chopped fresh herbs such as chervil, mint or basil and lemony red-stemmed wood sorrel can perk up a supermarket salad instantly. And what could make a quicker lunch than your own young broad beans mixed with plenty of chopped mint and parsley with feta cheese crumbled on top?

Pesticide-free fruit: your own cherry orchard

The advantage of fruit is that the plants are easier to look after than vegetables and can work well in limited spaces or large containers. They tend to like rich, well-drained soil and sunny spots. Sun-loving fig trees can be difficult to coax ripe fruit out of, but try the hardiest outdoor fig variety such as Brown Turkey.

Trees: apple, pear, cherry, plum and greengage.

Bushes: blackberry (Loch Ness, Kotata), raspberry, blueberry, gooseberry (Invicta). Organic gardening expert Bob Flowerdew recommends Royal Sovereign and Gariguette strawberry varieties for their flavour.

What you need to know

Buy from a specialist supplier who will give you the advice you need to help your plant off to a good start.

▶ **Varieties** The National Fruit Collection at Brogdale in Kent (brogdale.org) has six hundred different UK tree varieties, all with a subtly different taste, texture and colour. Contact them for a list of your regional varieties and to order a plant a year before delivery.

▶ **Rootstocks** These are made by grafting a fruit tree onto the root of another tree with desirable characteristics (for example, "M27" rootstock is short, compact and disease-resistant). The type of rootstock your new tree was grown on determines its height.

Home-grown salad all year round

Tomatoes	Sow: Seeds (March–April) for planting out as small hardened-off plants (May/June)
Harvest	July–October
Likes	Fertile, well-drained soil, plant food and sun (a south-facing wall is perfect), regular light watering (to prevent splitting of skin)
Dislikes	Shade, white fly (plant marigolds to deter them)
Varieties	Alicante, Green Zebra (green/yellow stripes). Cherry: Cherry Belle, Sungold (yellow), Gardener's Delight. Hanging baskets: Tumbler or Pearl; mix historic varieties
Tips	Keep plants focused on fruit (not leaf) production: pinch off non-flowering sideshoots and the top of plant when fruiting. Green tomatoes make excellent chutney
Rocket	Sow: all year round indoors; and in summer outside
Harvest	3–4 weeks after sowing; year round
Dislikes	Heat: bolts in hot weather
Varieties	Avanti
Tips	Very easy to grow; minimal pest problem
Spinach	Sow: regular small sowings every three weeks from March–September
Harvest	April–November
Likes	Cool conditions
Varieties	Galaxy, Bloomsdale

The secret of a really good salad is variety in taste, texture, colour and freshness. This is where **successional sowing** of different plants and packets of mixed leaves come into their own. With planning, salad leaves can be grown all year round and are easy to cultivate outside (in polytunnels, coldframes or greenhouses) and inside (in conservatories or on bright windowsills) in containers (with stones and gravel for drainage and rich compost).

Cut-and-come-again is a convenient and productive harvesting method which is increasingly popular. It's especially suited to indoor and windowbox growing. **Lambs lettuce, endive, mizuna, rocket, mustard, spinach or lollo rosso** can all be grown in this way. Three to four weeks after sowing you can cut your first salad, taking leaves from the outside to preserve growth from the centre of the plant. Cut each leaf a few centimetres above the base, as that is where regrowth will occur. You should expect three or four harvests from each plant. These leaves normally grow too quickly for diseases and pests to be a problem.

Lettuce	Sow: germinate seeds indoors for planting out February–September
Harvest	All year
Likes	Very rich soils with lots of nitrogen
Varieties	Cos: Corsair, Little Gem (takes over two months to develop a heart). Loose-leaved: Lollo Rosso, Lamb's lettuce (small rounded green leaves), Catalogna (serrated leaves), Salad Bowl (green and dark red oak leaves
Mizuna	March–August (outside); September–February (under cover)
Harvest	3–8 weeks after sowing; all year
Likes	Moist soil (keep well watered)
Dislikes	Dry conditions (will rot if not protected against heavy rain and snow)
Varieties	Tokyo Beau and Tokyo Belle
Tips	Sow some to harvest as whole plants (25cm apart) and some to cut-and-come-again (10cm apart, you will get about five pickings). Can be grown through winter.
Endive	Sow: February–September
Harvest	7–13 weeks after sowing; all year
Likes	Moist soil
Dislikes	Slugs
Varieties	Curled or frisée: Pancalieri, Monaco; or broadleaved varieties: Scarola
Tips	Easier to grow than chicory

Find out more

Salad Leaves for all Seasons, Charles Dowding (Green Books, 2008) **Detailed advice and examples about growing through the year.** charlesdowding.co.uk

The Organic Salad Garden, Joy Larkham (Frances Lincoln, 2003) **By the author of** bestselling *Grow Your Own Vegetables*; this book is very easy to follow with step-by-step instructions and useful identification charts for salad leaves, edible flowers, and vegetables.

Salads, Hugo Arnold (Avoca) is a concise collection of tasty, varied salad recipes from the Dublin-based food emporium Avoca.

When you can't be bothered to grow your own salads, you can order top-quality salad leaves from popular restaurant supplier Secretts Farm in Surrey (secretts.co.uk).

▶ **Planting** Walcot Nursery (walcotnursery.co.uk) will send you bare-rooted (Soil Association-approved) organic trees in November. Make sure you dig a hole much larger than the roots, hold the tree in the hole while filling it with a mix of compost and topsoil, allowing the roots to spread out. Check with the supplier about any special nutritional requirements.

Chicken run

Wandering down the garden to the chicken shed to collect an egg for your breakfast may sound enticing, but make sure you've got enough room to keep chickens unless you fancy a smelly swamp outside your back door. You'll need:

▶ **A cosy wooden or plastic house** with an attached rat- and fox-proof run (it should be entirely enclosed). These usually cost £250–400.

▶ **At least 6×8 metres of free garden or allotment space** with either grass or bark chippings for flooring (most recommend 120cm² per bird on the outside and 30cm² to nest on the inside).

▶ **Someone to feed your chickens** when you're away.

▶ **The plastic all-enclosed "eglu"** made by Omlet is a modern chicken-housing solution especially for the city garden. It looks a bit like a long rabbit run (3×1.5m). You can move it about to allow your grass to recover. It's designed for two chickens, which the company can also supply.

Chicken care

▶ Chickens live for about four years and are enjoyable to have around. Children love watching them flap about in dust baths (often in your flower borders). Keeping their surroundings clean by moving them around is the key to avoiding nasty chicken coop smells.

▶ Chickens love warmed-up meal mixed with water and any scraps you have (the ultimate in recycling).

How many eggs will I get?

▶ It varies according to the weather (they lay fewer eggs in winter) and the chicken, but four to five a week should be the minimum you'd expect. Chickens are most productive in their first year; after that they lay bigger eggs less often.

Omlet omlet.co.uk

▶ **Pollination** This is essential for trees to produce fruit and is carried out by bees (which can travel up to three miles) and often requires the presence of nearby compatible tree varieties.

▶ **Pruning** Do this once a year to create optimum conditions for fruiting and to catch and treat disease. It can seem something of a black art to the novice, but with advice from other gardeners or detailed step-by-step photographic guides, you can learn the basics quickly. You do need to know when to do it (usually winter) and where on the branch or stem to snip. Espaliers and fans need careful pruning to retain their shape (check the Royal Horticultural Society pruning guides online).

▶ **Disease** Read up on likely problems for your particular variety as disease can kill trees. Give your plants a regular health check: unexpected changes in leaf colour can indicate disease.

Find out more

Growing advice and gardens to visit

Royal Horticultural Society (RHS) rhs.org National horticultural charity. Good for general advice (online) on all aspects of fruit and vegetable growing. Also accredits horticulture courses run regionally around the country. They have an extensive library collection and a historic plant and tree collection to visit at their headquarters in Wisely, Surrey.

Garden Organic gardenorganic.org.uk (previously the Henry Doubleday Research Association or HDRA). A charitable organic research association which dates back to 1954. Visitors can see organic growing in action at their large display gardens at Ryton near Coventry.

Allotment organizations

National Society of Allotment and Leisure Gardeners (NSALG) natsoc@nsalg.org.uk The oldest allotment organisation (1930) with the stated aim to "Protect, Promote, & Preserve allotment gardening". They provide practical and legal advice about the running of allotment sites and dealing with local councils.

National Allotments Gardens Trust nagtrust.org Promotes allotments and co-runs the National Allotment Week with NSALG.

Scottish Allotment Garden Association sags.org.uk Advice and the latest news on local allotments.

Books

The Allotment Handbook Caroline Foley (New Holland, 2004) The perfect first-timer's guide to everything from getting an allotment to deciding what to plant and how to grow it.

The Vegetable and Herb Expert and **The Fruit Expert** Dr D. G. Hessayon (Expert series, both 1997) Illustrated and easy-to-use classics with sections on diagnosing problems.

The Allotment Keeper's Handbook Jane Perrone (Guardian Books/Atlantic, 2007) Very readable guide to finding an allotment and keeping it, and growing tips. Also a useful monthly planner.

The Great Vegetable Plot Sarah Raven (BBC Books, 2005) Creating a kitchen garden from a cook's point of view with plenty of useful photographs and plant information.

21st-Century Smallholder Paul Waddington (Eden Project Books, 2006) A good first book for a succinct overview of all areas of plant-growing and animal-keeping.

Seed and plant suppliers

Order seed and plant catalogues in good time (they make good New Year reading) for deliveries at sowing time. Look for traditional and/or organic varieties as well as compact varieties for pots and window boxes.

Organic Gardening Catalogue organiccatalog.com/catalog Organic pest control and plant feed, green manure, fruit and vegetable seeds and plants (including asparagus, mushrooms and rhubarb). Their **Heritage Seed Library** (HSL) contains thousands of old and unusual varieties, many of which have been dropped from commercial seed catalogues.

Jekka's Herb Farm jekkasherbfarm.com Specialist organic (Soil Association accredited) herb nursery supplying a vast range of individual plants and mixed salad pots by mail order. Winner of dozens of RHS gold medals.

Suffolk Herbs suffolkherbs.com Specialist organic and natural seed supplier of herbs, special mixes of wildflowers, green manures and sprouting seeds.

Suttons Seeds suttons.co.uk Your dad's favourite. Amazingly long list of conventionally produced seeds which will keep you busy during the dark days of January.

Blogs

Allotments UK blogs.allotments-uk.com The UK's largest online allotment community bringing together blogs by allotment growers for as-it-happens updates and photographs. Look out for "Allotment Garden" by Tony the Hoe, "The Pumpkin Patch" and "John's Garden".

Soilman soilman.net Regular updates on trials and tribulations of growing your own and links to other blogs. Useful (and entertaining) videos about how to grow certain plants such as asparagus and how to net broccoli.

Part V

The directory

Listings and books

Lift the lid on the global food system and it's easy to get depressed at the sight of transnational corporations gaining greater and greater control of what we eat. But powerful though they are, their way is not the only way. The good news is, the way you shop and eat every day can make a difference. Zoom in on any region of the country and you'll find individuals, businesses and groups who have a different vision of the future of food.

This final chapter is a celebration of some of those people and the food they make. It's beyond the scope of this guide to do more than scratch the surface of the wealth and diversity that is out there. Use it as a launch-pad and you'll soon discover quality producers of your own. Remember that good food will often (though not always) cost a bit extra. Never be afraid to ask to try before you buy. People who make food take a pride in what they do and are invariably ready to share their knowledge, enthusiasm and recipe ideas. Every time you buy some food from a small-scale producer, you're helping to make a small shift in the food economy. And in time that could add up to a change in the way people eat.

If that sounds too worthy and political, remember that for those lucky enough to have been born in the affluent west and able to exercise choice, food probably affords more hours of pleasure than any other activity in the course of our lives. Now go and get your (recycled) shopping bag and start discovering.

Entries are arranged by region, and telephone numbers are given only for those businesses which don't have a website.

Eastern England

Alby Clements The Fish Shack, Aldeburgh Beach, Suffolk thefishshack.co.uk **Get your freshly caught fish and shellfish on the beach from Alby and other local fishermen.**

Arthur Howell Burnham Market ▷ 01328 738230 **Local chain of family butchers dating back to 1889, selling their own home-smoked bacon, local game and venison from Holkham Park. Also a shop and abattoir in nearby Wells-next-the-Sea.**

Bakers and Larners Holt, Norfolk bakersandlarners.com **"The Fortnum and Mason of Norfolk" stocks 700 deli items including award-winning cheeses. (Visit Byfords Deli a few doors down for artisan breads.)**

The Cambridge Cheese Company All Saints' Passage, Cambridge ▷ 01223 328672 **Buy your Nelson's Glory, a local ash-coated goat's cheese, here.**

Chisnalls Delicatessen Saffron Walden, Essex ▷ 01799 528239 **Fifty-year-old family business specializing in cheese and everything you need to go along with it.**

Clark & Ravenscroft St. Gregory's Alley, Norwich clarkandravenscroft.com **Emphasis on local food (Narborough smoked meat and fish, local cheeses),**

homemade tarts and pesto as well as Mediterranean goodies.

Cookies Crab Shop Weybourne, Norfolk ▷ 01263 740352 **You can see the samphire growing on the salt marshes from this tiny shop-cum-café. They've been selling affordable home-smoked fish and freshly cooked lobsters and crabs since 1956, all caught a few miles away. (The Cley Smokehouse a mile away is great for traditional bloaters and smoked salmon pâté.)**

Daily Bread Co-operative King's Hedges, Cambridge dailybread.co.uk **Ethical shop selling organic fruit and vegetables and locally made bread from Cobs Bakery, made from Chelmsford-based Marriage's Mill flour.**

The English Grocer Buntingford, Hertfordshire englishgrocer.co.uk **All-local fruit and veg and a wide range of deli items including Braughing sausages, coffee and walnut cake and smoked fish. Stylish high street grocers owned by former Tesco man, Peter Durose, now a "champion of small, specialist producers".**

The Food Company Marks Tey, Colchester, Essex thefoodcompany.co.uk **All the local, sustainable and organic produce you could want, with a butcher selling local game, fishmonger, greengrocer,**

delicatessen and artisan bakery under one roof.

The Green Grocers Earlham Road, Norwich thegreengrocers.co.uk Organic supermarket with a stunning range of local bread (from three artisan bakers), meat including saddleback porkpies, cheese and all the usual nuts, grains and pulses of a health food shop. Fortnightly farmers' market on Sundays.

Loaves and Fishes Woodbridge, Suffolk ▷ 01394 384040 Local fish and shellfish, artisan bread and cheese.

North Elmham Bakery Dereham, Norfolk ▷ 01362 668577 One of a number of really good new Norfolk artisan bakeries. Look out for others (**All Natural, Metfield** and **Pye Bakery**) in local delis and bakers.

Picnic Fayre Cley-next-the-Sea, Norfolk picnic-fayre.co.uk Stop here before heading off to nearby beaches for all your picnic neads: local bread (try the lavender bread), artisan cheeses, wine and smoothies (even takeaway coffee). Allotment-grown vegetables are piled into baskets outside and

Buying cheese

Cheesemongers (see p.237) are the best place to buy cheese as they are knowledgeable and will select and keep cheeses perfectly. They are happy to let you try before you buy and also sell good-quality chutneys and oatcakes. Ask them to stock the best rough oatcakes by Adamsons of Pittenweem, Fife.

Credit crunch cheese

▶ **Buy in small quantities** and make one of them a cheaper variety like farmhouse cheddar.

▶ **Look for local cheeses at farmers' markets** where they can be cheaper. You also get to meet the producer.

▶ **Don't waste anything** Keep mixed ends of cheese to add to Tamasin Day-Lewis's gruyère and herb tart recipe (in *The Art of the Tart*, the best book on tarts both savoury and sweet).

Supermarkets have a good range of cheeses for cooking or adding to salads: **feta** is perfect in a Puy lentil salad with roasted red peppers, thin-sliced red onion, handfuls of chopped parsley and mint; **haloumi** can be grilled and drizzled with

dressing made of olive oil, lime, leaf coriander, capers and black pepper. Own-label block Cheddar or organic versions are fine for macaroni cheese; packet **gorgonzola** can make a five-minute blue cheese, cream and tarragon pasta sauce.

locally made tarts, pies, and delicious cakes adorn the front counter.

Rainbow Wholefoods Labour In Vain Yard, Norwich rainbowwholefoods.co.uk **Long-established health food shop selling 2500 products from seaweed to vegetarian pies and organic popping corn. GM-free zone.**

Salters Family Butcher Aldeburgh saltersfamilybutchers.co.uk **Sells local naturally reared Linden Farm beef, poultry from Sutton Hoo and local salt-marsh lamb.**

Shelford Deli Great Shelford, Cambridge shelforddeli.co.uk **Popular for fresh fish, local meats, cheeses and puddings (raspberry and almond cake), as well as home-made ready meals, salads and pies.**

Southern and SE England

Artisan Bread Original Whitstable, Kent artisanbread-abo.com **Organic, biodynamic breads suitable for a range** of free-from diets (such as rice, quinoa and spelt breads) made with flour that is freshly milled daily.

Bill's Produce Store Lewes and Brighton www.billsproducestore.co.uk **Café and shop all rolled into one, all driven by the founder's enthusiasm for the best fresh produce.**

Bona Foodie St James's Street, Brighton (also in Kemp Town and Hove) bonafoodie.com **Popular mini-chain of delis, with wide choice of lunchtime and other options.**

Bonne Bouche Hamble, Hampshire bonne-bouche.co.uk **Delicatessen and caterer which specializes in sourcing from small specialist producers.**

Brighton Sausage Company Gloucester Road ▷ 01273 676677 **Wide range of sausages, all made from Sussex free-range meat.**

Corbin's Uckfield, East Sussex corbinsdeli.co.uk **Sussex produce includes Flower Marie ewe's cheese,**

There's more to breakfast than Rice Krispies

Forget the big commercial brands: they're over-priced, full of salt, added sugar and sometimes artificial additives. Far better (and cheaper) to make your own muesli from health food shop loose ingredients (dried apricots, prunes, raisins and figs, hazel, almond, brazil and walnuts, sunflower and pumpkin seeds, milled flaxseed, and oats).

Supermarkets stock two excellent examples of the new breed of unadulterated wholegrain cereals: **Dorset Cereals** (lots of great recipes including: Spelt flakes with dried figs and grapes), and **Pertwood Farm**'s wheat-free, organic mueslis made from cereals grown on the Mole family's organic farm, with no added salt or sugar. Pricewise Pertwood is good value: try their bestselling Fruit and Seed Muesli or the subtle and light banana and walnut variety.

Porridge might not be as quick to make as muesli, but it is cheap and a good slow-energy-release breakfast (especially with sliced banana). Try Dorset Cereal's fruity porridge with cranberries and raspberries.

Golden Cross goat's cheese and pungent Scrumpy Sussex cheese.

The Ethical Food Company Verney Junction, Buckingham ethicalfoods. co.uk **This company aims to provide a range broad enough to provide a realistic alternative to supermarket shopping, with an emphasis on local, organic, Fairtrade and sustainable.**

The Goods Shed Station Road, West Canterbury, Kent thegoodsshed.net **A sort of permanent farmers' market situated in a converted railway shed by Canterbury station. On-site butcher and fishmonger and plenty of other fresh produce. There's even a restaurant, supplied entirely from the market.**

Infinity Food Shop And Bakery North Road and Gardner St, Brighton infini-tyfoods.co.uk **A workers' cooperative which has been selling organic foods for three decades. Extensive list of own-label ingredients including beans, nuts and grains. They claim the largest selection of organic and vegetarian food in the South East.**

Judges Bakery Hastings judgesbakery. com **Jo Fairley and Craig Sams of Green & Black's fame now sell organic artisan breads.**

The Natural Store Rochester Gardens, Hove, East Sussex thenaturalstore.co.uk **Stocks 3000 products, ranging from food to interior design and clothing.**

Norbiton Fine Cheese Company Kingston, Surrey norbitoncheese.co.uk **Wide range of cheeses by post.**

Pallant of Arundel Arundel, Sussex pallantofarundel.co.uk **Fine selection of local produce.**

The Real Eating Company branches in Hove, Lewes, Bournemouth and Horsham real-eating.co.uk **South-east foodies flock to these café-cum-delis that have won national acclaim for their accent on fresh local flavours.**

The Real Pâtisserie Trafalgar Street, Brighton (also Hove) realpatisserie. co.uk **French bread and cakes.**

Room for Food Bedford Place, Southampton, Hampshire ▷ 023 80233523 **This central Southampton deli stocks a wide range of local organic produce, including cheese from Lyburn farmhouse, cold meats, speciality breads, organic fruit and veg, soups and local honey.**

Sandy's Fishmonger King St, Twickenham ▷ 020 8892 5788 **Staunch supporter of sustainable fishing and British suppliers.**

Sussex and the City Meeting House Lane, Brighton sussexandthecity.co.uk **Fishmonger, cheesemonger and grocer which sources its food from within fifty miles of Brighton.**

London

Clarke's Kensington Church Street, W8 ▷ 020 7229 2190 **The deli next to the restaurant sells their own chocolate truffles and unusual breads (fig and fennel, chollas), Monmouth coffee and artisan cheeses.**

As Nature Intended Chiswick High Road, Chiswick asnatureintended.co.uk **Organic supermarket chain which stocks a wide range from the excellent Manna frozen ready meals to fresh meat and fish and organic tortillas. Also branches in Balham and Ealing.**

Port and Stilton ... in a chocolate!

Paul A. Young (paulayoung.co.uk), who has shops in Islington and the City, is an outstanding, relative newcomer in the world of fine chocolate. All his chocolates are hand-made fresh each day in his kitchens, and he never uses preservatives or artificial flavourings of any sort, meaning that they will keep for just seven days. The *Sunday Telegraph* called his brownies "the gooiest in Britain", but his range goes far beyond that. For the lover of classics, there are champagne truffles, sea salted caramels and milk chocolate rochers. But there is also an ever-changing selection of seasonal flavours; the autumn range, for example, includes spiced pumpkin, woody rosemary, and ginger and cardamom. And for the adventurous chocolate explorer, there are even Marmite and port and Stilton chocolates; they may sound revolting, but in fact they work astonishingly well.

Paul told Rough Guides that making fine chocolates involves finding the finest, ethically sourced ingedients and respecting their characteristics. All the same issues that are becoming important to consumers in general – ethics, provenance and quality

– also increasingly matter to chocolate lovers. And the high-end chocolatiers are a spur to the high street to raise its game, though Stilton chocolate may be some time off at Thorntons.

Brendan Olley tempering chocolate in Paul A. Young's kitchen. Tempering is a critical element of the chocolatier's art, involving fine judgement of just how much heat to apply to melt the fat crystals and give the chocolate its stability and texture.

Baker and Spice Denyer Street, Chelsea, SW3 bakerandspice.com Renowned bakers (their croissants are legendary) and freshly prepared deli foods. Branches in Belgravia, Maida Vale and Queen's Park.

The Barnes Fish Shop SW13 ▷ 020 8876 1297 Scottish organic salmon is a speciality, as are their home-made fish pies and fishcakes.

Bluebird King's Road, SW3 conran. com Conran's deli sells quality cured hams, cheese and pâtés, as well as Voisin chocolate and salads.

Brindisa Borough Market, SE1 brindisa. com Unbeatable range of Iberian delicacies: paprikas, excellent oils, organic chorizo, salted almonds and Catalan cheeses. Also at Exmouth Market, EC1.

Bumblebee Natural Foods Holloway, N7 bumblebee.co.uk One-stop ethical natural food shop with a local box scheme and delivery service.

Bushwacker Whole Foods Hammersmith, W6 ▷ 020 8748 2061 Vegetarian shop selling local organic fruit and veg, organic eggs, dairy and breads, meals and salads made on site.

La Cave à Fromage South Kensington, SW7 la-cave.co.uk **Expert cheese-mongers which supplies Le Manoir aux Quat' Saisons. Wide range of British and continental artisan cheeses.**

The Cheeseboard Greenwich, SE10 cheese-board.co.uk **An excellent web-site describes almost every cheese on offer. Creamy seasonal Vacherins and fresh goat's cheese "buttons".**

Mr Christian's Notting Hill, W11 mrchristians.co.uk **Wonderful neigh-bourhood deli on Elgin Crescent which offers incredible choice and high-quality, home-prepared foods (shepherd's pie and broad bean, asparagus & goat's cheese salad). Particularly good bread, artisan cheese, charcuterie, oils and vinegars.**

Condon Fishmonger's Wandsworth Road, SW8 ▷ 020 7622 2934 **Hundred-year old fishmonger's with its own smoke-house. Fresh fish daily.**

East Dulwich Deli Lordship Lane, Dulwich, SE22 ▷ 020 8693 2525 **English cheeses and ham and Italian fresh pasta. Their in-house bakery makes organic bread in a wood-fire oven.**

Euphorium Bakery Islington, N1 ▷ 020 7704 6905 **Wide range of breads (wholemeal baguette, Scandinavian seed breads) and cakes including Mousseline Roule (posh chocolate swiss roll). Branches at Belsize Park and Hampstead.**

Farm W5 The Green, Ealing, W5 farmw5. co.uk **An ethical urban farm shop with a vast and varied stock: organic dairy, meat and fish, fruit and veg; breads from local Born and Bread bakers, artisan cheeses and unusual deli items.**

F.C. Soper's Peckham, SE15 ▷ 020 7639 9729 **Traditional fishmongers selling sustainably caught fresh fish.**

FishWorks Marylebone High Street, W1 fishworks.co.uk **High-quality fresh fishmongers (and restaurant). Other London branches and Bath, Bristol.**

Flâneur Farringdon Road, EC1 flaneur. com **Sophisticated, wide-ranging food hall selling their own bread, artisan cheeses, antipasti, wild boar and salami, fruit and vegetables, tea and coffee, and traiteur for your lunch or supper.**

Flour Power City Bakery Hoxton, N1 flourpowercity.com **Wide range of organic artisan breads (made from Shipton Flour) including their signature Hoxton Rye Levain and croissants sold through London's delis and Borough Market.**

Forman and Field Stratford, E15 formanandfield.com **Well-stocked deli in the old East End near the new Olympic stadium site, selling Alderton ham and game pie, Maldon oysters, potted shrimp and salmon cured with natural salt, oak-smoked and hand-sliced, as well as deli items**

(Bloody Mary salsa, artisan cheeses), hand-made almond and other cakes.

Fresh and Wild Soho, Camden, Battersea and Stoke Newington wholefoodsmarket.com Cross between a health food shop and smart deli selling organic meat and fish, good bread (look out for Flour Power City Bakery) and cakes, vegetarian and vegan foods. Now part of the US **Whole Foods Market** chain, which has its flagship store in Kensington High Street.

Ginger Pig Moxon St, W1 thegingerpig. co.uk Organic butcher known for its addictive sausage rolls. Also at Borough Market.

A. Gold Brushfield Street, Shoreditch, E1 agold.co.uk Comprehensive range of traditional British produce from pink sugar mice to Lancashire Eccles cakes, Cumbrian bacon to Stinking Bishop cheese. Cappuccino and at the **Market Café** a few doors down.

The Grocery Kingsland Road, E2 thegroceryshop.co.uk New York deli-style organic and Fairtrade supermarket.

Hamish Johnston Fine Cheeses Battersea, SW11 hamishjohnston.com British farmhouse cheeses and many continental foods from preserved lemons to salted anchovies.

Hampstead Tea and Coffee NW11 ▷ 020 8731 9833 Organic and Fairtrade tea specialists. Mail order.

Hampstead Seafood NW3 ▷ 020 7435 3966 Organic Scottish salmon, Greek sea bass and tuna.

Handmade Foods 40 Tranquil Vale, Blackheath, SE3 handmadefood.com Pretty Blackheath village shop with a great deli range (artisan cheeses) and meals to go, including organic rare roast beef, fresh tuna empanadas, asparagus and cream tart and home-made puddings. They also sell great coffee (Monmouth) and cakes.

Just Natural Muswell Hill, N8 ▷ 020 8340 1720 Over 3000 organic and Fairtrade products under one roof including Inverawe smoked fish and Graig Farm meats.

Konditor & Cook Cornwall Road, Waterloo, SE1 konditorandcook.com Excellent bakers and cakeshop (try the lemon poppyseed cake, curly whirly chocolate and vanilla cake or the spinach and cream cheese muffin). Branches at Borough Market, Chancery Lane, Curzon Soho Café and the Gherkin.

Kennards Good Foods Bloomsbury, WC1 kennardsgoodfoods.com Excellent cheeses, Graig Farm meats, bread and dairy and organic veg from Secretts Farm.

James Knight of Mayfair Notting Hill Gate, W11 james-knight.com The Royal Family's fishmonger, selling lobster and crab spring rolls, salmon en-croûte, sustainably caught Cornish wild black breen and Loch Crinan scallops.

La Fromagerie Marylebone, W1 lafromagerie.co.uk Great British artisan cheeses and French, too, such as Comté, a firm, mature cheese with a crystalline texture and nutty flavour, as well as chutneys and teas. Also Highbury Park branch.

Steve Hatt, Islington, N1 ▷ 020 7226 3963 Traditonal fishmonger's widely reckoned to be the best in London.

Artisan bread

Artisan bread with its crisp crust and deep flavour has made a comeback in the last ten years with many good bakers selling slowly proved real bread made from stone-ground, unbleached, untreated flours (wheat, rye or spelt) and baked in a wood-fired oven. Some of the excellent organic artisan flours used include those milled by **Shipton Mill** (shipton-mill.com), Gloucestershire; **Letheringsett Mill** (letheringsettwatermill.co.uk), Norfolk and **Bacheldre** in Wales (bacheldremill.co.uk).

Good bread is easy to make: all you need is strong bread flour, dried or preferably fresh yeast (from a baker's or health food shop), a big bowl, damp tea towel, a few loaf tins and a little patience. There are many bread recipes to try yourself: Bertinet's French **sourdough** (good with pork rillettes and gherkins) or Avoca's quick and easy **multiseed wholemeal**, which goes straight into the oven without proving. It has a wonderful cake-like texture, perfect with Keen's cheddar and homemade chutney (*Avoca Cookbook*, Hugo Arnold, 2002).

Real bread pioneers

Crust Richard Bertinet (Kyle Cathie, 2007) thebertinetkitchen.com French baker's step-by-step guide to exceptional sourdough, spelt, brioche and more. He also runs sell-out bread-making courses in Bath.

English Bread & Yeast Cookery Elizabeth David (Penguin, 1977) A classic book, widely used by emerging 1970s breadmakers which also gives coverage of the bread of other cultures.

The Handmade Loaf Dan Lepard (Mitchell Beazley, 2008) danlepard.com A guide to traditional bread-making by the baker whom Fay Maschler called "the bread supremo".

Bread Matters Andrew Whitley (Fourth Estate, 2006) realbreadcampaign.org Whiteley, a life-long bread activist, is adamant real bread must be made with "no additives or 'processing aids' like added enzymes … it must be allowed time to ferment".

L.S. Mash Brixton SW9 ▷ 020 7274 6423 Family-run fishmongers: fresh scallops, rock salmon and other native fish.

Macfarlane's Clapham SW4 ▷ 020 8673 5373 Dorset bacon and ham, freshly baked bread, artisan cheeses and chocolates and a weekly organic fruit and veg box delivery.

Melrose & Morgan Primrose Hill, NW1 melroseandmorgan.com High-quality grocers selling reasonably priced cheese tarts, fish pies, sausage rolls and cakes prepared on site, Neal's Yard cheeses and organic chicken from Sutton Hoo.

Moxon's Clapham, SW4 ▷ 020 8675 2468 Fish from Newlyn market in Cornwall and Billingsgate Market (and samphire in the summer). Also at East Dulwich, SE22.

Neal's Yard Dairy Covent Garden nealsyarddairy.co.uk Handmade, traditional cheeses as well as cream, yoghurt and butters. Try Stichelton blue from Nottinghamshire for Christmas. Also at Park Street, Borough Market, SE1.

Ottolenghi Islington, N1 ottolenghi. co.uk A bakery, deli and café selling irresistible and imaginative Mediterranean-inspired salads,

breads and cakes to eat in or take away. Smaller outlets in Notting Hill, Belgravia and Kensington.

Panzer's Deli St John's Wood, NW8 panzers.co.uk Food from around the world as well as Clarke's bread and Poilâne's sourdough, home-made cakes, hand-sliced smoked salmon, organic soups and a greengrocers.

Planet Organic Westbourne Grove, W2 planetorganic.com One of the earliest organic supermarket chains. Large range including ready-made food and sustainable fish. Branches Fulham, Muswell Hill, Islington and Bloomsbury.

Rippon Cheese Stores Upper Tachbrook Street, SW1 ripponcheese.com Five hundred cheeses squeezed into a small shop and expert staff on hand to guide you through them.

Source Foods Richmond, Surrey, TW9 ▷ 0208 439 9866 Home-made fish-cakes and other prepared foods offer an alternative to supermarket ready meals. Also stocks local veg, artisan bread and cheese.

Trinity Stores Balham SW12 trinitystores.co.uk A true foodie deli where you'll find fig jam, organic

Tea time

There are more and more quality teas on sale on the high street and in supermarkets now, and as tea is light and travels well, it's suited to online shopping, too. So here are some alternatives to dunking a Tetley tea-bag in your mug:

▶ **Dragonfly** dragonfly-teas.com are a UK-based tea company with high ethical standards. Their breakfast rooibos tea is widely stocked in supermarkets.

▶ **Clipper teas** clipperteas.com have a wide range of Fairtrade and organic teas (and also coffees and hot chocolate).

▶ **Teapigs** teapigs.co.uk has a very imaginative range of ethically sourced teas, including tung ting oolong. The website lists UK stockists and also sells direct.

▶ **Equal Exchange** equalexchange.co.uk Fairtrade since 1981, a workers' cooperative with a range of teas (such as Darjeeling), coffees and other products.

▶ **Solaris Botanicals** solarisbotanicals.com an award-winning Galway-based organic tea specialist. Their website has useful information on brewing tea.

▶ **Taylors of Harrogate** taylorsofharrogate.co.uk long-established, family-owned firm with international reach which buys its teas direct and follows a sustainable sourcing policy.

▶ **Dr Stuart's** drstuarts.com emphasis is on the health benefits in this widely stocked range of herbal, fruit and "functional" teas with names such as Tranquillity and Detox.

▶ **Wilkinson's Tea & Coffee Merchants** wilkinsonsofnorwich.com Incredible range from hand-sewn Chinese green tea balls and loose nettle tea to seasonal First Flush Darjeeling and Liquorice tea. They have a shop on Lobster Lane, Norwich.

Treat tea with respect: **black teas** such as Darjeeling and Assam can take boiling water, but **green and white teas** are more delicate, so let the water cool for a couple of minutes in the kettle. Remove tea (especially strong black teas such as Lapsang Souchong) from the water after around three minutes and you can brew up from it a second and even third time.

If you enjoy tea but want to avoid **caffeine**, you can get rid of most of it by swirling the leaves for 20 seconds in a little freshly boiled water. Then discard the water and brew your tea as normal. Or try **rooibos** (redbush), a naturally caffeine-free tea from South Africa.

dairy, Fine Cheese Co. biscuits and Inverawe organic smoked salmon.

Walter Purkis & Sons Muswell Hill, N10 purkis4fish.com They've been selling fresh fish (much of it wild) to Londoners for almost two hundred years. Their Crouch End branch houses the old smokery for haddock, kippers and salmon.

Verde Delicatessen Brushfield Street, Shoreditch, E1 ▷ 020 7247 1924 Jeanette Winterson's lovely shop

Coffee with a clear conscience

At 42%, instant coffee accounts for the lion's share of the hot drinks market, but **Fairtrade coffee** is one of the fastest-growing sectors, with the big multinationals wanting a piece of the action alongside the specialist roasters. The small companies have the advantage of being able to forge close relationships with growers at ground level. **Union Hand-Roasted**'s Steven Macatonia told Rough Guides that his company carries out a lot of painstaking work to find the best growers' cooperatives and also small family farms, and works with them both on the quality of the coffee and the conditions of the workers. But coffee will only sell long-term if it tastes good, too, so the sourcing is only half the story; careful artisanal (rather than computer-controlled) roasting is what brings out the character and flavour of each batch of beans.

Cafedirect cafedirect.co.uk The biggest Fairtrade hot drinks company in the UK. It re-invests around 60% of its profits in producer countries. You'll find its products in supermarkets, independents and Oxfam shops.

Union Hand-Roasted unionroasted.com This site has detailed tasting notes on all their coffees on their website. Try their award-winning Ethiopian coffee, available at Waitrose and in delis.

Monmouth Coffee Company monmouthcoffee.co.uk Roasters of consistently excellent coffee from single estates and cooperatives: organic espresso blend, Colombian decaff and a host of other distinctive flavours from around the world. Sample and buy at Monmouth Street in Covent Garden and at Borough Market.

Around 15% of coffee drunk is decaff. **Decaffeination** by the **Swiss water method** is chemical-free, unlike the alternatives, which use solvents such as methylene chloride or ethyl acetate to strip out the caffeine (which can, confusingly, be referred to as a "water method"). If the coffee doesn't advertise the fact that the Swiss water method was used, you can be sure that a chemical process was involved.

Find out more

swisswater.com/decaff/

selling a wide range of products and notably home-made pumpkin pasta (just add a few fried sage leaves, butter and parmesan).

Villandry Great Portland Street, W1 villandry.com French breads and pastries baked on site, herbs and vegetables from the excellent Secretts Farm, cheese counter, charcuterie, cakes and chocolates, and takeaway foods.

South-West Engand

Better Food Company Sevier Street, Bristol betterfood.co.uk This (nearly) 100% organic supermarket sells meat, fruit and veg from their walled garden in Somerset, dairy produce. Also delicatessen and dried goods.

Blacks Delicatessen Chagford blacks-deli.co.uk Stylish deli in a pretty Dartmoor town near Exeter, which offers ready-made foods, their own cooked meats, local cheeses and a wide range of continental items.

Bon Goût Deli Magdalen Road, Exeter bongoutdeli.co.uk **Wide range of foods including local Devon Chili Company sauces. They will send you local Langage Farm clotted cream by post if you feel the urge.**

Browse Seafoods Brixham, Devon browseseafoods.co.uk **The last fishmongers in this traditional fishing port. All fish is sourced locally and their famous crab is cooked and picked on site.**

Chandos Deli Whiteladies Road, Bristol chandosdeli.com **Three branches in Bristol as well as in Bath and Exeter. Carefully selected range of local and continental cheeses, oils and vinegars, smoked fish and game, local honey and jams; excellent take-away coffee. Delicious cakes (their lemon drizzle slice is very good).**

The Cheese Shed Bovey Tracy, Devon thecheeseshed.com **West Country cheese specialists (over one hundred varieties) including Devon Oke, Elmhirst, Harbourne Blue, Vulscombe and White Nancy goat's cheeses, all sold at their Deli Mann's Delicatessen on Fore Street. Mail order.**

The CheeseWorks Cheltenham thecheeseworks.co.uk **Award-winning shop specializing in British, French and Spanish cheeses, with plenty of local varieties such as Double Gloucester, chutneys and biscuits. Also olives and cold meats.**

Country Cheeses Tavistock, Devon countrycheeses.co.uk **Specializes in Westcountry cheese, some made** specially for the shop. Branches in Topsham (Exeter) and Totnes.

Daylesford Farm Shop near Stow-on-the-Wold, Gloucestershire daylesfordorganic.com **A destination deli and café. You won't be disappointed by the trek to find it. Artisan breads, biscuits, tarts and cakes baked on the premises, vegetables, dairy and Cheddar from Daylesford farm as well as a carefully chosen selection of excellent cheeses (and delicious homemade cheese biscuits) and Serrano ham on the bone. There is also a wide range of organic coffee, tea and chocolate.**

Effings Totnes, Devon effings.co.uk **Well-stocked with local and world foods (Lebanese, Spanish, Italian), including freshly baked baguettes, deli counter with exceptional olives, local and continental cheeses, cooked meats and pâtés (try the seasonal game pâté), and cakes.**

The Fine Cheese Company Walcot Street, Bath finecheese.co.uk **Over one hundred carefully sourced and stored cheeses as well as excellent own label chutneys (try their fig), cold meats and flavoured cheese biscuits.**

Goodies Deli Larkhall, Bath goodiesdeli.co.uk **Supplying local shoppers with cheese, meats, fish and bread for twenty years. Part of a thriving old-fashioned high street, which still boasts its own butcher and greengrocer.**

Harvest Walcot Street, Bath harvest-bath.coop **Long-running health food shop cooperative and co-founder of Essential Foods (suppliers of dry goods, natural foods to health food shops throughout the UK). Good selection of dry goods, spices, vegetarian and vegan foods and locally made bread.**

Hobbs House Bakery Chipping Sodbury hobbshousebakery.co.uk **Delicious traditionally made organic bread (especially their wild wheat white and G-stone) made from Shipton Flour and delivered to regional delis. Branches in Nailsworth and Tetbury shops, too, where you can buy their yummy coffee and walnut and Old Sodbury cakes and doughnuts.**

House of Cheese Tetbury, Gloucestershire houseofcheese.co.uk **The Prince of Wales's local. Award-winning cheese supplier specializing in hard English cheeses such as Godsells mature Single Gloucester and soft-rind French cheeses.**

Sharpham Park Shop Shepton Mallet, Somerset kilvercourt.com **Organic food produced within a fifty-mile radius, including their own excellent spelt grains, flour, bread and biscuits. Also has a proper butcher's and cheese counter.**

Moby Nicks Dartmouth, Devon ▷ 01803 839070 **Locally caught fish and shell-fish and locally smoked fish at affordable prices from expert fishmonger Nick. You can also pick your lobster from the tank!**

Papadeli Alma Road, Bristol papadeli. co.uk **Small well-stocked Italian deli (and Spanish produce): charcuterie, smoked fish and artisan cheeses. Homemade foods including salads, moussaka and beef en daube.**

Phil Bowditch Fishmongers Taunton, Somerset ▷ 01823 253500 **Fish is expertly sourced by this former fisherman at the nearby Brixham auction. Specialities include**

Rice and grains

Say farewell to boil-in-the-bag and plastic trays of rice, and explore the wonderful world of grains. Rice, the staple food of half the world's population, comes in dozens of forms. Delis, health food shops and ethnic grocers are all good sources.

▶ **Basmati** Aromatic long-grain from Northern India and Pakistan. Benefits from short soaking period before cooking.

▶ **Thai jasmine** A white smooth rice with gently perfumed flavour.

▶ **Risotto rice** Short-grained Italian rice that is designed to soak up plenty of liquid in cooking (like Spanish paella rice). Aficionados swear by Vialone nano.

▶ **Wild rice** A native North American marsh grass with long dark grains that split in cooking. Good mixed with other plainer rices. Also try nutty Camargue red rice.

And alternatives...

▶ **Quinoa** South American grain with very high protein content.

▶ **Couscous** North African staple. Good in salads and with stews and rich sauces.

▶ **Bulgur** Chunky wheat kernels. Quick to prepare and good for soaking up sauces. High in fibre and protein.

▶ **Spelt** Low-gluten alternative to rice in risottos or to barley in soups. Seek out Sharpham Park's organic pearled spelt.

▶ **Polenta** Italian cornmeal which can be eaten "wet" (runny) or "dry" (set and then grilled in slices). Excellent with mushrooms or blue cheese sauce.

Find out more

The Rice Book Sri Owen (Frances Lincoln, 2003) for everything you could want to know about the history and culture of rice, plus hundreds of recipes.

---

incredibly fresh scallops, Dover sole, red mullet and wild sea bream.

Quayside Fish Porthleven, Cornwall quaysidefish.co.uk Fishmongers and deli selling oak-smoked crevettes and salmon, Cornish fish straight off the day boats, as well as award-winning chutneys and preserves.

River Cottage Stores Ltd Axminster, Devon rivercottage.net Local dairy, meat, cheese and bread sourced by Hugh Fearnley-Whittingstall along

with jams, chutneys, chocolate and all manner of snacks.

Williams Fish Market and Food Hall Nailsworth, Gloucestershire williamsfoodhall.co.uk Does what it says and extremely well. Brilliant fish counter and generous bunches of fresh herbs (including hard to find chervil), exquisite white peaches, plenty of deli items and homemade foods, including fish pie.

Wyndhams Delicatessen Poundbury, Dorchester wyndhamsfood.com A deli

Home-made cake by post

If you hanker after the taste of home-made cakes and are too busy (or lazy) to get into the kitchen, **Meg Rivers'** Cotswold cakes could be the answer. They are not cheap, but they are good value: made of natural ingredients and free-range eggs in small batches, using traditional methods (and a mixer three times the size of Nigella's Kitchen Aid). Their flapjack and nutty brownies can be passed off as your own in your child's lunchbox (small pieces work out at about 50p each) and Christmas guests will be impressed with the Christmas cake loaded with dense fruit and nuts and topped with real toasted marzipan. The bestselling **chunky chocolate cake**, made with hazelnut flour and gianduja, is satisfyingly homely. Keep a few pieces in the freezer which can be warmed up as an emergency pudding with a dollop of cream. They also do a "Starving Student" box. Order online (megrivers.com).

Other cake companies to try (available in supermarkets and health food shops):

▶ **Village Bakery** (village-bakery.com) Organic award-winning brownies and gluten-free Rich Fruit Cake Slices.

▶ **Honeybuns** (honeybuns.co.uk) A small company based in Dorset which makes readymade cake slices, including wheat- and dairy-free versions.

▶ **Sussex-based Organic Cake Company** (theorganiccakecompany.co.uk) Try this Sussex-based bakery's carrot and walnut cake and traditional Victoria sponge.

with a local food focus selling a wide range of organic fresh and cooked meats, including bestselling cooked ham with honey and mustard glaze.

Central England

Appleyards Shrewsbury, Shropshire ▷ 01743 240180 English cheese and locally cured ham are a speciality.

Aubrey Allen Leamington Spa, Warwickshire aubreyallen.co.uk Award-winning butcher which sells free-range pork, Cornish lamb and inventive range of sausages.

R. Browne Lonsdale Road, Harborne ▷ 0121 427 2057 Birmingham's award-winning butcher sells Tamworth pork and Longhorn beef from Quenby.

The Cheese Society St Martin's Lane, Lincoln thecheesesociety.co.uk Huge selection of cheeses and a café. An imaginative monthly selection of five cheeses can be sent to mail-order customers.

Colston Bassett Store Colston Bassett, Nottinghamshire colstonbassettstore.com Sells Colston Bassett Stilton straight from the maturing room at the dairy. Also by mail order.

Cotswold Fine Foods Chipping Norton, Oxfordshire ▷ 01608 642843 Good traditional deli with fine range of Cotswold cheeses.

Deli Flavour Stoneygate, Leicester deliflavour.net This deli has a particularly extensive range of Leicestershire foods, organic foods and Fairtrade teas and coffees.

Deli on the Square Ludlow, Shropshire delionthesquare.co.uk A traditional delicatessen in one of England's pre-eminent food towns.

Delilah Fine Foods Middle Pavement, Nottingham delilahfinefoods.co.uk This shop only opened in 2005 but quickly gained national recognition for the quality and range of its stock. Winner of the 2007 *BBC Good Food* magazine Independent Delicatessen of the Year, it was praised as setting "a template for delis of the future".

Elliott's Kitchen and Butcher's Towcester, Northants ▷ 01327 350454 Traditional deli and butcher's which sells their own beef and lamb.

M. Feller, Son & Daughter The Covered Market, Oxford ▷ 01865 251164 One of the first organic butchers in the country, who also sells in season game. Check out the other butchers and the **Oxford Cheese Company** in Oxford's covered market.

Field Fayre Ross-On-Wye, Herefordshire field-fayre.co.uk Local organic fayre.

Fish in a Box Newport, Shropshire www.fishinabox.co.uk As the name suggests, sustainably sourced, very fresh fish delivered to your door.

Fresh Basil Belper, Derbyshire freshbasil.co.uk Deli that promotes local producers from Derbyshire.

The Granary Delicatessen Watlington, Oxfordshire granarydeli.co.uk Prides itself on a selection of cheeses that tastes unlike their supermarket equivalents. Also online ordering.

Gonalston Farm Shop Gonalston, Nottingham gonalstonfarmshop.co.uk Fish from South Coast day boats, well-hung beef reared on their own pastures, and lamb and pork from farms within an eight-mile radius of the shop are just some of the highlights here.

Hay Wholefoods and Delicatessen Hay-on-Wye, Herefordshire ▷ 01497 820708 Organic meat and other local produce.

Haymans Fisheries The Covered Market, Oxford haymansfisheries.co.uk This fishmonger has been trading for eighty years. Fish sourced daily from inshore boats from Brixham in Devon and the Cornish ports.

Honeysuckle Wholefoods Cooperative Oswestry, Shropshire honeysuckle-wholefoods.co.uk Traditional health food shop.

Reg Martin Ludlow, Shropshire ▷ 01584 872008 This is just one of several butchers in the small market town of Ludlow. Reg Martin's shop stocks marbled sides of beef, venison, free-range chickens and award-winning

Real chocolate

Forget the mass-produced "Belgian chocolates" of the high street; there's no short-age of innovative and often ethically right-on chocolate-makers if you know where to look for them. Here are some of the best:

▶ **Montezuma chocolate** monetzumas.co.uk was founded in Brighton by two ex-lawyers. Much of their imaginative range is organic and hand-made. Try their **choco:block** for a serious slab of chocolate or their geranium and orange flavour.

▶ Brussels-based **Pierre Marcolini** (marcolini.be) manufactures his *grand cru* chocolate himself using cocoa beans that he selects personally, very much a rarity these days. You can find his chocolates in London at **Verde and Company** in Spitalfields.

▶ **Organic Seed and Bean Company** organicseedandbean.co.uk Organic and largely Fairtrade chocolate. As well as bars flavoured with mint, lavender or rose, they also make chocolate-covered pumpkin and sunflower seeds.

▶ **Artisan du chocolat** artisanduchocolat.com State-of-the-art high tech chocolatiers whose range includes delectable liquid salted caramels and incredible thin chocolate wafers filled with fruit *coulis*.

▶ **Divine** divinechocolate.com The first Fairtrade chocolate bar launched in the UK in 1998. The company is co-owned by the cocoa farmers cooperative Kuapa Kokoo in Ghana, who not only receive a fair price for their cocoa but also share in the company's profit. Try their orange milk chocolate or mint wafers.

▶ **Valrhona** valrhona.com is the chocolate of choice for many chefs. The French company's no-nonsense, high-quality blocks of white, dark and milk chocolate are available from many delis as well as Fresh and Wild.

▶ **Cocoa Loco** cocoaloco.co.uk is a Sussex-based family firm with strong ethical credentials, famous for its Kilner jars full of irresistible giant chocolate buttons.

▶ **James Chocolates** jameschocolates.co.uk Hand-made chocolates from Somerset stocked in John Lewis, Fortnum & Mason, Harvey Nichols and independents. Try their chocolate discs flavoured with aromatic essential oils.

▶ **Rococo Chocolates** rococochocolates.com is the home of the **Chocolate Society**. Try their exotically flavoured chocolate wafers, such as coffee and cardamom, cocoa-dusted roasted almonds and wide range of truffles. Shops on the King's Road and Marylebone High Street.

---

sausages. Also check out **D.W. Wall and Son**, a rare breed specialist.

Melton Cheeseboard Melton Mowbray, Leicestershire meltoncheeseboard.co.uk **Specializes in Stilton**.

Mousetrap Cheese branches in Leominster, Hereford and Ludlow mousetrapcheese.co.uk They not only sell but also make cheese from their own local herd: crumbly Monkland and creamy Little Hereford.

Staffordshire Organic Cheese Acton, Newcastle-under-Lyme, Staffordshire staffordshireorganic.com **Farm shop and maker of Staffordshire organic cheese, a traditional Cheddar made from raw cow's milk.**

Rossiters Organic Butchers Mary Vale Road, Bourneville ▷ 0121 458 1598 **The first certified organic butcher in Birmingham, Rossiter's is family run and sells a wide range of fully traceable meat, poultry and fish.**

Ryan & Son Much Wenlock, Shropshire ▷ 01952 727409 **Butcher who sources all his meat from within five miles.**

Wild & Free Rugby, Warwickshire wildandfree.net **Organic fruit, veg, meat and other groceries.**

Wenlock Edge Farm Longville in the Dale, Shropshire wenlockedgefarm.com. **Artisan makers of traditional award-winning bacon, ham, charcuterie and Shropshire black pudding.**

T.O. Williams of Wem four shops in Shropshire williamsofwem.co.uk **Their cheese buyer is the chief judge of the World Cheese Awards. That says it all.**

North-West England

Alston Wholefoods Alston, Cumbria ▷ 01434 381588 **Cooperative in the highest market town in England, which sells local Moody Baker breads, Wild & Fruitful preserves and local cheeses such as Doddingtons Cheddar.**

Barbakan Chorleton-cum-Hardy, Manchester barbakan-deli.co.uk **Long-established deli with a famous bakery producing 15,000 loaves a week from roast potato bread to fruit** soda as well as Polish cheesecake. **Artisan cheeses and meats from Germany, Poland and Italy.**

The Cheese Hamlet Didsbury, Manchester cheesehamlet.co.uk **South Manchester cheese-lovers' haven, well-stocked with deli goods, too.**

The Cheese Shop Chester chestercheeseshop.co.uk **Foodie landmark with over two hundred local (Lancashire a speciality) and continental cheeses ripened in the shop's cellars. Rose Prince has called it "one of the best cheese shops outside London".**

Churchmouse Cheeses Kirkby Lonsdale churchmousecheeses.com **Small shop with perfect cheeses, especially local Cumbrian Croglin, Ribblesdale Blue and Lancashire varieties. Also try their delicious quiches and curd tarts. Named best independent cheese shop in Britain in 2007.**

Delifonseca Stanley Street, Liverpool delifonseca.co.uk **Excellent well-stocked deli selling regional cold meats (including Cheshire Smokehouse's air-dried prosciutto) and cheeses such as Applebys cloth-wrapped Cheshire.**

The Great Tasting Meat Company Nantwich, Cheshire greattastingmeat.co.uk **Farmer Andrew Jackson is a founder of the Cheshire Slow Food group and sells his Hereford and Dexter beef from his farm shop and at local markets.**

Growing with Grace Clapham, Lancaster growingwithgrace.co.uk **Organic food shop which sells freshly picked salad leaves from its own greenhouses along with bread, milk and veg boxes to local addresses.**

Howbarrow Organic Farm Grange-over-Sands, Cumbria howbarroworganic.co.uk **Online delivery service for local organic products (meat, bread, vegetables) including organic trout and salmon from Hawkshead Trout Farm as well as dried goods from natural foods wholesaler, Suma.**

J & J Graham Penrith, Cumbria ▷ 01768 862281 **Sells locally made pies, quiches and bread (including organic bread from nearby Village Bakery). Local cheeses a speciality, including Blengdale Blue and brie-like Keldthwaite Gold.**

Katsouris Deli Deansgate, Manchester ▷ 0161 8191260 **Popular Mediterranean specialist: excellent meze, roast meats and salads.**

Low Sizergh Barn Kendal, Cumbria lowsizerghbarn.co.uk **Award-winning organic dairy farm used for local Kendal cheese varieties and organic eggs, a farm shop full of local hedgerow jams and ice-creams, Borrowdale tea bread, Cumbrian meat and a varied artisan cheese counter.**

Mossley Organic and Fine Foods Mossley, Manchester mossleyorganicandfine-foods.co.uk **Organic family-run grocery store selling over 3000 different products including local Saddleworth Grandpa Green's banoffee ice cream. Veg box scheme for Glossop, Oldham and Tameside.**

On the Eighth Day Oxford Road, Manchester eighth-day.co.uk **Co-operative shop since 1970 keeps local university students in vegetarian and vegan foods as well as bread and cakes baked on site.**

Organicfair Chester organicfair.co.uk **Award-winning organic supermarket (open seven days a week). It also stocks the excellent Dr Hauschka skincare range.**

The Real Food Company Alsager, Cheshire ▷ 01270 873322 **Organic meat, fish (salmon, sustainably farmed smoked haddock, herring and prawns), dairy, wholefoods and fruit and veg.**

Unicorn Grocery Chorlton, Manchester unicorn-grocery.co.uk **Award-winning trendy co-op deli selling vegan foods, locally grown fruit and veg, and gluten-free cakes as well as the local and continental delicacies.**

Wild Carrot Buxton, Derbyshire wild-carrot.co.uk **Vegetarian co-op selling a wide range of local produce (it also has a box scheme) including bread and honey, vegan and speciality foods.**

Windmill Wholefoods Smithdown Road, Liverpool windmillorganic.co.uk **Organic cooperative selling locally baked bread from the German Bakery (try the rye sourdough bread with ginger and sesame seeds).**

North-East England

Alligator Fishergate, York alligatorwholefoods.co.uk **Independent organic wholefoods shop specializing in fresh fruit and veg, locally sourced where available.**

Arcimboldo's Delicatessen King's Road, Harrogate, Yorkshire ▷ 01423 508760 **Italian, Spanish and local produce.**

The Balloon Tree Farm Shop, Gate Helmsley, York theballoontree.co.uk

Spice up your life

Spices bring a touch of exoticism to cooking as nothing else can. But visit the supermarket spice aisle and you're confronted with a sad array of identical jars of dried spices, ground and packed months ago, their subtle flavours already fading. And most of us have a dusty shelf of out-of-date spices in our kitchen. But it needn't be this way: imagine receiving a package of spices through the post that were ground and blended just days before, the volatile flavours still powerful. That's the service offered by a number of companies such as **Sambava Spices**. Company founder James Ransome, a former chef, set up the business in order to bring into the British kitchen some of the intense flavours he'd encountered on his travels overseas.

His range has now grown to 190 different spices, many of them sourced direct from suppliers overseas. He told Rough Guides that the secret is to use them when they're fresh and not to be afraid of them. He reckons that every kitchen should have a basic stock of aromatic black peppercorns, Aleppo chili flakes, allspice (for Caribbean and Middle Eastern dishes), cumin, coriander, turmeric and paprika. Not forgetting his aromatic black peppercorns. Beyond that, you should have fun experimenting with the inexhaustible world of spice combinations. To provide inspiration, James has a subscription service in which you receive a package of spices and recipe ideas every month.

Sambava Spices sambavaspices.com

Seasoned Pioneers seasonedpioneers.co.uk
Site with a high reputation for its wide range of spices. Mail order available.

The World of Spice Michael Bateman (Kyle Cathie, 2006) **A book bursting with spicy recipes from around the world.**

Rare breed meats, seasonal fruit and veg, and quality ready meals.

Beano Wholefoods North Street, Leeds beanowholefoods.co.uk **Leeds' only 100% vegetarian shop. Much of its produce is locally sourced.**

Blacker Hall Farm Shop Wakefield, W. Yorks blackerhall.com **Beef, pork and lamb from the farm and home-baked bread and quiche.**

The Blagdon Farm Shop Blagdon theblagdonfarmshop.co.uk **"What's good for you is good for the country-side" is this farm shop's philosophy.**

Here you'll find local and rare breed meats from Northumberland, local cheeses, and Craster kippers.

Bondgate Bakery Otley, West Yorkshire ▷ 01943 467516 **Baking both traditional (Yorkshire curd tarts) and exotic (potato, pumpkin seed and sage loaves).**

Bradford Wholefoods Shipley, Bradford, ▷ 01422 202648 **Organic produce from a farm run by mental health charity, the Cellar Project.**

Café Royal bakery and delicatessen Nelson Street, Newcastle www.sjf.co.uk

One of the top artisanal bakeries in the country.

The Cheeseboard Harrogate, North Yorkshire britnett-carver. co.uk/thecheeseboard **Renowned Yorkshire's cheese shop. Around two hundred different types on display.**

Cranstons Butchers Cattle Market, Hexham ▷ 01434 602271 **Meat products from Northumberland, Cumbria and Yorkshire.**

Cross of York Newgate Market, York ▷ 01904 627590 **Wet fishmonger on the marketplace every day, selling fresh fish from the Yorkshire coast, including Whitby crab.**

Daniela's Jesmond, Newcastle-upon-Tyne ▷ 0191 2811142 **Deli that stocks Italian, Greek and Spanish food.**

Deli at Darras Ponteland, Northumberland deliatdarras.co.uk **An "eclectic mix of regional, British and international fine foods" in smart surroundings.**

Fine Foods of Yorkshire Easingwold finefoodsofyorkshire.com **One of the owners of this deli used to be a butcher, so meat is a particular strength.**

Food Therapy Northgate, Halifax ▷ 01422 350826 **Wholefoods and organic are all part of the therapy. Good selection of breads, too, and a local veg box scheme.**

The Green Shop Berwick Upon Tweed, Northumberland ▷ 01289 305566 **Wide range of all-organic products.**

Henshelwood's Deli Newgate Market, York ▷ 01904 673877 **Good selection of Yorkshire cheeses and prepared dishes using local ingredients.**

The Honey Tree Heaton Road, Newcastle thehoneytree.org **A social enterprise which reinvests profits in the community, and sells the widest range of local and organic foods that the region has to offer.**

Lewis & Cooper Northallerton lewisandcooper.co.uk **Award-winning independent gourmet food store since 1899.**

Love Organic! Chapel Allerton, Leeds ▷ (0113) 266 3030 **Organic store with wide range of produce on offer as well as a box scheme.**

McConnell Thomas Hovingham and Kirkbymoorside, North Yorkshire mcconnellthomas.co.uk **These are general stores "with an eco-twist", which means lots of organic, Fairtrade and low-carbon footprint products.**

Moorhouse Farm Shop Stannington, Morpeth moorhousefarmshop.co.uk **Local products include lamb and pork direct from the farm.**

Org Great George Street, Leeds org-organics.org.uk **Leeds' first all-organic store, offering "the best in organic, sustainable, ethical and locally sourced goods". You can also shop online.**

Out of this World Nottingham, Leeds and Newcastle outofthisworld.coop **Out of this World is a cooperative with 16,000 members and shops in three cities. They claim to stock the country's widest range of ethically sourced goods.**

Ridley's Fish & Game Corbridge, Northumberland ridleysfishandgame. co.uk **Top quality fresh fish, seafood, poultry and local wild game.**

A nation of snackers

According to *The Grocer* magazine "one in every three meals is now a snack." So if you're going to eat snacks, make sure you choose really good ones with high-quality ingredients, low salt and no artificial additives. Order online, avoid mass-produced versions and you may discover some new favourites.

▶ **Olives Et Al** olivesetal.co.uk This small independent producer sells carefully sourced, top-quality olives in a wide range of marinades (popular varieties are chilli, garlic and black pepper and rosemary oil and sundried tomato). They also kiln-roast their own nuts in a variety of spice mixes to create very addictive snacks. Try the wonderful Siena nut and seed mix or the harissa kiln-roasted almonds. Habas Fritas are unusual, very tasty dried broad beans and their tapenade maroaine (olive pâté) is excellent on toast as a quick starter. They supply delis, Harvey Nichols and restaurants, but you can also buy direct from their website.

▶ **Liberation** chooseliberation.com This 100% Fairtrade company, sells a range of really fresh-tasting oven-baked, lightly salted or unsalted cashew and peanut mixes (as well as a tasty lemon and chilli variety). Comedian Harry Hill worked with Liberation to produce his own Fairtrade "Harry's Nuts" from small producers in Malawi. Liberation are 42%-owned by the nut farmers of Brazil, Malawi, Nicaragua, Peru and India. Buy them at the **Ethical Superstore** (bulk buy discount) or from supermarkets such as Waitrose and Oxfam shops. The company also supplies Fairtrade nuts for Tesco, Sainsbury's, the Co-op and Morrisons.

▶ **Burts** and **Tyrells** If you enjoy crisps, buy brands which make them properly, where they end up as close to a potato slice as possible. (According to a 2008 High Court ruling, Pringles are not crisps as they contain only 42% potato and are a shape "not found in nature".) Kettle Chips are now a big supermarket premium crisp category with sales of £60m a year. Try Burts or Tyrells potato (and other root vegetable) crisps. Both companies produce some of the crunchiest, tastiest real potato crisps in low-salt and weird and wonderful flavours. They're available in some supermarkets and from delis.

Salt's Delicatessen Swinegate, Leeds saltsdeli.co.uk **Popular Spanish-style delicatessen, also to be found at local farmers' markets.**

Stewart & Co Fine Food and Butchery West Jesmond stewartandcofinefood. co.uk **An attractive large shop selling** organic meats, handmade cheese, freshly baked bread, handmade cakes and local fruit vegetables.

Valley Garden Organics Hebden Bridge ▷ 01422 846651 **A community enterprise that gives priority to local produce from surrounding farms.**

Weeton's West Park, Harrogate weetons.com Deli set up by three dairy farmers, stocking twelve hundred Yorkshire products from fifty local farms. As their website says: "No middle men. No corporate HQ. No food miles. No misleading special offers."

Wensleydale Cheese Shop Hawes, North Yorkshire wensleydale.co.uk You can see their range of traditional waxed and muslin-bound cheeses being made, and take them home with you.

Wales

Blas ar Fwyd Llanrwst, Conwy blasarfwyd.com Award-winning deli specializing in Welsh cheeses and meats, their own home-made bread and ready-meals, and organic and continental foods.

Barita Delicatessen Llandeilo, Carmarthenshire barita.co.uk Well-stocked with local Welsh ham, cheeses (try Caws Cenarth organic brie) and Llanfaes ice cream along with homemade bread and tarts.

Beanfreaks St Mary's Street, Cardiff beanfreaks.com Chain of traditional health food shops since the 1970s offering dried nuts, cereals, pulses and rice along with vegetarian and vegan foods. Branches in Bridgend, Cwmbran and Newport.

Blasau Delicatessen Machynlleth, Powys ▷ 01654 700 410 Selection of organic vegetables and a well-stocked deli counter with olives, stuffed peppers, cakes and single estate chocolate.

Castle Kitchen Montgomery, Powys ▷ 01686 668795 Home of the famous Montgomery cheddar, this deli sells plenty of local produce as well as store-cupboard basics.

Clement & Cosgrove Mumbles, Swansea ▷ 01792 363006 Seaside deli with all you'd need for a beach picnic: Perl Las cheese, locally baked herb breads, hams, pink lemonade and meze.

Face of Flowers Llambed Business Park Lampeter face-of-flowers-organic. co.uk Shop in their Aladdin's cave of a warehouse or online for Welsh mountain lamb, organic burgers and sausages, local preserves (try H&P's green bean relish or carrot and caraway chutney) and cheeses. Also dried goods from Essential.

Foxy's Deli Penarth foxysdeli.com Locally made foods include Snowdonia Cheddar, Welsh patties and wild fig ice-cream. Also continental items. Branch at Newport.

Goodies Swansea Market Hall ▷ 07793 589596 Welsh (Caerfai Cheddar) and continental cheeses, chorizo and pork pies, olives and fresh pasta.

The Organic Stores Ruthin, Denbighshire ▷ 01824 705796 Organic shopping at its best: fruit and veg, Graig Farm meat and fish, Welsh cheeses and pies to go.

Pop Ty-r Dref Town Bakery Dolgellau, Gwynedd ▷ 01341 422507 Bread, cakes and tarts, local bacon, ham and cheese; preserves and honey.

St David's Food and Wine St David's, Pembrokeshire ▷ 01437 721948 Well-stocked cheese and cold meats counter, delicious Welsh Bara-Brith fruit loaf and other local products.

Sarah's Delicatessen Beaumaris, Anglesey sarahsdelicatessen-coffeehouse.co.uk Diverse range of regional (smoked Anglesey bacon) and continental meats and deli items, over one hundred cheeses, herbs and spices, and traditional produce such as laver (seaweed) bread.

The Source Caerphilly, Glamorgan ▷ 029 2088 3236 Vegetarian and organic deli with pâtés and salads as well as healthy ready meals.

Ultracomida Deli Narberth, Dyfed ultracomida.com Good range of continental deli items, Welsh cheeses (try the creamy blue Gorau Glas) and meats. Ready meals made from local produce and Spanish tapas also available. Aberystwyth branch.

Wally's Deli Cardiff wallysdeli.co.uk Continental-style deli in a Victorian shopping arcade, which is still run

by the Austrian family who founded it in 1948. Amazing range of salamis such as Hungarian Czabi pepperoni with paprika and Spanish morcilla, Eastern European specialities and an olive bar.

Wenallt Stores Llanbedr, Gwynedd ▷ 01341 241220 Sells bread and local produce: Welsh cheese, cooked meats, fruit and veg.

Wholefoods of Newport Pembrokeshire ▷ 01239 820773 Traditional health food shop selling dried goods alongside organic veg and eggs and a wide range of local honeys. Look out for the Celtic Crunch ice-cream with local toffee brittle.

Scotland

Armstrongs of Stockbridge Raeburn Place, Edinburgh armstrongsofstockbridge.co.uk Traditional fishmonger which has been in business for over sixty years, with a reputation for super-fresh fish and its own smokehouse on site.

Berits & Brown Kippen, Stirlingshire beritsandbrown.com Launched in rural Stirlingshire, this company now has delis throughout the country. The accent is on "high quality, fresh and honest produce from all over the UK".

Chisolms of Ayr Carrik Street, Ayr chisholmsofayrdeli.com Award-winning family deli with big cheese selection and local Ayrshire lamb.

Cocoa Mountain Durness, Sutherland cocoamountain.co.uk Located in the most north-westerly village in the country, Cocoa Mountain makes delicious preservative-free chocolates and truffles. Also mail order.

Cockles Delicatessen Lochgilphead ▷ 01546 606292 Local cheeses (including Isle of Mull brie), olives, smoked salmon and organic breads.

The Corner on the Square Beauly, Inverness-shire corneronthesquare. co.uk Village deli, favourites include featuring Fairtrade, organic and locally sourced foods such as Highland herb hams and local heather honey.

Crombies Broughton Street, Edinburgh ▷ 0131 557 0111 Butcher famous for its free-range pork sausages and haggis.

Damhead Organic Food Lothianburn, Edinburgh damhead.co.uk Organic farm shop and veg box scheme which delivers throughout Scotland.

Delizique Hyndland Street, Glasgow delizique.co.uk Probably Glasgow's finest deli, now with a café. Much of the food is prepared on site, including the excellent bread and cakes.

Falko Bruntsfield Place, Edinburgh falko.co.uk Award-winning German cakes by the eponymous Falko. Also a regular at Edinburgh farmers' market. Also in Gullane, East Lothian.

Fletchers of Auchermuchty seriouslygoodvenison.co.uk Mail order venison and farm shop, acclaimed by the likes of Gordon Ramsay.

Grassroots Woodlands Road, Glasgow grassrootsorganic.com A Soil Association award-winning organic wholefoods supermarket which sells home-produced fruit and veg.

Heart Buchanan Byres Road, Glasgow heartbuchanan.co.uk Everything is made on-site by a team of chefs in this West End deli, so that you can discover "the joy of not cooking".

Henderson's Farm Shop Hanover Street, Edinburgh hendersonsofedinburgh. co.uk Vegetarian organic fare.

Kathellan Home Farm Kelty, Fife kathellan.co.uk Rare-breed meat from the farm plus local fruit and veg, and bread baked on the premises.

The Manna House Easter Road, Edinburgh manna-house-edinburgh. co.uk Open-plan bakery and pâtisserie which uses all natural local ingredients. Also stocks other Scottish produce.

McCallums Houldsworth Street, Glasgow ▷ 0141 204 4456 Fresh fish and shellfish still gleaming from the sea. The most reasonable place in town for langoustines, lobster and a host of other sea food. They also have an oyster bar on the coast in Troon.

Charles MacLeod Stornoway, Isle of Lewis charlesmacleod.co.uk Best Butcher in Scotland 2008 according to the *Scotsman*. Certainly the finest black pudding, widely stocked in Scotland and available by mail order.

I.J. Mellis Cheesemonger Great Western Road, Glasgow ▷ 0141 339 8998 Probably Scotland's pre-eminent

cheesemonger. Excellent selection of British cheeses from small producers, as well as well kept continental selection. Branches in Edinburgh and Aberdeen.

Menzies of Dunkeld Dunkeld, Perthshire menziesofdunkeld.co.uk Local smoked salmon and honey as well as fine wine in this delicatessen situated between Perth and Pitlochry.

Phoenix Community Stores Findhorn Bay, Forres, Moray phoenixshop.co.uk Findhorn is an eco-village community, so Phoenix specializes in local, organic, Fairtrade and artisan foods and products.

Puddledub Pork & Fifeshire Bacon Co. Auchtertool, Fife puddledub.co.uk Dry-cured bacon, fine hams, delicious sausages and fresh tasty pork delivered to your home from this small family business.

Real Foods Broughton Street and Brougham Street, Edinburgh realfoods. co.uk Long-established and good old-fashioned health food shops with extensive range.

The Really Garlicky Company reallygarlicky.co.uk Under the slogan "It's chic to reek!" this Farm Entrepreneur of the Year 2008 supplies shops throughout the UK with top-notch garlic. Website is full of garlicky tips and facts.

Roots and Fruits Great Western Road and Byres Road, Glasgow ▷ 0141 339 3077 Organic meat, bread and over 200 other organic products at reasonable prices.

John Saunderson Leven Street, Edinburgh johnsaunderson.co.uk Rated by the cognoscenti as the best butcher in the capital.

The Store branches in Edinburgh and Ellon, Aberdeenshire thestorecompany.co.uk Dry-aged Aberdeen Angus beef and grass-fed lamb are the specialities here plus high-quality, locally produced poultry, fish, deli products, field grown vegetables and cheeses.

The Taste of Moray near Nairn, Inverness-shire tasteofmoray.co.uk Highland food specialist, whose range includes Inverawe smoked fish and seafood.

Valvona & Crolla Elm Row, Edinburgh valvonacrolla.co.uk Scotland's world-famous delicatessen, crammed full of the finest Italian produce, bread baked on site and dishes made with local produce. They also have a VinCaffè at Multrees Walk.

Northern Ireland

Ballylagan Organic Farm Ballyclare, Belfast ballylagan.com This was the first organic farm in Northern Ireland to open a farm shop. They sell a variety of organic fruit and vegetables, meat from native British breeds of sheep, pigs and cattle and eggs, including our own home-grown seasonal produce.

Causeway Cheese Company Loughgiel, Co. Antrim causewaycheese.com Based near the famous Giant's Causeway, this traditional cheesemaker's products are sold throughout Northern Ireland. Try their Ballyveely goat's cheese and the dulse (seaweed-flavoured) cheese.

Drumgooland Smokehouse Ballyward, Co. Down ▷ 028 4065 0720 A wide variety of hot-smoked fish is produced by this traditional smokehouse, including Guinness and turf-smoked salmon, smoked organic eel and smoked trout pâté with orange.

Dublin

Although full listings for Ireland are beyond the scope of this book, here are some favourite addresses in the Irish capital:

Avoca Suffolk Street avoca.ie The best bread in the city: delicious cake-like multi-seed and cheese-streaked white loaves. Also cakes, ready-made salads and quiches.

Fallon & Byrne Exchequer Street fallonandbyrne.net Enormous gourmet foodhall selling meat, locally caught fish, vegetables and fruit.

Sheridans South Anne Street sheridanscheesemongers.com Local and regional artisan cheeses, such as the delicious St Tola goat's cheese (and a good selection of wines, too).

Fivemiletown Creamery Fivemiletown, Co. Tyrone fivemiletown.com Maker of the multi-award-winning Ballyoak cheese, smoked with oakwood from local forests.

Pheasants' Hill Farm Shop Downpatrick, Co. Down pheasantshill.com UK TV food hero finalist sells meat from rare breeds: sausages, old-fashioned dry-cured hams and bacon.

Primacy Meats Bangor, Co. Down primacymeatsfoodvillage.co.uk A butcher's shop, bakery and green-grocer's all rolled into one. A wealth of locally sourced produce in this "food village".

Sawers Fountain Centre, Belfast sawersbelfast.com The oldest deli in town and generally reckoned to be the best, it excels particularly in sea-food and cheeses.

Swanton's Gourmet Foods Lisburn Road, Belfast swantons.com Irish and imported foods, plus homemade dishes.

Yellow Door Deli Woodhouse Street, Portadown yellowdoordeli.co.uk This deli now has a Lisburn Road branch in Belfast, too. Breads are baked on the premises (such as treacle breads and fruit soda loaf), as is the pâtisserie and there are lots of upmarket ready meals on offer, too.

Shopping online

Artisanal cheese

Neal's Yard Dairy nealsyarddairy.co.uk

The Fine Cheese Co. finecheese.co.uk

Paxton & Whitfield paxtonandwhitfield.co.uk

Fish

Andy Race andyrace.co.uk Organic smoked salmon and langoustine, as well as the delectable Finnan haddock and hot-smoked mackerel.

Hebridean Smokehouse hebrideansmokehouse.com Peat-smoked salmon and sea trout; smoked scallops and hot-smoked salmon pâté.

Graig Farm graigfarm.co.uk Sustainable fish as well as a wide range of organic meat (mutton, goat as well as more usual chicken and pork) reared by this mid-Wales farm or by other small producers.

Loch Duart Salmon lochduart.com Delicious sustainable salmon and smoked fish.

Organic Smokehouse organicsmokehouse.com Delicate oak-smoked naturally pale smoked salmon and mousse, smoked Herefordshire Cheddar and Halen Môn Sea Salt.

Inverawe Smokehouse smokedsalmon.co.uk Traditional smokehouse selling oak-smoked salmon, pâtés and fresh fish.

Organic meat

Clare's Organics Faringdon, Oxfordshire claresorganics.co.uk Locally reared chicken beef, lamb, mutton and pork.

Churchtown Farm Organic Produce County Down, Northern Ireland churchtownfarmorganicproduce.com Award-winning beef, lamb and pork.

Elan Valley Organic Mutton elanvalley-mutton.co.uk Award-winning joints and oak-smoked mutton hams from four-year-old Welsh mountain sheep.

Langley Chase Organic Farm Wiltshire langleychase.co.uk Jane Kallaway specializes in an ancient rare breed, the spectacularly horned Manx Loaghtan sheep, to produce her multi-award-winning lamb and mutton.

Helen Browning Eastbrook Farm, Swindon, Wiltshire helenbrowningorganics.co.uk Wide range of organic meat including bacon and sausages.

Higher Hacknell Organic Meat Umberleigh, Devon higherhacknell.co.uk Local breeds butchered on site. Also sells chickens.

Hindon Organic Farm Exmoor, Somerset hindonfarm.co.uk Aberdeen Angus beef, Gloucestershire Old Spot pork and Exmoor ham.

Sheepdrove Meat Hampers Hungerford, Berkshire sheepdroveshop.com Multi-award-winning organic chicken (alpacas protect the flocks from foxes), turkey, lamb, beef and pork (shops in Bristol and Maida Vale).

Rhug Estate Organic Farm Denbighshire, Wales rhug.co.uk Joints, salt marsh lamb, gammon and artisan sausages as well as organic turkeys.

Pipers Farm Cullompton, Devon pipersfarm.com Award-winning beef from naturally fed, slow-growing Ruby Red cows, hams and bacon from cider-orchard-grazing pigs. Chickens are kept in small flocks and killed on the farm.

My Boxed Roast London myboxedroast.co.uk Free-range meat for a tradi-tional Sunday lunch or a barbecue.

Books

Trolley Wars: The Battle of the Supermarkets Judi Bevan (Profile, 2005) A broadly sympathetic account of the rise of the supermarkets, fascinating for its portrayal of the personalities and the behind-the-scenes power struggles.

Bad Food Britain: How a Nation Ruined its Appetite Joanna Blythman (Fourth Estate, 2006) We're filling our faces with rubbish: campaigning journalist's indictment of what's gone wrong with the way the nation eats.

Shopped: the Shocking Power of Britain's Supermarkets Joanna Blythman (Harper Perennial, new edition 2005) Everything the supermarkets would rather you didn't know about how they became a multi-billion pound industry and top dogs in the food chain.

The Oxford Companion to Food Alan Davidson (Oxford, 1999) A vast compendium of food knowledge from throughout history, taking in both the practical and the bizarre.

Not on the Label: What Really Goes into the Food on Your Plate Felicity Lawrence (Penguin, 2004) *Guardian* journalist's eye-opening investigation of the hidden stories of everyday foodstuffs such as bread, bananas and chicken.

Eat Your Heart Out: Why the Food Business is Bad for the Planet Felicity Lawrence (Penguin, 2008) How big business benefits from feeding us processed foods full of corn, soya and sugar, and what its true cost may be.

On Food and Cooking Harold McGee (Scribner, new edition, 2004) The modest title belies the wealth of information on food science and how to treat ingredients in this legendary reference book.

What to Eat Marion Nestle (North Point Press, 2006) An aisle-by-aisle exposé of what's really in our food to help you tell the good from the bad.

Food Politics: How the Food Industry Influences Nutrition and Health Marion Nestle (University of California Press, 2nd edition, 2007) US-focused study of how the food industry markets its products and lobbies government to ensure that it can.

Stuffed and Starved: Markets, Power and the Hidden Battle for the World Food System Raj Patel (Portobello, 2007) A billion of us eat too much while another billion go hungry. The effects of globalization on world food and the people who are trying to change things.

The Omnivore's Dilemma: The Search for a Perfect Meal in a Fast-food World Michael Pollan (Penguin, 2006) Highly respected US journalist's investigation of the food chain: what we eat, how it came to our table and what it's true cost is.

In Defence of Food: The Myth of Nutrition and the Pleasures of Eating Michael Pollan (Penguin, 2008) In the words of the *Independent*, "a watertight case for wholesome real food rather than gimmicky diets as the road to health".

The End of Food Paul Roberts (Bloomsbury, 2008) Roberts argues in impressive detail that our food system is unsustainable and that we face a "a perfect storm of sequential or even simultaneous food-related calamities".

Tescopoly: How One Shop Came Out on Top and Why It Matters Andrew Simms (Constable and Robinson, 2007) Simms' book is a grim warning of what a country of "Tesco-towns" would be like.

The Ethics of What We Eat: Why Our Food Choices Matter Peter Singer and Jim Mason (Rodale, 2008) Hands-on exploration of contemporary food choices from a leading moral philosopher. The examples are American, but the ethical thinking is international.

So Shall We Reap: What's Gone Wrong with the World's Food – and How to Fix it Colin Tudge (Penguin, 2003) An appeal for a new "enlightened agri-cuture" to feed the world's growing population rather than unbridled globalization, big agribusiness and biotech gene patenting.

Other resources

On BBC Radio Four, the **Food Programme** covers both the pleasures and the politics of food in an intelligent way. Early risers can keep up to date with what's going on in farming six mornings a week with **Farming Today** at 5.45am; for the rest of us there is a podcast. **The Archers** presents contemporary food politics (and much else besides) in fictional form; the series' agricultural story editor, Graham Harvey's book, **We Want Real Food** (Robinson, 2006), tackles the issue of where he thinks agricultural policy has gone wrong.

You can subscribe to free updates on the latest in the world of food retailing at **The Grocer** (thegrocer. co.uk.) The magazine itself comes out weekly and is an invaluable window on the world of corporate food manufacturing and retailing.

For a US slant on the world of environmental politics, with plenty of articles on food, try the Seattle-based website, **Grist** (grist.org). Unusually, and refreshingly, Grist provides, in its own words, "gloom and doom with a sense of humour".

Picture credits

4, Rough Guides, adapted by Gemma Matthews; 5, redrawn by Mike Lewis; 13, Archiv der Max-Planck-Gesellschaft, Berlin-Dahlem; 16, Pesticide Action Network; 18, Pesticide Action Network; 22, Assured Food Standards; 23, The Independent; 24, Brown Cow Organics; 27, Stock Xchange; 29, Katharine Reeve; 34, kevinzim/sxc; 35, Rare Breeds Survival Trust/Jon Durrant; 37, Katharine Reeve; 37, Compassion in World Farming; 39, Compassion in World Farming; 41, weyriver.co.uk/Phil Kemp; 42, Freedom Food Limited; 45, Defra; 48, Greenpeace/Christian Aslund; 49, Katharine Reeve; 50, Fish4Ever; 51, MFA; 52, MFA; 56, Katharine Reeve; 57, Mitch Tonks; 58, Iraklis Klampanos; 63, Marine Stewardship Council ; 66, Hormel Foods; 70, Ethical Investment Research Services, drawn by Gemma Matthews; 71, Baker Perkins; 74, Katharine Reeve; 76, Robert Owen-Wahl; 77, Clearspring; 92, Matt Hains; 93, Soil Association; 98, Katharine Reeve; 99, Compassion in World Farming; 102, Environmental Working Group; 105, TNS Worldpanel; 105, Katharine Reeve; 119, Mary's Meals ; 132, Bananalink; 134, commons.wikimedia.org; 136, Katharine Reeve; 137, Fairtrade Foundation; 139, Marcus Lyon/Fairtrade Foundation; 142, Phytotrade Africa; 145, Greenpeace; 162, from Raj Patel, Stuffed and Starved (Portobello, 2007) redrawn by Gemma Matthews; 163, Robert Owen-Wahl; 165, Slow Food; 170, buythesea.co.uk; 173, Katharine Reeve; 176, WRAP; 185, adapted from Patrick Holford, Optimum Nutrition Made Easy; 193, Katharine Reeve; 195, Brita; 202, Archive of the Musuem of London; 203, Defra; 207, TNS Worldpanel; 212, Stock Xchange; 217, Katharine Reeve; 219, National Consumer Council, redrawn by Gemma Matthews; 221, J. Sainsbury's; 222, George Miller; 224, J. Sainsbury's; 227, Katharine Reeve; 229, Katharine Reeve; 235, Katharine Reeve; 236, George Miller; 237, Neal's Yard Dairy; 240, Abel & Cole; 244, Gemma Matthews; 245, Riverford Organics; 246, Katharine Reeve; 247, Katharine Reeve; 248, Katharine Reeve; 250, Katharine Reeve; 253, Katharine Reeve; 257, Katharine Reeve; 258, Katharine Reeve; 262, Katharine Reeve; 266, Katharine Reeve; 267, Katharine Reeve; 270, omlet.com; 275, Livia Miller; 276, Katharine Reeve; 277, Katharine Reeve; 280, George Miller; 281, Katharine Reeve; 282, Katharine Reeve; 283, Katharine Reeve; 284, Neal's Yard Dairy; 287, Daylesford Organics; 288, The Fine Cheese Company; 288, Katharine Reeve; 289, Meg Rivers' Cakes; 290, George Miller; 295, Stock Xchange; 296, Weeton's; 297, Katharine Reeve; 299, Ultracomida; 300, Falko; 301, George Miller.

Index

A

Abel & Cole 143, 197,
  239, 240, 242
acid–alkaline balance 190
acrylamide 71
Action Aid 143
additives 80–82
ADM (Archer Daniels
  Midland Co) 67
Adrià, Ferran 168
Africa 12, 115, 118, 121,
  142
air-freight 125, 138, 241
Aldi 204, 205, 206, 215,
  216
allergies, food 194
allotments 255–258
anaemia 191
anaphylaxis 194
animals
  diseases 40–41
  domestication of 6
animal welfare 32–43,
  96, 220
anorexia nervosa 184
antioxidants 80, 191
apples 28–29, 126
Asda 36, 46, 76, 80, 194,
  204–205, 207, 209,
  211, 217, 219–220,
  225, 228, 235
aspartame 85
Australasia 121

B

baby food 17
Bacheldre Mill 283
bakers, artisan 235, 283
bananas 130–133, 171
baobab 142
Barry Callebaut 135
bees 98
Big Barn 254

biofuels 44, 122–124
Bird flu 41
bivalves 55
bluetongue disease 41
Blumenthal, Heston 168
Blythman, Joanna 231
BMI (Body Mass Index)
  180
Booths 218
Borlaug, Norman 113
Borough Market, London
  247
bread 72, 213, 283
breakfast cereal 278
Brogdale Horticultural
  Trust 29
Brown Cow Organics 24
BSE 40
bulgur 289
Bunge 67
butchers 233–234
butter 74
bycatch 50

C

Cadbury Schweppes 68,
  70, 135, 136
Cafédirect 139
caffeine 285
cakes 290
calcium 189
calories 156, 180
canning 65
cappuccino 134, 182
carbohydrates 187
carbon-footprint label-
  ling 127
carbon offsetting 128
carbon counting 128
carbon dioxide 12, 31, 49,
  87, 128, 176
carbon footprint 166
Carbon Trust 127
Cargill 67, 86
Carrefour 116, 201, 207
Carson, Rachel 18
catering industry 169

celebrity chefs 166–167
Chatsworth farm shop
  251
cheese 237, 277
cheesemongers 237
Cheestrings 192
chicken 22, 32, 38, 211
  keeping 270
  Tesco 42
children's food 191–192
China 119, 154
Chiquita 130
chocolate 135–137, 171,
  280, 292
chocolate cake 290
cholesterol 187
Chorleywood Bread
  Process 72
Clearspring 77
climate change 44, 49,
  120–129, 176–177
Co-operative Wholesale
  Society 204
Coca-Cola 70, 86
cod 49, 51, 54
coeliac disease 194
coffee 113, 133–134, 182,
  286
coleslaw 244
colourings 81
Common Agricultural
  Policy 21
Common Ground 29
Compassion in World
  Farming 22, 33, 38, 97,
  211, 220, 221
Competition Commission
  209, 233
convenience stores 203,
  232
cookery books 197
corn 66
Corporate Watch 68
couscous 289
cows 34
crab 55
cream teas 253

NOTES